This is the first complete new translation of Bernstein's most famous and influential work. It will provide students with an accurate and unabridged edition of what has come to be recognised as the classic defence of democratic socialism and the first significant critique of revolutionary Marxism from within the socialist movement. First published in 1899, at the height of the Revisionist Debate, it argued that capitalism was not heading for the major crisis predicted by Marx, that the revolutionary rhetoric of the German Social Democratic Party was out of date, and that socialism could, and should, be achieved by piecemeal reform within a democratic constitutional framework. The historical significance of Bernstein's work lies in its being the focal point of one of the most important political debates of modern times. Its contemporary relevance lies in the light it casts on 'the crisis of Communism'.

The introduction sites Bernstein's work in its historical and intellectual context, and this edition also provides students with all the necessary reference material for understanding this important text.

D0322498

CAMBRIDGE TEXTS IN THE
HISTORY OF POLITICAL THOUGHT

═══

EDUARD BERNSTEIN
The Preconditions of Socialism

CAMBRIDGE TEXTS IN THE
HISTORY OF POLITICAL THOUGHT

Series editors

RAYMOND GEUSS

Reader in Philosophy, University of Cambridge

QUENTIN SKINNER

Regius Professor of Modern History, University of Cambridge

Cambridge Texts in the History of Political Thought is now firmly established as the major student textbook series in political theory. It aims to make available to students all the most important texts in the history of western political thought, from ancient Greece to the early twentieth century. All the familiar classic texts will be included, but the series seeks at the same time to enlarge the conventional canon by incorporating an extensive range of less well-known works, many of them never before available in a modern English edition. Wherever possible, texts are published in complete and unabridged form, and translations are specially commissioned for the series. Each volume contains a critical introduction together with chronologies, biographical sketches, a guide to further reading and any necessary glossaries and textual apparatus. When completed, the series will aim to offer an outline of the entire evolution of western political thought.

For a list of titles published in the series, please see end of book.

EDUARD BERNSTEIN

The Preconditions of Socialism

EDITED AND TRANSLATED BY

HENRY TUDOR
*Senior Lecturer in the Department of Politics,
University of Durham*

CAMBRIDGE
UNIVERSITY PRESS

PUBLISHED BY THE PRESS SYNDICATE OF THE UNIVERSITY OF CAMBRIDGE
The Pitt Building, Trumpington Street, Cambridge, United Kingdom

CAMBRIDGE UNIVERSITY PRESS
The Edinburgh Building, Cambridge CB2 2RU, UK
40 West 20th Street, New York, NY 10011–4211, USA
477 Williamstown Road, Port Melbourne, VIC 3207, Australia
Ruiz de Alarcón 13, 28014 Madrid, Spain
Dock House, The Waterfront, Cape Town 8001, South Africa

http://www.cambridge.org

First published 1993
Reprinted 2004

Printed in the United Kingdom at the University Press, Cambridge

A catalogue record for this book is available from the British Library

Library of Congress Cataloguing in Publication data
Bernstein, Eduard, 1850–1932.
[Voraussetzungen des Sozialismus und die Aufgaben der
Sozialdemokratie. English]
The preconditions of socialism / Eduard Bernstein : edited and
translated by Henry Tudor.
p.   cm. – (Cambridge texts in the history of political
thought)
Includes bibliographical references and index.
ISBN 0 521 39121 0 (hardback). – ISBN 0 521 39808 8 (paperback)
1. Socialism. 2. Democracy. 3. Sozialdemokratische Partei
Deutschlands. I. Tudor, H. (Henry), 1937– . II. Title.
III. Series.
HX273.B55313 1993   92–23175 CIP
320.5′31 – dc20

ISBN 0 521 39121 0 hardback
ISBN 0 521 39808 8 paperback

WV

Hence the Ten Hours' Bill was not only a great practical success; it was the victory of a principle.

Karl Marx, Inaugural Address of the International

Contents

Contents

Editor's note

Eduard Bernstein's famous polemic, *Die Voraussetzungen des Sozialismus*, was first published in 1899. It was reprinted several times in subsequent years and then, in 1921, Bernstein produced a revised and enlarged second edition. However, it was the first edition of 1899 that was at the centre of the controversy known as the Revisionist Debate, and that is the one that I have translated. There is already an English translation done by Edith C. Harvey and published in 1909 with the title *Evolutionary Socialism*. It reappeared in 1961 as a Schocken paperback, and two years later it was reprinted with an introduction by the late Sidney Hook.

Harvey's translation was not intended as a scholarly work and she did not feel it necessary to supply the usual apparatus. Nor, for that matter, did she translate the whole book. Chapter 2 was omitted, as were large sections of the remaining four chapters. Indeed, something between a quarter and a third of the book was left out. Furthermore, in the parts of the book which Harvey did translate, many inaccuracies and other defects crept in. Nevertheless, her translation has served as a good first draft, and if the present translation is an improvement, then it is largely because I have been able to build on her labours.

The Introduction inevitably covers much the same ground as my Introduction to *Marxism and Social Democracy; The Revisionist Debate 1896–1898* (ed. H. and J. M. Tudor, Cambridge, 1988) and my short piece on Bernstein in Robert Benewick (ed.), *Dictionary of Twentieth Century Political Thinkers* (London, 1992). I have, however, taken this opportunity to bring in some new material and to develop the analysis a bit further.

Material I have inserted in the text is enclosed in square brackets. Footnotes in the original are indicated by lower-case italic letters; my own notes are indicated by arabic numbers: both will be found at the foot of each page. I am very grateful to Raymond Guess and to my wife, Jo Tudor, for their helpful comments on various parts of this text. They have saved me from committing many errors. I am sure that at least as many remain, and for these I am, of course, entirely responsible.

Abbreviations

Adler *BW*	Victor Adler, *Briefwechsel mit August Bebel und Karl Kautsky, sowie Briefe von und an I. Auer, E. Bernstein, A. Braun, H. Dietz, E. Ebert, W. Liebknecht, H. Muller und P. Singer*, collected and with commentary by F. Adler, Vienna, 1954
Capital I	Karl Marx, *Capital: A Critique of Political Economy*, vol. I, trans. Ben Fowkes, Harmondsworth, 1976
Capital III	Karl Marx, *Capital: A Critique of Political Economy*, vol. III, trans. David Fernbach, Harmondsworth, 1981
LVZ	*Leipziger Volkszeitung*
MECW	Karl Marx and Frederick Engels, *Collected Works*, 50 vols. (incomplete), London, 1975–
MESC	Karl Marx and Frederick Engels, *Selected Correspondence*, Moscow, n.d.
MESW	Karl Marx and Frederick Engels, *Selected Works*, 2 vols., Moscow, 1958
MEW	Karl Marx and Friedrich Engels, *Werke*, 39 vols., Berlin, 1972–8
NZ	*Die Neue Zeit*
Protokoll	*Protokoll über die Verhandlungen des Parteitages der Sozialdemokratischen Partei Deutschlands*, Berlin, 1890–1913
RLGW	Rosa Luxemburg, *Gesammelte Werke*, 5 vols., Berlin, 1974–80

Tudor and Tudor *Marxism and Social Democracy: The Revisionist Debate 1896–1898*, ed. and trans. by H. Tudor and J. M. Tudor, with an introduction by H. Tudor, Cambridge, 1988

Introduction

When, in the spring of 1899, Bernstein's *Preconditions of Socialism* appeared, it caused a sensation. In effect, the book was a restatement and elaboration of the reformist standpoint Bernstein had been developing in a series of articles published during the previous two years. The controversy which these articles provoked had culminated in the rejection of Bernstein's position at the Stuttgart Conference of the German Social Democratic Party in October 1898. However, many felt that the issue had not yet been laid to rest. Karl Kautsky in particular was profoundly dissatisfied and he therefore urged that Bernstein produce 'a systematic, comprehensive, and carefully reasoned exposition of his basic conceptions, insofar as they transcend the framework of principles hitherto accepted in our party'.[1] Bernstein agreed, and the result was *The Preconditions of Socialism and the Tasks of Social Democracy*. Hastily written and flawed as it was, it was to become the classic statement of democratic, non-revolutionary socialism.

The background

Bernstein was born in Berlin on 6 January 1850. His father was a locomotive driver and the family was Jewish though not religious. When he left school he took employment as a banker's clerk. In 1872, the year after the establishment of the German Reich and the suppression of the Paris Commune, he joined the 'Eisenach' wing of

---

[1] Karl Kautsky, 'Tactics and Principles', 13.10.1898, Tudor and Tudor, p. 312.

the German socialist movement and soon became prominent as an activist. In 1875 he attended the Gotha Conference at which the Eisenachers united with the Lassalleans to form what was to become the German Social Democratic Party.[2] It was not long before the party reaped the benefit of its newly found unity. In the Reichstag elections of 1877 it gained 493,000 votes. However, two assassination attempts on the Kaiser in the following year provided Bismarck with a pretext for introducing a law banning all socialist organisations, assemblies, and publications. As it happened, there had been no Social Democratic involvement in either assassination attempt, but the popular reaction against 'enemies of the Reich' induced a compliant Reichstag to pass Bismarck's 'Socialist Law'.

For nearly all practical purposes, the party was outlawed and, throughout Germany, it was actively suppressed. However, it was still possible for Social Democrats to stand as individuals for election to the Reichstag, and this they did. Indeed, despite the severe persecution to which it was subjected, the party actually increased its electoral support, gaining 550,000 votes in 1884 and 763,000 in 1887. Party conferences could still be held outside Germany, and party papers – such as, the official party organ, *Der Sozialdemokrat*, and Karl Kautsky's political and literary review, *Die Neue Zeit* – could still be published abroad and smuggled across the frontier. In short, the party survived and, in certain respects, it even flourished.

Shortly before the 'Socialist Law' came into effect, Bernstein himself fled to Switzerland to take up a post as secretary to Karl Höchberg, a wealthy supporter of Social Democracy. A warrant subsequently issued for his arrest ruled out any possibility of his returning to Germany, and he was to remain in exile for more than twenty years.

It was shortly.after his arrival in Switzerland that he began to think of himself as a Marxist.[3] In 1880, he accompanied Bebel to London in order to clear up a misunderstanding over his involvement in an article published by Höchberg and denounced by Marx and Engels

---

[2] See Bernstein's account in his *Sozialdemokratische Lehrjahre* (Berlin, 1978), pp. 41ff; Roger Morgan, *The German Social Democrats and the First International 1864–1872* (Cambridge, 1965), gives an excellent account of the German socialist movement prior to the Gotha Conference.
[3] Bernstein, *Sozialdemokratische Lehrjahre*, p. 72; Bernstein to Bebel, 20.10.1898, Tudor and Tudor, p. 324.

as being 'chock-full of bourgeois and petty bourgeois ideas'.[4] The trip was a success. Engels in particular was impressed by Bernstein's zeal and the soundness of his ideas.

Back in Zurich, Bernstein became increasingly active in working for *Der Sozialdemokrat*, and in the following year he succeeded Georg von Vollmar as the paper's editor, a post he was to hold for the next ten years. It was during these years that Bernstein established his reputation as a leading party theoretician and a Marxist of impeccable orthodoxy. In this he was helped by the close personal and professional relationship he established with Engels. This relationship owed much to the fact that he shared Engels's strategic vision and accepted most of the particular policies which, in Engels's view, that vision entailed.

Engels, being convinced that the transition from capitalism to socialism could never be achieved by peaceful parliamentary means, argued that the main task of the party was to prepare for the inevitable revolution. However, to do this the party had first of all to survive, and that meant avoiding any action that might provoke the state into further acts of repression. It also meant using all available means to build up the strength of the party and increase its popular support. In the Reichstag, Social Democratic deputies should, therefore, adopt a position of intransigence within a framework of strict legality. Engels agreed that there was no harm in supporting measures that might improve the lot of the working man. But any measures that might strengthen the government against the people should be resisted.[5] These included the programme of welfare legislation which Bismarck initiated in the 1880s and also such apparently innocuous measures as state subsidies for the construction of steamships.[6]

For Engels, the danger was that a concentration on peaceful parliamentary activity might cause Social Democrats to forget their revolutionary objective. He therefore saw it as an important part of Bernstein's task as editor of the official party organ to halt the spread of 'philistine sentiment' within the party. Bernstein was glad to oblige.

[4] MESC, pp. 388 ff; MEW, vol. XXXIV, pp. 394ff.
[5] Engels to Bebel, 24.11.1879, MEW, vol. XXIV, p. 424.
[6] The party opposed the 'steamship subventions' because they formed part of Germany's policy of colonial expansion. At the same time, the subventions gave employment to dockyard workers and were, for that reason, supported by many Social Democrats. For Bernstein's account of the controversy see *Sozialdemokratische Lehrjahre*, pp. 155ff.

In one leading article after another, he spelled out the case for intransigence.[7]

In 1887, the German government persuaded the Swiss authorities to close down *Der Sozialdemokrat*. Bernstein moved to London where he resumed publication from premises in Kentish Town. His relationship with Engels soon blossomed into friendship. He also made contact with various English socialist organisations, notably the Fabian Society and Hyndman's Social Democratic Federation. It is clear that he was impressed by the liberal political climate that prevailed in England at the time.[8] Indeed, in later years, his opponents routinely claimed that his 'Revisionism' was due to his having come to see the world 'through English spectacles'. It is, of course, impossible to determine how far the charge was justified. For what it is worth, Bernstein himself denied it.[9]

In 1890 Bismarck fell from power. One of the factors that contributed to his downfall was the remarkable success the Social Democrats scored in the Reichstag elections of that year. They gained nearly one and a half million votes. Bismarck proposed to respond with further repressive measures, but the new Kaiser, Wilhelm II, favoured a policy of reconciliation. Bismarck accordingly resigned. Shortly afterwards, the 'Socialist Law' was allowed to lapse, and it was once again possible for Social Democracy to operate openly as a political organisation in Germany. However, the warrant which had been issued for Bernstein's arrest remained in force, and Bernstein therefore stayed in England until 1901 when it was finally withdrawn.

The electoral success of the party opened up new prospects and caused many Social Democrats to reconsider their strategy. This caused a certain amount of turmoil within the party. On the left, a group of intellectuals, known as the Youngsters, mounted a campaign in which they warned against opportunism, deplored the party's obsession with parliamentary success, and insisted that socialism could be achieved only by revolutionary means. They had reason to be concerned. The fall of Bismarck and the conciliatory attitude of the Kaiser had led many Social Democrats to think that socialism

---

[7] For instance, the three articles by Bernstein from the *Sozialdemokrat* in Tudor and Tudor, chapter 1.
[8] This is particularly evident in Bernstein's *My Years of Exile: Reminiscences of a Socialist* (London, 1921).
[9] Bernstein to Bebel, 20.10.1898, Tudor and Tudor, pp. 325–6.

might, after all, be achieved by legislation and peaceful reform.

At the Erfurt Conference, held in the autumn of 1891, the leadership of the party managed to stave off the assaults from both left and right. The new party programme which the conference eventually accepted had been drafted mainly by Kautsky and Bernstein. It is therefore not surprising that the theoretical assumptions on which it was based and the general political strategy it prescribed were basically those of Engels. Engels himself did have one or two criticisms, but in the main he was profoundly satisfied with the result.[10]

Der Sozialdemokrat had ceased publication soon after the 'Socialist Law' lapsed. However, Bernstein's distinguished record as editor, together with his restlessly active mind and his ready pen, brought him more than enough work as a journalist and author. His literary output during the 1890s was prodigious. At the same time, his views underwent a fundamental change. The change was slow, piecemeal, and difficult to detect. Engels, for one, noticed nothing.[11] Neither did Kautsky. Indeed, Bernstein himself did not realise that he had shifted his ground until early in 1897. On his own account, the light dawned while he was giving a lecture to the Fabian Society on 'What Marx Really Taught'. As he later put it in a letter to Bebel:

> as I was reading the lecture, the thought shot through my head that I was doing Marx an injustice, that it was not Marx I was presenting . . . I told myself secretly that this could not go on. It is idle to attempt to reconcile the irreconcilable. The vital thing is to be clear as to where Marx is still right and where he is not.[12]

By this time, Bernstein had concluded that the main point on which Marx was 'not right' was his theory that the capitalist economy, riven by its own inner contradictions, would inevitably founder, thus providing the occasion for the revolutionary proletariat to seize political power and establish a socialist order of society. The difficulty was that, in the mid 1890s, the inner contradictions of capitalism were not much in evidence. Certainly, the terminal crisis so confidently predicted by marx and engels had not occurred and, so far as

[10] Engels, 'Zur Kritik des sozialdemokratischen Programmentwurfs 1891', MEW, vol. XXII, pp. 227–38.
[11] It is true that in the 1890s Engels did occasionally express doubts about some of Bernstein's articles but, as I have observed elsewhere, he objected to their tone and timing rather than to their content. Tudor and Tudor, p. 9.
[12] Bernstein to Bebel, 20.10.1898, Tudor and Tudor, p. 325.

Bernstein could see, it was not going to occur. It might well be that capitalism had a built-in tendency to suffer periodic dislocations. However, the development of a sophisticated credit system, the emergence of trusts and cartels, and improved means of transport and communication, had all enabled capitalism to eliminate, or at least control, the trade crises that had been so marked a feature of the economy in the earlier part of the century. Besides, Bernstein argued, there was no evidence that the means of production were being concentrated in fewer and fewer hands, or that cut-throat competition was eliminating large sections of the bourgeoisie, or that the proletariat was being progressively reduced to abject poverty. Indeed, capitalism seemed to be in rude good health and was likely to remain so for the foreseeable future. It was therefore idle for socialists to pin their hopes on an imminent collapse of the bourgeois social and economic order.

On the other hand, Bernstein observed, the advance of democracy in most industrialised countries had enabled working-class parties to enter the political arena, and there was a real prospect that significant progress could be achieved by parliamentary means. Indeed, the 'victory of socialism' might well be accomplished by the steady implementation of socialist principles through legislation and institutional reform. However, Bernstein was careful to insist that by 'socialism' he did not mean the communist ideal entertained by certain elements of the radical left. A modern industrial economy was, he argued, far too complex to be managed effectively by the state or by 'society', whatever that might mean.[13] The state could regulate private enterprises but it should not own them. And it should not own them because it could not run them – or, at least, nothing like all of them. Loose talk about expropriating the expropriators was therefore dangerous nonsense. A socialist economy would inevitably include a large and thriving private sector.

It was also nonsense, Bernstein argued, to suggest that social care be extended to the point where the individual was completely relieved of any personal responsibility for his own welfare.[14] Socialism, for

---

[13] Bernstein, 'The Social and Political Significance of Space and Number' and 'The Theory of Collapse and Colonial Policy', Tudor and Tudor, pp. 83–98 and pp. 159–70.

[14] Bernstein, 'The Social and Political Significance of Space and Number', Tudor and Tudor, pp. 93–4; also present volume, p. 148.

him, entailed extending the individual's control over his own circumstances, and this meant 'the implementation of cooperation across the board'.[15] Socialists should therefore take a constructive view of the possibilities offered by trade unions, cooperative societies, and local government institutions. The objective of cooperative activity in these various organisations should be, not the class interest of the proletariat, but 'the common good'. Bernstein never doubted that there were clashes of class interest in modern industrial societies, but he always insisted that there was also a fundamental common interest, or good, which took precedence over any 'sectional' interests.[16] There was, incidentally, nothing particularly recondite about Bernstein's notion of the common good. It was simply a parcel of goods ranging from freedom of speech down to efficient street lighting. Bernstein was, in short, what Hyndman liked to call a 'gas and water socialist'.

Starting in 1896, the year after Engels died, Bernstein developed these views, partly in a series of articles published in *Die Neue Zeit* under the title 'Problems of Socialism' and partly in an extended polemical exchange with the English socialist, Ernest Belfort Bax. The controversy soon became general. Parvus, Franz Mehring, Rosa Luxemburg, and many others joined in; and, at the Stuttgart Conference in October 1898, Bebel came out against Bernstein, and Kautsky broke his silence with a powerful speech denouncing Bernstein's views.[17] It was, as I have already remarked, in response to this that Bernstein wrote *The Preconditions of Socialism*.

I do not intend to go through the book point by point. However, it might be helpful if I said something about the general nature of the political doctrine the book contains. In particular, are we to regard Bernstein's 'Revisionism' as a form of Marxism or as something completely different? Let us begin by looking at Bernstein's own account of the matter.

---

[15] Bernstein, 'A Statement', Tudor and Tudor, p. 193.
[16] For instance, in 'The Social and Political Significance of Space and Number', Tudor and Tudor, p. 93; see also his discussion of the 'productivity vs jobs' dilemma, 'The Conflict in the English Engineering Industry', Tudor and Tudor, pp. 129ff.
[17] Tudor and Tudor, pp. 287ff.

Bernstein's critique of Marxism

In his letter to the Stuttgart Conference (reproduced in the preface to his *Preconditions*) Bernstein cited Marx and Engels in support of his position, emphasising particularly the views Engels had expressed in his introduction to the 1895 edition of Marx's *The Class Struggles in France*. Here, Bernstein observed, Engels had argued that the time for violent revolution had passed and that Social Democracy would flourish 'far better on legal methods than on illegal methods and overthrow'. Indeed, he went on, 'Engels is so thoroughly convinced that tactics geared to a catastrophe have had their day that he considers *a revision to abandon them* to be due even in the Latin countries where tradition is much more favourable to them than in Germany.'[18]

This was, at best, misleading. Engels had not abandoned his conviction that a violent revolution was inevitable. He had, however, come to the conclusion that a decisive political crisis would occur before capitalism suffered its otherwise inevitable economic collapse; and his main concern was that the party should not be provoked into taking any action which might enable the authorities to carry out a pre-emptive strike.[19]

In other words, Engels was thinking in terms of strictly legal and parliamentary activity within the framework of a revolutionary strategy; and he was clear that the strategy had to be a revolutionary one because, for him, it was axiomatic that the bourgeoisie would not sit back and allow the proletariat to legislate capitalism out of existence. His expectation was that, if anything of the kind looked likely, the authorities would try to prevent it by staging a *coup d'état*. It would then fall to Social Democracy to stage a popular uprising in the name of constitutional legality. However, any such uprising would be crushed if the army came out on the side of the government. It was therefore imperative that Social Democracy use the electoral system to increase its popular support, particularly in areas of heavy military recruitment. Hence the importance of universal suffrage.[20]

It is true that the revolutionary basis of Engels's position was not

[18] Present volume, p. 4.
[19] The main reason for his caution was that recent developments in military technology meant that, as he put it: 'The era of barricades and street fighting has gone for good; *if the military fight*, resistance becomes madness', Frederick Engels, Paul and Laura Lafargue, *Correspondence* (Moscow, n.d.), vol. III, p. 208.
[20] Ibid., pp. 98 and 393, and vol. II, pp. 366–7.

made explicit in the 1895 Introduction. At the time, the German government was actively considering legislative measures against the Social Democrats; and Engels accordingly tried 'not to say anything which might be used as a means to assist in the passing of the *Umsturzvorlage* in the Reichstag'.[21] Indeed, the embattled leaders of the party subjected the text to yet further editing before they published it in the party press.[22] However, even the text thus bowdlerised was capable of interpretations other than the one Bernstein proffered in his letter to the Stuttgart Conference. Rosa Luxemburg, for one, was able to detect its revolutionary intent; and she did not have the benefit of personal acquaintance with its author.[23]

In fact, Bernstein was well aware that he had put forward a one-sided account of Engels's position. Accordingly, in the first two chapters of *The Preconditions of Socialism*, he tried to provide a more adequate analysis of the relationship between his own standpoint and that of Marx and Engels; and he began by examining what could be meant by calling socialism 'scientific'.

Any science, he argued, consists of a pure and an applied part. Pure science is 'constant' in the sense that it consists of principles which are 'universally valid'. Applied science, however, consists of propositions which are generated by applying the principles of pure science to particular sets of circumstances; and these propositions are valid only so long as the circumstances remain unchanged. Applied science is thus 'variable' in that its claims can be rendered invalid by a change in circumstances.

At this point we would have expected Bernstein to characterise the theory of the inevitable collapse of capitalism as part of Marx's applied science. This would have enabled him to reject the theory as having been superseded by recent economic and social developments while still insisting that the principles of Marx's pure science (the materialist conception of history, the theory of surplus value, etc.) remained intact. He could then have vindicated himself as a good Marxist by arguing that he rejected, not the principles of Marxism, but only the obsolete applications of those principles to particular

---

[21] Ibid., p. 368.
[22] Engels himself felt that the changes made him 'appear as a peaceful worshipper of legality at any price', and this, he declared, created 'a disgraceful impression'. Engels to Kautsky, 1.4.1895, MESC, p. 568; MEW, vol. XXXIX, p. 452.
[23] Rosa Luxemburg, *Selected Political Writings*, ed. Dick Howard (New York and London, 1971), p. 120; RLGW, vol. I, 1, p. 432.

cases. This, however, he did not do. Indeed, he went out of his way to reject this strategy and to insist that Marx's general theory of capitalist development belonged squarely 'in the domain of pure science'.[24] So to reject this theory was to reject a fundamental principle of scientific socialism.

Bernstein, however, saw this apparently drastic conclusion as being subject to one important qualification. For him, the activity of the pure scientist was necessarily open-ended. As he put it: 'Even the principles of pure science are subject to changes which, however, occur mostly in the form of limitations. With the advancement of knowledge, propositions previously regarded as having absolute validity are recognised as conditional and are supplemented by new cognitive principles which, while limiting their validity, simultaneously extend the domain of pure science.'[25] In other words, the principles of pure science could be modified without being rejected. Thus Marx's claim that the contradictions of capitalism lead inexorably to its downfall is true of capitalism today no less than it was when Marx first formulated it. However, we now know that it is true only as a 'tendency', for subsequent scientific investigation, much of it conducted by Marx and Engels themselves, has revealed other tendencies which counteract, but do not eliminate, the contradictions of capitalism. Similarly, Marx and Engels had often made the materialist conception of history look like a form of economic determinism. But, particularly in their later work, they recognised that political and ideological factors could influence economic developments and that economic factors were the determining force only 'in the last instance'. And so forth.

Bernstein's general point was that scientific truths are not to be regarded as doctrines cast in bronze. Science is an activity of investigation in which certain criteria are acknowledged, namely, 'empirical experience and logic',[26] and which is therefore a critical and continuing activity. So to treat even the purely theoretical parts of Marx's doctrine as being authoritative is to be not scientific but doctrinaire. Marx and Engels themselves had revised their theory, thus demonstrating its scientific character; and the scientific socialist should, Bernstein suggested, follow their example. In Bernstein's view, therefore, 'the further development and elaboration of Marxist doctrine

[24] Present volume, p. 11.
[25] Ibid., p. 9.   [26] Ibid.

must begin with criticism of it'.[27] It was only by virtue of such criticism and development that scientific socialism could vindicate its character as being genuinely scientific. In this sense, Bernstein argued, we can say that 'it is Marx who in the end carries the point against Marx'.[28]

The difficulty was that Marx himself had, in fact, *not* 'carried the point against Marx'. Neither he nor Engels had seen what was, on Bernstein's analysis, the plain implication of the various modifications they had introduced into their original theory. To the very end they had continued to insist that capitalism was doomed to collapse and that socialism could be achieved only by revolution. Why was this?

According to Bernstein, the answer was simple. It was because they were never able to free their thinking from the straitjacket of Hegelian dialectics. Time and again the results of their painstaking scientific research were annulled by an a priori deduction dictated by the Hegelian logic of contradiction. It was this, Bernstein argued, that accounted for the Blanquist element in Marxist thinking.[29] Class conflict and revolution were, quite simply, built into the intellectual presuppositions of Marx and Engels. Had they been able to transcend these presuppositions they would, Bernstein hinted, have come to much the same conclusions as he himself had done.

However, while Bernstein was right to draw attention to the place of dialectics in Marx's thinking, there was something odd about his depiction of it as an extraneous element incompatible with any genuinely scientific approach. For Marx and Engels, it was precisely its dialectical character which made their theory scientific rather than ideological. Reality itself was inherently dialectical, and any thinking which did not reflect this fact could not be called scientific. But Bernstein was clearly operating with a different notion of science. His paradigm was the natural sciences, not (as it was for Marx and Engels) history; and his view of science was distinctly positivist in character. However, as he himself was well aware, this raised the question of the relationship between scientific theory and political practice. In particular, it raised the question whether the objectives or goals of a political movement, such as socialism, could be scientifically established. And this brings us to the core of the difference between Bernstein and his Marxist opponents.

---

[27] Ibid., p. 28.   [28] Ibid.   [29] Ibid., pp. 37–8.

The movement and the final goal

For Marx and Engels, revolution was a structural feature of the bourgeois order of society; and it was a feature which, according to Engels, had been revealed when philosophical idealism had been 'driven from its last refuge, the philosophy of history', thus clearing the way for 'a materialistic treatment of history'. Henceforth, 'socialism was no longer an accidental discovery of this or that ingenious brain, but the necessary outcome of the struggle between two historically developed classes – the proletariat and the bourgeoisie'.[30] This outcome was 'necessary' for two closely related reasons.

First, on Marx's analysis, capitalism, being based on the private ownership of the means of production, could maintain itself only by constantly undermining the very conditions of its own existence. In particular, 'the centralisation of the means of production and the socialisation of labour' would become increasingly incompatible with 'capitalist private property' until the point was reached at which the system would simply collapse.[31] Since the root cause of the collapse was private property, capitalism could be replaced, if it was to be replaced at all, only by an economic and social order based on the common or social ownership of the means of production.

Second, since the proletariat was the exploited class in bourgeois society, the class interest of the proletariat could be nothing other than the replacement of the system in which it was exploited with one in which it was not. This meant abolishing private property in the means of production (which enabled surplus value to be extracted) and putting some form of common ownership in its place. However, this objective was not a mere ideal, a moral yearning for a better world. It coincided with the 'necessary outcome' of the historical development of capitalism. Like the coming of spring, it might gladden the heart, but it required no moral justification. It was simply an inevitability. In this sense, socialism was scientific. The final goal of the socialist movement could be shown to be 'necessary' by scientific analysis.

This view carried with it a number of implications for the way Marx and his followers understood political activity. To begin with,

[30] Engels, 'Socialism: Utopian and Scientific', MESW, vol. II, p. 135; MEW, vol. XIX, p. 208.
[31] *Capital* I, p. 929.

because the proletariat was the revolutionary class in bourgeois society, any party representing the proletariat was necessarily a revolutionary party. It was revolutionary in the sense that its final goal was the final goal of the proletariat, namely, the seizure of political power and the establishment of a socialist society on the ruins of capitalism. If the party decided to represent other classes as well as, or indeed instead of, the proletariat, it would acquire a different class interest and therefore cease to be revolutionary. Conversely, if it abandoned the final goal it would cease to represent the proletariat and would, whatever its protestations, become the representative of some other class. In either case, it would lose its identity. The class character of the party and its revolutionary end were, in this way, meshed. The one entailed the other.

Furthermore, since the final goal lay in the future, political activity in the present could only consist in using whatever means lay to hand in order improve the party's readiness to act when the time came. For most German Marxists in the 1890s this meant taking part in local and national elections, contributing to Reichstag debates, and promoting trade-union activity with a view to increasing the organisational strength and popular support of the party and heightening the revolutionary consciousness of the working class. However, it was repeatedly stressed that such activities were to be regarded as means and not as ends in themselves.[32] They were, in other words, not inherently right or wrong. They were right or wrong depending on whether, in the given circumstances, they contributed to the achievement of the final goal. The final goal, however, remained constant, and it was the final goal that determined the character of the activity in question. As Liebknecht put it at the Erfurt Conference: 'What is revolutionary lies, not in the *means*, but in the *end*.'[33] Taking part in a Reichstag election could therefore be a legitimate revolutionary tactic. It was, however, only a tactic, a temporary expedient which implied no commitment whatsoever to parliamentary democracy.

The notion of the final goal was therefore central to the way

---

[32] 'For Social Democracy, democratic institutions are essentially means to an end, not ends in themselves', anon., but probably Kautsky, 'Das demokratische Prinzip und seine Anwendung', *NZ*, 15, 1 (1896), 19. Or as Rosa Luxemburg put it: 'For Social Democracy, there exists an indissoluble tie between social reforms and revolution. The struggle for reform is the *means*; the social revolution is its *end*', *Selected Political Writings*, p. 52. See also Engels to Bernstein, 24.3.1884, MESC, p. 445; MEW, vol. XXXVI, p. 128.   [33] *Protokoll*, 1891, p. 206.

German Marxists in the 1890s understood their political activity. It united revolutionary theory with day-to-day political practice; it vindicated the party's characteristic tactic of taking full part in the political process while resolutely avoiding any entanglement with other parties or classes; and it helped sustain morale in times of stress and persecution. So it is hardly surprising that party activists throughout the land sat up and took notice when, in January 1898, Bernstein declared: 'I frankly admit that I have extraordinarily little feeling for, or interest in, what is usually termed "the final goal of socialism". This goal, whatever it may be, is nothing to me, the movement is everything.'[34] Bernstein was dismissing as irrelevant the very notion which, for Marxists at least, made sense of everything the party was doing.

Dismayed by the outcry which his declaration provoked, Bernstein made several attempts to explain himself. In a statement published in *Vorwärts*, he said that he saw the final goal of socialism not as a future state of affairs but as the set of principles that governed the day-to-day political activity of the party. What he had really meant, he said, was therefore that 'The movement is everything to me because it bears its goal within itself.'[35]

As this clarification failed to satisfy his critics, he returned to the topic in his letter to the Stuttgart Conference, and again in the final chapter of *Preconditions*. His point in both places was essentially the same. He did not, he said, intend to express any 'indifference concerning the final carrying out of socialist principles'.[36] Indeed, he would 'willingly abandon the form of the sentence about the final goal as far as it allows the interpretation that every general aim of the working-class movement formulated as a principle should be declared valueless'.[37] But, while it was one thing to speak of the final goal as the implementation of certain principles, it was quite another to think of it as a future event or state of affairs. The future, Bernstein argued, was uncertain and could not be predicted. At some point in the future, the capitalist system might well collapse. But then again, it might not. In any case, the idea was at best a hypothesis – intellectually interesting, but of no practical import for current political problems. 'I am', Bernstein said, 'not concerned with what will happen

---

[4] 'The Theory of Collapse and Colonial Policy', Tudor and Tudor, pp. 168–9.
[5] 'A Statement', Tudor and Tudor, p. 194.
[6] Present volume, p. 5.   [37] Ibid., pp. 5, 192.

in the more distant future, but with what can and ought to happen in the present, for the present and the nearest future.'[38] The question of tactics was, in other words, a question of assessing present circumstances with a view to determining what could be done by way of implementing the 'general principles of Social Democracy'.

However, for Marx and his followers, political activity in a society riven by class conflict was not, and could not be, a matter of implementing a set of general principles. Principles might be paraded about on the public stage, but they were essentially a cover for class interest. In the last analysis, political activity was governed by the long-term strategic objectives of the various conflicting classes. And this, as we have noted, meant that a tactical move could not be understood as being inherently either right or wrong. What was right today could, if the circumstances changed, become wrong tomorrow. Political activity was therefore not a matter of following fixed rules or implementing principles regarded as valid in themselves; it was a matter of finding the means to a predetermined end, and ultimately it was the end that justified the means.

However, the various glosses Bernstein put upon his rejection of 'the final goal' made it clear that, for him, political activity was indeed governed by timeless principles which functioned as moral imperatives. Ends could therefore not be separated from means in the way his Marxist opponents supposed. For Bernstein, the end was not a remotely future consequence of what was done in the present; it was achieved directly *in* what was done. Thus a particular social reform, insofar as it implemented one of the principles of Social Democracy, was of value not just as a means but as an end in itself. As Bernstein put it, 'There can be more socialism in a good factory act than in the nationalisation of a whole group of factories.'[39]

In other words, for Bernstein, ends and means were implicated in one another such that the ends pursued could be inferred from the means adopted, for the end of a political act was nothing other than the principle manifest in it. It therefore made perfectly good sense for Bernstein to conclude that there was a contradiction between Engels's advocacy of strict legality, on the one hand, and his revolutionary rhetoric on the other. And it also made sense for him to suggest that, since the party had adopted the peaceful tactics Engels

[38] Ibid., p. 5.
[39] 'The Theory of Collapse and Colonial Policy', Tudor and Tudor, p. 168.

recommended, it ought to 'find the courage to emancipate itself from an outworn phraseology' and 'make up its mind to appear what it is today: a democratic, socialistic party of reform'.[40]

Bernstein never went as far as Peuss who, at the Stuttgart Conference, roundly declared: 'I find the whole concept of a final goal repugnant, for there are no final goals.'[41] As Bernstein saw it, political activity properly understood was a union of realism and idealism, of pragmatism and principle; and where principle was involved there was indeed room for talk about final goals. But, he felt, even then such talk should be cautious and qualified.

Bernstein's political vision

It is evident that Bernstein's view of political activity presupposed an understanding of modern industrial societies that was radically different from that of Marx and his followers. Marx always insisted that, under capitalism, politics were ultimately and inevitably governed by class conflict. Bernstein was not prepared to be quite so categorical. He accepted that conflicting class interests were a factor in the politics of modern industrial societies, but, as we have already observed, he maintained that all classes also had a common interest in the maintenance and furtherance of civilised values, and it was this common interest which was, or ought to be, the objective of political activity. As he put it in one place, 'while modern civilisation is much indebted to the capitalist economy, it is by no means exhausted by it'[42] and elsewhere he declared that 'the morality of developed civil society is by no means identical with the morality of the bourgeoisie'.[43] For Bernstein, in short, the values of 'developed civil society' embraced and transcended all sectional interests and points of view.

He was, however, aware that a particular class might obtain a monopoly of political power and use its monopoly to enforce its class interest against the interests of other classes and against the common interest. Indeed, a conspicuous example of this had been Germany at the time of the 'Socialist Law'. And he accepted that when the

[40] Present volume, p. 188.
[41] *Protokoll*, 1898, p. 89.
[42] 'The Struggle of Social Democracy and the Social Revolution: Polemical Aspects', Tudor and Tudor, p. 151.
[43] 'The Realistic and the Ideological Moments in Socialism', Tudor and Tudor, p. 243.

working class was, in this fashion, systematically excluded from the political arena, then it had no option other than revolutionary class struggle. However, where democracy had been achieved and all classes enjoyed the same civil and political rights, then it was possible for the legitimate demands of the workers to be satisfied by ordinary political means and for compromises to be struck on the basis of the common interest. The first objective of the socialist movement should therefore be the achievement of full democracy, and it is significant that Bernstein defined democracy as 'the absence of class government'.[44]

So, while Bernstein agreed that class conflict might be a feature of a developed civil society, he denied that it was in any way the definitive feature. For him, the state was not necessarily, or even normally, the instrument of class rule. Instead, it was the means by which barbarism and inhumanity could be eliminated and the moral principles of advanced civilisation could be imposed on all aspects of public life. This, for Bernstein, was the ultimate political objective of Social Democracy. It was an objective which differed from that of the liberals only in being more comprehensive and consistent in its conception. Socialism was, according to Bernstein, 'the legitimate heir' of liberalism, and, he added, there is 'no really liberal thought which does not also belong to the elements of the ideas of socialism'.[45]

As Bernstein himself remarked, one of his ablest critics was Rosa Luxemburg.[46] In the run-up to the Stuttgart Conference, she had attacked his position in a series of articles under the title 'Social Reform or Revolution?', and when his *Preconditions* appeared she returned to the fray. Her object was to show that Bernstein's enterprise was not to be understood as a 'revision' or up-dating of Marx's 'proletarian' standpoint. It was, rather, a defection to the standpoint of 'the progressive, democratic petty bourgeoisie'.[47] That this was not immediately obvious was, she argued, due largely to the fact that any new movement 'begins by suiting itself to the forms already at hand, and by speaking the language which was spoken'.[48] For this reason, she suggested, differences in substance tended to be obscured by

[44] Present volume, pp. 140, 143.
[45] Ibid., p. 147.
[46] Ibid., p. 200.
[47] *Selected Political Writings*, p. 134; RLGW, vol. I, 1, p. 445.
[48] Ibid., p. 53; ibid., p. 370.

similarities in form and language. Although she frequently mentioned this feature of the debate, she gave only one example by way of illustration. In *Preconditions* Bernstein drew attention to the fact that the word *bürgerlich* means both 'civil' and 'bourgeois', and that this ambivalence had given the false impression that, in calling for the abolition of 'bourgeois' society, socialists were demanding an end to 'civil' society. In fact, he said, nothing could be further from the truth. 'Social Democracy does not wish to break up civil society and make all its members proletarians together; rather, it labours incessantly to raise the worker from the social position of a proletarian to that of a citizen, and thus to make citizenship universal.'[49] To this, Rosa Luxemburg replied: 'When he uses, without distinction, the term "citizen" in reference to the bourgeois as well as the proletarian, thus intending to refer to man in general, he in fact identifies man in general with the bourgeois, and human society with bourgeois society.'[50] Her description of Bernstein's standpoint as 'bourgeois' begged the question, for it presupposed the very point he was questioning, namely, the class character of civil society. However, she was quite right in suggesting that Bernstein's attempts at linguistic clarification were symptoms of a profounder change in his standpoint. They were, she argued, symptoms of the fact that his view was no longer scientific but ideological, and by this she meant that it was an idealist view.

Bernstein's idealism, she contended, was a direct and necessary consequence of his denial that capitalist development inevitably leads to a general economic collapse, for this amounted to denying that socialism was 'objectively necessary', and it was precisely the 'objective necessity' of socialism that constituted its scientific character.[51] Bernstein had certainly argued that, with the rejection of the breakdown theory, socialism would lose none of its persuasive force. 'For', he said, 'what are all the factors we have mentioned as tending to suppress or modify the former crises? Nothing else, in fact, than the preconditions, or even in part the germs, of the socialisation of production and exchange.'[52] This, Rosa Luxemburg argued, was misleading. If cartels, trade unions, and the credit system were

---

[49] Present volume, p. 146.
[50] *Selected Political Writings*, pp. 127–8; RLGW, vol. I, 1, p. 440.
[51] *Selected Political Writings*, p. 58; RLGW, vol. I, 1, p. 376.
[52] 'The Theory of Collapse and Colonial Policy', Tudor and Tudor, p. 166.

'means of adaptation' which would enable capitalism to maintain itself, then, although they might express the social character of production, they could not be described as preconditions of socialism. Indeed, by maintaining production in its capitalist form, they would render the transformation of socialised production into socialist production unnecessary. 'That', she said,

> is why they can be the germs or preconditions of a socialist order only in a conceptual sense and not in a historical sense. They are phenomena which, in the light of our conception of socialism, we *know* to be related to socialism but which, in fact, not only do not lead to a socialist revolution, but, on the contrary, render it superfluous.

According to Bernstein's account, she continued, the class consciousness of the proletariat would cease to be 'the simple intellectual reflection of the ever growing contradictions of capitalism and its approaching decline' and become instead 'a mere ideal whose force of persuasion rests only on the perfections attributed to it'. It was by thus seeing socialism not as a historical necessity but as a rational possibility which could be made a matter of moral commitment that Bernstein had, she argued, offered 'an idealist explanation of socialism'.[53]

In *Preconditions* Bernstein himself had tentatively explored the idealist implications of his position. He had stressed that he wished to strengthen 'equally the realistic and the idealistic elements in the socialist movement'; he had argued that 'the point of economic development attained today leaves the ideological and especially the ethical factors greater space for independent activity than was formerly the case', and he had closed his work with an appeal for a 'return to Kant'.[54] However, he had not in plain terms rejected materialism and declared himself an idealist. He may, indeed, have had political reasons for being cautious, but it is reasonable to suppose that his caution also owed something to the fact that he had not yet fully clarified his thoughts on the relationship between science and ethics. In *Preconditions* he had, in effect, avoided the issue. He had said that socialism was scientific in the sense that it formulated its aims in accordance with a body of scientifically established knowledge.[55]

---

[53] *Selected Political Writings*, p. 59; RLGW, vol. I, 1, p. 377.
[54] Present volume, p. 209.   [55] Ibid., p. 9.

However, he had not said that the aims themselves were scientifically established; and indeed the account he had given of scientific method made it very difficult to see how any such scientific establishment of aims was possible.

Two years later, he published a lecture with the Kantian title 'How is Scientific Socialism Possible?', in which he finally made his position clear. After reiterating his claim that the collapse of capitalism, and hence the necessity of socialism, is incapable of scientific proof, he went on to argue that, in any case, no system of thought is scientific 'when its aims and presuppositions include elements that fall outside the pale of unbiassed knowledge', and that socialism is a system of thought that contains precisely such elements, namely, a set of aims which expresses, not the results of scientific investigation, but the interests of the working class.[56] Science, being mere cognition, can not move men to action; and for this reason socialism, insofar as it is an end to be striven for, a movement towards what ought to be, could not, for Bernstein, be scientific.

It is, I think, clear that Bernstein and Rosa Luxemburg were talking at cross-purposes. Bernstein's positivist view of science left no room whatsoever for the scientific determination of the ends of action. 'Ought' could not be derived from 'is'. For Rosa Luxemburg, however, science was a matter of showing what is 'objectively necessary' in the historical sense, and practical activity was scientific insofar as it was guided by a recognition of objective necessity as opposed to some preconceived idea of what ought to be. Hence her point about the class consciousness of the proletariat. It was not sufficient that the proletariat recognise that, measured by certain ethical principles, the capitalist system is defective. For her, the deficiencies of capitalism had to be demonstrated by capitalism itself, and it had to demonstrate them by showing that it was in fact incapable of carrying on. A social system, in other words, could not be justified or condemned on grounds that were somehow independent of that system. A social system justified or condemned itself by the way in which it objectively developed; and insofar as men's opinions were scientific, that is, objective, they were 'the simple intellectual reflections' of that development. In the end, history was the judge.

[56] 'Wie ist wissenschaftlicher Sozialismus möglich?', in *Ein revisionistisches Sozialismusbild*, ed. Helmut Hirsch (Stuttgart, 1976), pp. 75ff.

The aftermath

Rosa Luxemburg was not alone in finding Bernstein's views unacceptable. The spring and summer of 1899 saw a flood of articles against Bernstein in the party press. Kautsky led the campaign, but many others of lesser eminence contributed. Bernstein stoutly maintained his position, concentrating his efforts on rebutting Kautsky's detailed criticisms. At the party conference held at Hanover that autumn, the Revisionism question was virtually the only item on the agenda. Bebel introduced the topic by giving his reasons for rejecting Bernstein's views. His speech lasted six hours. Although Bernstein himself was once again absent – he was still under threat of arrest – his position was ably defended by Eduard David. However, the tide of opinion was clearly against him, and his position was decisively rejected.

Two years later, the warrant issued for Bernstein's arrest was at last withdrawn and he returned to Germany. In 1902 he was elected Reichstag deputy for Breslau, a seat he held until 1906 and again from 1912 to 1918. During these years he added nothing significant to the position he had developed in the 1890s. However, he continued to advocate his views and, although he never formed his supporters into an organised political group, his influence within the party and the trade-union movement continued to grow.

In 1903 he again found himself at the centre of a controversy. The issue that sparked it off was his recommendation that the party should accept the position in the Reichstag praesidium to which its numerical strength entitled it. In itself the issue was a minor one, but behind it lay the more general, and more important question of the relationship of the party to the established political and social order. Once again the annual party conference was dominated by the Revisionist debate, and once again the party maintained its stance of revolutionary intransigence.

During the First World War, Bernstein's opposition to the voting of war credits placed him, a bit artificially, on the radical left of the party. When the war ended, however, he resumed his place in the mainstream of German Social Democracy. In 1920 the party suffered an electoral setback, and Bernstein became a member of the commission appointed to redraft the party's programme. The resulting Görlitz Programme of 1921 abandoned much of the Marxist analysis embodied in the Erfurt Programme of 1891 and was widely regarded as owing much to Bernstein's influence. However, this belated triumph of Revisionism was short-lived. The Heidelberg Programme of 1925 restored many of the basic principles of Erfurt. In 1928 Bernstein retired from active politics, and in 1932 he died.

Principal events in Bernstein's life

1850 Born 6 January in Berlin.

1872 Joins Social Democratic Workers' Party.

1875 Gotha Conference.

1878 Anti-socialist legislation. Bernstein, employed as secretary to Karl Höchberg, goes into exile in Switzerland.

1879 Foundation of *Der Sozialdemokrat*.

1881 Bernstein editor of *Der Sozialdemokrat*.

1887 Expelled from Switzerland, Bernstein takes *Der Sozialdemokrat* to London.

1890 S.P.D. (Sozialdemokratische Partei Deutschlands) victory in Reichstag elections. Fall of Bismarck. Anti-socialist legislation allowed to lapse. *Der Sozialdemokrat* ceases publication.

1891 Erfurt Conference.

1895 Engels dies. Bernstein, with Bebel, named as literary executor.

1896 Controversy with Belfort Bax on colonialism. First article in the series 'Problems of Socialism', published in *Die Neue Zeit*.

1897 Marries Regina Schattner.

1898 Further controversies with Belfort Bax, Parvus, and others. In October, 'Revisionism' rejected at the Stuttgart Conference.

1899 Publication of *Die Voraussetzungen des Sozialismus*, followed by controversies with Karl Kautsky, Rosa Luxemburg, and others. Bernstein's position debated at length and rejected at the Hanover Conference in October.

1901 Returns to Germany. Selected articles published as *Zur Theorie und Geschichte des Sozialismus*.

1902 Elected Reichstag deputy for Breslau, a position held until 1906 and again from 1912 to 1918.

1903 'Revisionism' rejected again at the Dresden Conference.

1914 Outbreak of First World War.

1916 Bernstein, having opposed war credits, joins the radical SAG (*Sozialdemokratische Arbeitsgemeinschaft*).

1917 Joins the newly formed USPD (*Unabhängige Sozialdemokratische Partei Deutschlands*).

1918 End of First World War. Bernstein rejoins the majority SPD.

1920 Succeeds Georg von Vollmar as Reichstag deputy for the third electoral district in Berlin.

1921 The Görlitz Conference accepts a new party programme strongly influenced by Bernstein's 'Revisionism'.

1928 Retires from active politics.

1932 Dies.

Bibliographical note

Intellectual and political background

For a general historical account of the background to the Revisionist Debate, see Gordon A. Craig, *Germany 1866–1945* (Oxford, 1981). Carlton J. H. Hayes, *A Generation of Materialism 1871–1900* (New York, 1941), provides a good and comprehensive account of the intellectual milieu within which the debate took place. There are several useful analyses of the history and structure of the German Social Democratic Party. Roger Morgan's *The German Social Democrats and the First International 1864–1872* (Cambridge, 1965) is still the best study (in English) of the origins and early years of German Social Democracy; and Carl E. Schorske's *German Social Democracy 1905–1917: The Development of the Great Schism* (2nd edn, Cambridge, Mass., 1983) has yet to be superseded. Students should also consult G. Roth, *The Social Democrats in Imperial Germany* (Totowa, N. J., 1963); W. L. Guttsman, *The German Social Democratic Party 1875–1933; Ghetto to Government* (London, 1981); Richard Geary, *Revolution and the German Working Class, 1848–1933* (Brighton, 1985); and Helga Grebing, *History of the German Labour Movement: A Survey* (Leamington Spa, 1985). There are some interesting contributions in Richard J. Evans (ed.), *Society and Politics in Wilhelmine Germany* (London, 1978), and Alex Hall, *Scandal, Sensation and Social Democracy: The SPD Press and Wilhelmine Germany, 1890–1914* (Cambridge, 1977), deals with a neglected but important aspect of the background to the debate.

Bernstein and Revisionism

Apart from the present volume, the only other books by Bernstein that are available in English are: *Ferdinand Lasalle as a Social Reformer* (London, 1893), *My Years of Exile* (London, 1921), and *Cromwell and Communism* (London, 1931). However, particularly in the 1890s, Bernstein published a number of articles (in English) in *Justice*, the organ of the Social Democratic Federation; and the main articles that initiated the Revisionist Debate are translated in H. and J. M. Tudor (eds.), *Marxism and Social Democracy: The Revisionist Debate 1896–1898* (Cambridge, 1988).

Peter Gay's excellent *The Dilemma of Democratic Socialism* (New York, 1962) is still the only book-length study of Bernstein and Revisionism in English. However, the following are probably the best of the many books that include substantial discussions of Bernstein and the Revisionist Debate: R. Fletcher, *Revisionism and Empire: Socialist Imperialism in Germany, 1897–1914* (London, 1984); L. Kolakowski, *Main Currents of Marxism: Its Rise, Growth and Dissolution*, 3 vols. (Oxford, 1978); Leopold Labedz (ed.), *Revisionism: Essays on the History of Marxist Ideas* (London, 1962); George Lichtheim, *Marxism* (London, 1964); and David McLellan, *Marxism after Marx: An Introduction* (London and Basingstoke, 1979). There are some useful pieces, particularly on Bernstein's later career, in Roger Fletcher (ed.), *Bernstein to Brandt: A Short History of German Social Democracy* (London, 1987). There are also one or two articles that are worth consulting, e.g. Sydney D. Bailey, 'The Revision of Marxism', *Review of Politics*, 16 (1954); Charles F. Elliott, 'Quis custodiet sacra? Problems of Marxist Revisionism', *Journal of the History of Ideas*, 28 (1967); Harry J. Marks, 'Sources of Reformism in the Social Democratic Party of Germany, 1890–1914', *Journal of Modern History*, 11 (1939); D. W. Morgan, 'The Father of Revisionism Revisited: Eduard Bernstein', *Journal of Modern History*, 51 (1979); and J. P. Nettl, 'The German Social Democratic Party 1890–1914 as a Political Model', *Past and Present*, 30 (1965).

Bernstein's critics

Some extracts from Kautsky's counterblast to Bernstein's book are included in Karl Kautsky, *Selected Political Writings*, ed. and trans.

Patrick Goode (London and Basingstoke, 1983). Rosa Luxemburg's articles against Bernstein, which were subsequently reissued as a book, are translated in Rosa Luxemburg, *Selected Political Writings*, ed. Dick Howard (New York and London, 1971). Georgi Plekhanov's articles against Bernstein will be found in volume II of his *Selected Philosophical Works* (Moscow, 1976–81). For discussion of Kautsky's contribution see: Gary P. Steenson, *Karl Kautsky 1854–1938: Marxism in the Classical Years* (Pittsburg, 1978); M. Salvadori, *Kautsky and the Socialist Revolution, 1880–1938* (New York, 1979); and Dick Geary, *Karl Kautsky* (Manchester, 1987). The authoritative work on Rosa Luxemburg is J. P. Nettl, *Rosa Luxemburg*, 2 vols. (Oxford, 1966). The best, indeed the only, study of Plekhanov is still Samuel H. Baron, *Plekhanov: The Father of Russian Marxism* (London, 1963).

Biographical notes

The information contained in these notes is culled from the standard sources (e.g. *The Dictionary of National Biography* and *Biographisches Wörterbuch zur Deutschen Geschichte*) and from the very similar, and useful, notes to be found under the heading 'Personenverzeichnis' at the end of each volume of Marx and Engels, *Werke* (Berlin, 1978). I have not included Marx and Engels themselves, nor figures such as Descartes, Spinoza, Shakespeare, Charles Dickens, and Kant. (Readers to whom these names are unfamiliar will have other and vastly more important difficulties with Bernstein's text.) At the other end of the spectrum, I have omitted a few figures too obscure to appear in any work of reference other than a fairly recondite bibliography.

ADLER, Victor (1852–1918). Physician and journalist. Co-founder and leader of the Austrian Social Democratic Party. At first one of Bernstein's critics, he became an influential exponent of the democratic and reformist road to socialism.

BABEUF, François Noel, known as Gracchus (1760–97). Revolutionary communist and editor of *Tribun du peuple* during the French Revolution. His conspiracy to overthrow the Directory and establish a communist society in France was discovered, and he was executed.

BARBES, Armand (1809–70). French revolutionary democrat. Associate of Blanqui and leading member of the *Société des saisons*. Involved in the uprising of 1839 and in the attempt to overthrow the National Assembly on 15 May 1848.

BARTH, Ernst Emil Paul (1858–1922). Philosopher and sociologist. Became professor at Leipzig University in 1890. Critic of Marxism.

BAX, Ernest Belfort (1854–1926). Barrister and journalist. With William Morris, founded the Socialist League. Was, for a while, a leading member of Hyndman's Social Democratic Federation. Launched the 'Revisionist Debate' with his critique of Bernstein in November 1896.

BEBEL, Ferdinand August (1840–1913). Master turner by trade and disciple of Marx. Founding member and, for much of his active life, leader of the German Social Democratic Party. Member of the Reichstag 1871–81 and 1883–1913.

BERTRAND, Louis (1866–1941). French novelist. Also wrote travel books and biographies. Elected to the Academy in 1925.

BLANC, Jean Joseph Louis (1811–82). French revolutionary socialist and historian. Founded the *Revue de progrès* in 1839. A year later he published his *Organisation du travail* advocating the establishment of cooperative workshops, subsidised by the state. Member of the provisional government in 1848. In exile (London) 1848–71. Elected to the National Assembly on his return to France, and to the Chamber of Deputies in 1876.

BLANQUI, Louis Auguste (1805–81). French communist and revolutionary. Took an active part in all Paris uprisings from 1830 to 1870. Founded several secret revolutionary societies. Leading member of the Paris Commune, 1871.

BÖHM-BAWERK, Eugen von (1851–1914). Austrian statesman and economist. Leading advocate of the marginal-utility theory of value, and prominent critic of Marx. Minister of Finance, 1900–4.

BRENTANO, Lujo (1844–1931). German professor of political economy. Leading *Kathedersozialist*. Critic of Marx.

BRIGHT, John (1811–89). English Liberal. Advocate of free trade. With Cobden, leader of the Anti-Corn-Law League.

BUCHEZ, Philippe Benjamin Joseph (1796–1865). Physician and socialist. Follower of Saint-Simon and advocate of the establishment of producers' cooperatives with state aid. Published works on history and philosophy. President of National Assembly in 1848.

CASTILLE, Hyppolyte (1820–86). Prolific French author and historian. Took active part in June insurrection, 1848. Later abandoned republicanism and supported the Empire.

CUNOW, Heinrich (1862–1936). Marxist historian and ethnographer. On editorial board of *Die Neue Zeit* from 1898. Subsequently supporter of Revisionism. On editorial board of *Vorwärts*, 1907–14. Author of several works on the history of primitive society.

DESTUTT DE TRACY, Antoine-Louis-Claude (1754–1836). French materialist philosopher and economist. Author of *Eléments d'idéologie* and *Traité de la volonté*.

DÜHRING, Karl Eugen (1833–1921). German philosopher and political economist. Became *Privatdozent* at the University of Berlin in 1863. Had considerable influence on German Social Democracy in the 1870s and was the object of Engels's critique, *Anti-Dühring*.

ECCARIUS, Johann Georg (1818–89). German worker and revolutionary. Member of Communist League, active member of First International, Secretary of General Council (1867–71). Supported the Bakuninists at the Hague Congress. Later, active in British trade-union movement.

FEUERBACH, Ludwig Andreas (1804–72). German materialist philosopher. Author of *The Essence of Christianity* (translated by George Eliot). His critique of Hegel had a powerful influence on Marx and Engels in the early years of their collaboration.

FOURIER, François Marie Charles (1772–1837). French utopian socialist. Survived the 'Terror' by the skin of his teeth. Author of *Théorie des quatre mouvements* (1808), *Traité d'association domestique agricole* (1822), and *Le nouveau monde industriel et sociétaire* (1829).

GIFFEN, Sir Robert (1837–1910). Scottish economist and statistician. Became comptroller-general of the commercial, labour, and statistical department of the Board of Trade. Author of *The Growth of Capital* (1890) and *The Case against Bimetallism* (1892).

GUESDE, Jules (1845–1922). French socialist and co-founder of the French Workers' Party. Opponent of the Possibilists. Later acquired a reputation as an opportunist.

HASSELMANN, Wilhelm (b. 1844). A leading Lassallean. Subsequently (1880) expelled from the German Social Democratic Party for his anarchist tendencies.

HEBERT, Jacques René (1755–94). French Revolutionary, prominent Jacobin, editor of *Le Père Duchesne*. Played a prominent part in the September massacres and in the condemnation of Marie Antoinette. Was himself guillotined by Robespierre.

HEINE, Wolfgang (1861–1944). Lawyer, Reichstag deputy, Social Democrat. Strong advocate of social reform by parliamentary means. Served as minister of justice in Prussia for a few months immediately after the First World War.

HERKNER, Heinrich (1863–1932). German economist and prominent *Kathedersozialist*. At various times, professor at Freiburg, Karlsruhe, Zurich, and Berlin.

HÖCHBERG, Karl (1853–85). German journalist and philanthropist. Financed several Social Democratic publications. Employed Bernstein as his secretary in 1878.

HYNDMAN, Henry Mayers (1842–1922). English socialist and admirer of Marx. Leader of the Social Democratic Federation and editor of its organ, *Justice*.

JEVONS, William Stanley (1835–82). English economist and logician. Early proponent of the marginal utility theory of value. Professor of logic at Owen's College, Manchester, in 1866 and professor of political economy in the University of London in 1876. Author of *Theory of Political Economy* and *Principles of Economics*.

KAUTSKY, Karl Johann (1854–1938). Leading German Social Democrat and follower of Marx. Editor of *Die Neue Zeit*. Close associate of Bernstein, until the revisionist debate.

LANGE, Friedrich Albert (1828–75). German neo-Kantian philosopher and supporter of socialism. Author of *Geschichte des Materialismus*.

LASSALLE, Ferdinand (1825–64). Leading German Social Democrat and publicist. Strongly influenced by Hegel. Took part in the Revolution of 1848 and subsequently founded the General Association of

German Workers. His admiration for Marx was not reciprocated. Author of *System der erworbene Rechte* and *Bastiat-Schulze*.

LAW, John (1671–1729). Scottish financier, banker, and advocate of paper money. Settled in France where his idea for a national bank was adopted. Was made Comptroller-General for Finances in 1720. Became object of popular hatred when the bubble burst. Died in poverty.

LIEBKNECHT, Wilhelm (1826–1900). Leading German Social Democrat and follower of Marx. Took active part in the Baden insurrection in 1848–9. Went into exile, returning to Germany in 1862. Elected to Reichstag in 1874. Imprisoned several times. Editor of the party newspaper, *Vorwärts*.

LOUIS-PHILLIPPE (1773–1850). King of France from 1830 to 1848. The 'bourgeois monarch'. Abdicated in the course of the 1848 upheavals.

LUXEMBURG, Rosa (1871–1919). Prominent German left-wing socialist of Polish extraction. Leading opponent of Bernstein's Revisionism. Author of *Social Reform or Revolution* and *The Accumulation of Capital*.

MEHRING, Franz (1846–1919). Eminent German Social Democrat and historian. Critic of Bernstein. Editor of the *Leipziger Volkszeitung* (1906–11). Co-founder of the German Communist Party. Author of *Geschichte der deutsche Sozialdemokratie* and *Karl Marx, the Story of his Life*.

MULHALL, Michael George (1836–1900). Irish statistician and journalist. Founded an English newspaper in Buenos Aires. Chiefly noted for his *Dictionary of Statistics*.

NIEUWENHUIS, Ferdinand Domela (1846–1919). Dutch socialist, co-founder of the Social Democratic Labour Party of the Netherlands, and member of parliament.

OWEN, Robert (1771–1858). Distinguished British utopian socialist. Indefatigable advocate of social reform along the lines pioneered by himself at New Lanark. Author of *A New View of Society*.

PARVUS (Helphand, Alexander L.) (1867–1924). Russian journalist and revolutionary socialist. Active in the German Social Democratic Party in the 1890s. As editor of the *Sächsische Arbeiter-Zeitung* (1896–

8), he mounted a sustained attack on Bernstein's position. Member of the Petersburg soviet in 1905. Turned against communism after the October Revolution of 1917.

PLEKHANOV, Georg Valentinovich (1857-1918). Eminent Russian Marxist and revolutionary. Helped found the League for the Emancipation of Labour in 1883. From 1883 till 1917 in exile in Geneva. Active in criticising Bernstein's philosophical position. When Russian Social Democracy split, he became the leading Menshevik theorist.

POTTER, Beatrice. See Webb.

PROUDHON, Pierre-Joseph (1809–65). French socialist and revolutionary. Active in Revolution of 1848. Several prison sentences. Object of Marx's critique, *The Poverty of Philosophy*. Author of *Qu'est-ce que la propriété?* and *Système des contradictions économiques*.

RICARDO, David (1772–1823). Eminent English political economist and businessman. Main work: *Principles of Political Economy and Taxation* (1817).

ROBESPIERRE, Maximilien Marie Isidore de (1758–94). French revolutionary, Jacobin leader, and effective head of government during the Terror. Elected to States General in 1789 and executed when he fell from power in 1794.

RODBERTUS-JAGETZOW, Johann Karl (1805–75). German economist, lawyer, and advocate of state socialism. Elected to Prussian National Assembly in 1848.

ROGERS, James Edwin Thorold (1823–90). English economist, became professor of political economy at Oxford in 1862. Liberal member of parliament (1880–6).

SAINT-SIMON, Claude Henri, Comte de (1760–1825). French utopian socialist. Author of *Du système industriel* and *Nouveau christianisme*.

SAY, Jean-Baptiste (1767–1832). French political economist, disciple of Adam Smith. Active in government during the French Revolution. Became professor at the College de France in 1831. Main work: *Traité d'économie politique* (1803).

SCHAPPER, Karl (1813–70). One of the leaders of the League of the Just, member of Central Committee of the Communist League. In

1850, he and Willich headed the 'left' faction of the League which opposed Marx. In 1865, became member of General Council of First International.

SCHMIDT, Conrad (1863–1932). German Social Democrat and journalist. Editor of *Vossische Zeitung*, associate editor of *Vorwärts*, one of the founders of *Sozialistische Monatshefte*. Early supporter of Bernstein's position.

SCHULZE-DELITZSCH, Franz Hermann (1808–83). Economist and leading member of the Progressive Party. Opponent of Lassalle and initiator of various self-help organisations in Germany.

SCHULZE-GAVERNITZ, Gerhard von (1864–1943). German economist, member of the liberal Progressive People's Party, Reichstag deputy (1912–20).

SISMONDI, Jean Charles Leonard Simonde de (1773–1842). Swiss historian and economist. Author of *Histoire des républiques italiennes du moyen âge* and *Nouveaux principes d'économie politique*.

STIEBELING, George C. American statistician and member of the Socialist Workers' Party of North America. Published several articles on economics and economic history.

STIRNER, Max (1806–56). German anarchist philosopher, advocate of extreme individualism. Author of *Der Einziger und das Eigentum*.

VANDELEUR, John Scott. Irish land-owner and follower of Robert Owen. Founded an Owenite agricultural cooperative on his estate at Ralahine in County Clare.

VANDERVELDE, Emile (1866–1938). Leader of the Belgian Labour Party and member of parliament. Prominent member of the Second International.

VOLLMAR, Georg von (1850–1922). German Social Democrat, journalist, and Reichstag deputy. In 1890s became a leading advocate of piecemeal reform and compromise.

WEBB, Beatrice (1858–1943) and Sidney (1859–1947). English social reformers, historians, and political economists. Married in 1892, they became leading members of the Fabian Society. Founded *The New Statesman*, helped establish the London School of Economics. Sidney was Labour member of parliament (1922–9), President of the Board of Trade (1924), and Colonial Secretary (1929). In 1929 he became Baron Passfield. Joint authors of *History of Trade Unionism* and *Industrial Democracy*.

WILLICH, August (1810–78). Prussian officer and revolutionary. Commander of volunteer corps in Baden insurrection of 1849, member of Central Committee of Communist League and, with Schapper, leader of the 'left' faction opposed to Marx.

WOLFF, Julius (1862–1937). German economist. Professor at Zurich and subsequently (1898) at Breslau.

ZETKIN, Clara Josephine (1857–1933). Radical socialist, schoolteacher, and leading member of the German Social Democratic Party. Editor of the women's journal, *Die Gleichheit*. In 1919, joined the newly founded German Communist Party.

Foreword

The main object of the present work is to provide support for the views the author developed in a letter to the German Social Democratic Party conference held at Stuttgart from 3 to 8 October 1898.[1]

This letter reads:

'The views I expressed in the series "Problems of Socialism" have recently been discussed in socialist papers and at socialist meetings; and the German Social Democratic Party conference has been asked to state its position with regard to them. In case this happens and the party conference complies with the request, I feel obliged to make the following statement.

'The vote of a meeting, whatever its status, obviously cannot dissuade me from the views I have formed in the course of an investigation into social phenomena. I stated my views in *Die Neue Zeit*, and I see no reason to depart from them in any important particular.

'It is, however, equally obvious that I cannot be indifferent to a vote of the party conference. It will therefore be understood that I am particularly anxious to defend myself against misrepresentations and erroneous conclusions drawn from my remarks. Since I am prevented from attending the conference myself, I hereby do this in the form of a written communication.

'Certain parties have asserted that the practical implication of my essays would be that we abandon the taking of political power by the politically and economically organised proletariat.

'That is an arbitrary conclusion and I emphatically dispute its accuracy.

'I have opposed the view that we stand on the threshold of an imminent collapse of bourgeois society, and that Social Democracy *should allow its tactics to be determined by, or made dependent upon, the prospect of any such forthcoming major catastrophe*. I stand by this view in every particular.

[1] *Protokoll*, 1898, pp. 122–6.

1

'Supporters of this catastrophe theory base their view largely on the arguments of *The Communist Manifesto*. They are wrong in every respect.

'The prognosis for the development of modern society outlined in *The Communist Manifesto* was correct insofar as it sketched the general tendencies of this development. It was, however, mistaken in various specific conclusions, notably in its estimate of the *length of time* which this development would require. This latter point has been recognised without reservation by Friedrich Engels, the co-author of the *Manifesto*, in his preface to *The Class Struggles in France*.[2] But it is obvious that if the development of the economy took very much longer than originally envisaged, it would also assume *forms* and produce structures which were not, and could not have been, foreseen in *The Communist Manifesto*.

'The intensification of social relations has not in fact occurred as the *Manifesto* depicts it. It is not only useless but extremely foolish to conceal this fact from ourselves. The number of property-owners has grown, not diminished. The enormous increase in social wealth has been accompanied not by a fall in the number of capitalist magnates but by an increase in the number of capitalists of all grades. The middle classes are changing in character, but they are not disappearing from the social spectrum.

'The concentration of industrial production has still not taken place with consistently equal intensity and speed across the board. It does indeed bear out the prophecies of socio-political criticism in a great many branches of production, but in other branches it still lags behind them. In *agriculture*, the process of concentration is taking place even more slowly. Industrial statistics show an extraordinarily wide and varied range of enterprises. No class of enterprises shows any sign of disappearing from the scale. Significant changes in the internal structure of these industries and in their interrelations cannot conceal this fact.

'Politically, in all the developed countries, we are seeing the privileges of the capitalist bourgeoisie gradually giving way to democratic institutions. Under the influence of these institutions and driven by the growing vitality of the labour movement, a social reaction has set in against the exploitative tendencies of capital. It is as yet timid and

[2] MESW, vol. I, p. 125. MEW, vol. XXII, p. 515.

tentative, but it is there, and more and more sectors of economic life are coming under its influence. Factory legislation, the democratisation of local government and the expansion of its activities, the removal of legal restrictions on trade unions and co-operative organisations, the consultation of labour organisations in all work contracted by public authorities, all are signs of this stage of development. The fact that Germany still considers the possibility of gagging the unions indicates not its advanced but its *retarded* political development.

'The more the political institutions of modern nations are democratised, the more the necessity and opportunity for great political catastrophes will be reduced. Anyone who stands by the theory of catastrophe must seize every opportunity to resist and restrict the development I have outlined, as indeed the consistent supporters of this theory once did. But must the proletariat take power only by means of a political catastrophe? And does this mean the appropriation and use of state power exclusively by the proletariat against the whole non-proletarian world?

'If anyone wants to say that it does, let me remind him of two things. In 1872, Marx and Engels stated in their preface to the new edition of *The Communist Manifesto* that the Paris Commune in particular had proved that "the working class cannot simply lay hold of the ready-made state machinery and wield it for its own purposes".[3] And in 1895, Friedrich Engels explained in detail, in his preface to *The Class Struggles*, that the time for surprise political attacks, or "revolutions carried through by small conscious minorities at the head of unconscious masses" had now passed and that a large-scale confrontation with the military would be the means of *delaying*, even reversing for a while, the steady growth of Social Democracy; in short, that Social Democracy would flourish "*far better on legal methods than on illegal methods and overthrow*".[4] Accordingly, he defines the immediate task of the party as "to keep this growth [in electoral support] going without interruption", i.e. "*slow propaganda work and parliamentary activity*".[5]

'Thus Engels who, as his statistical examples show, nonetheless managed to overestimate somewhat the speed with which things

---

[3] MESW, vol. I, p. 22. MEW, vol. XVIII, p. 96.
[4] MESW, vol. I, pp. 134 and 136. MEW, vol. XXII, pp. 523 and 525.
[5] MESW, vol. I, pp. 135 and 134. MEW, vol. XXII, pp. 524 and 523.

would develop. Shall we be told that, because he wished to avoid a situation in which the steady growth of Social Democracy secured by legal propaganda was interrupted by a political catastrophe, he abandoned the seizure of political power by the working class?

'If no such objection is raised and his remarks are endorsed, then there are no reasonable grounds for offence at the statement that the task of Social Democracy, for a long time to come, will be, not to speculate on the great collapse, but to "organise the working class politically, train it for democracy, and fight for any and all reforms in the state which are designed to raise the working class and make the state more democratic".[6]

'That is what I said in my impugned article and what I still maintain with all that it implies. As regards the matter in question, it amounts to the same thing as Engels's proposition, for democracy means that *at any given time the working class should rule to the extent permitted by its intellectual maturity and the current stage of its economic development.* Incidentally, in the place just mentioned, Engels explicitly refers to the fact that even *The Communist Manifesto* "proclaimed the winning of . . . democracy as one of the first and most important tasks of the militant proletariat".[7]

'In short, Engels is so thoroughly convinced that tactics geared to a catastrophe have had their day that he considers *a revision to abandon them* to be due even in the Latin countries where tradition is much more favourable to them than in Germany. "If the conditions of war between nations have changed", he writes, "no less have those for the war between classes."[8] Have we forgotten this already?

'Nobody ever questioned the necessity for the working class to fight for democracy. The quarrel is about the theory of collapse and the question of whether, given the present economic development of Germany and the degree of maturity of its urban and rural working class, Social Democracy would benefit from a sudden catastrophe. I have answered this question in the negative and I shall continue to do so, because in my view a steady advance offers a more secure guarantee of lasting success than the chances offered by a catastrophe.

'And as I am convinced that important stages in the development

---

[6] Bernstein, 'The Struggle of Social Democracy and the Social Revolution', Tudor and Tudor, p. 169.   [7] MESW, vol. I, p. 129. MEW, vol. XXII, p. 518.
[8] MESW, vol. I, p. 134. MEW, vol. XXII, p. 523.

of nations cannot be leapt over, I set the greatest possible store by the immediate tasks of Social Democracy, viz. the struggle for the political rights of the worker, the political activity of workers in towns and municipalities for the interests of their class, as well as the work of organising workers economically. It is in this spirit that, at one point, I penned the statement that the movement was everything to me, that what is *normally* called the final goal of socialism was nothing; and in this spirit I still endorse it today. Even if the word "normally" had not shown that the proposition was to be understood only conditionally, it was quite obvious that it *could* not express indifference towards the ultimate implementation of socialist principles, but only indifference – or, more correctly, lack of anxiety – to "how" things would ultimately take shape. At no time has my interest in the future gone beyond general principles, and detailed depictions of the future were never something I could read through to the end. It is present tasks and those of the immediate future which occupy my thoughts and energies; perspectives beyond that concern me only insofar as they suggest guidelines for the most effective action in this regard.

'The seizure of political power by the working class and the expropriation of the capitalists are not in themselves final goals but merely the means to achieve certain goals and fulfil certain aspirations. As such, they are demands in the programme of Social Democracy, and nobody questions them. The circumstances in which they will be fulfilled cannot be predicted. We can only fight for their realisation. But the taking of political power cannot be achieved without political *rights*, and the most important tactical problem which Social Democracy has to solve at the present is, it seems to me, *the best way to extend the political and industrial rights* of the German working man. Unless a satisfactory answer can be found to this question, stressing the other one is ultimately no more than rhetoric.'

This statement was followed by a brief polemical exchange between myself and Karl Kautsky, an exchange to which Victor Adler, in the *Wiener Arbeiterzeitung*, also contributed.[9] This induced me to make a further statement, published in *Vorwärts* on 23 October 1898, from which the following extract might be of interest:

'In *Vorwärts*, Karl Kautsky and Victor Adler, replying to my article "The Conquest of Political Power", expressed a view they had

[9] Bernstein, 'The Conquest of Political Power', Kautsky, 'Tactics and Principles', and Adler, 'The Party Conference at Stuttgart', in Tudor and Tudor, pp. 305–19.

already conveyed to me by letter, namely, that a comprehensive exposition, in book form, of the standpoint I developed in "Problems of Socialism" was much to be desired.[10] I have, until now, resisted the advice of these friends, because I took the view (which I still hold) that the drift of these articles is completely in line with the general development of Social Democracy. However, as they have now restated it in public, and as various other friends have expressed the same wish, I have decided to give effect to the suggestion and to develop my conception of the aim and the tasks of Social Democracy systematically in a book . . .

'Adler and others have taken offence because I held out the prospect of a relaxation in class conflict as democratic institutions develop; and they believe that I am seeing things through English spectacles. This is most definitely not the case. Even assuming that the proposition that "the more highly developed country shows the less developed an image of its own future"[11] has suddenly lost its validity, and also taking full account of the differences between developments in England and on the Continent (of which I am, after all, not altogether ignorant), my view still rests on manifestations on the Continent, which may at most have been temporarily lost sight of in the heat of battle, but which can not be ignored for long. Everywhere in the more advanced countries we see the class struggle assuming more moderate forms, and our prospects for the future would hold little hope if this were not the case. Needless to say, the general course of development does not rule out periodic setbacks. But if, for example, we consider the attitude towards strikes adopted by a growing proportion of the bourgeois public, even in Germany, if we think how many strikes, even there, are dealt with in a quite different and much more sensible manner than was the case ten or twenty years ago, then it can not be denied that there is progress to be recorded here. While this does not mean that "miracles will happen tomorrow" – to use Marx's phrase – it does, in my judgment, indicate a more hopeful path for the socialist movement than the one provided by the catastrophe theory; nor need it impair either the enthusiasm or the energy of the activist. I am sure that Adler will not disagree with me on this point.

'There was a time when my ideas would have met with no opposi-

---

[10] Ibid., pp. 312 and 314.   [11] *Capital* I, p. 91.

tion in the party. If things are different today, I see in this only an understandable reaction to certain current phenomena, which will pass away when these phenomena themselves disappear and leave room for a return to the awareness that, with the growth of democratic institutions, the more humane attitude, which is slowly but surely gaining ground in the rest of our social life, cannot fail to extend to the more significant conflicts between the classes but will ensure that they too manifest themselves in a more moderate form. Today we use ballot papers, demonstrations, and similar means of exerting pressure to accomplish reforms which a hundred years ago would have required bloody revolutions.'

'London, 20 October 1898'

The following work has been composed in the same spirit as these remarks.

I am well aware that it deviates in several important particulars from the views to be found in the theory of Karl Marx and Friedrich Engels – whose writings have exercised the greatest influence on my views as a socialist, and one of whom – Friedrich Engels – not only honoured me with his personal friendship until his death but also showed beyond the grave, in his testamentary arrangements, a proof of his confidence in me.[12] This difference in our ways of seeing things is not of recent date; it is the product of an inner struggle which lasted for years, and I have in my hand the proof that this was no secret to Friedrich Engels. Moreover, although I must protect Engels from the imputation that he had become so narrow-minded as to exact from his friends an unconditional adherence to his views, it will be understood from the foregoing why I have, until now, done everything possible to avoid expressing my disagreement as a critique of the doctrine propounded by Marx and Engels. Until now, this was all the easier because, as regards the practical questions at issue here, Marx and Engels themselves considerably modified their views in the course of time.

All that has changed. I now find myself in dispute with socialists who, like myself, have come from the school of Marx and Engels, and I must, if I am to defend my views, show them the points where the doctrine of Marx and Engels seems to me to be particularly erroneous or self-contradictory.

---

[12] Bernstein was named, along with Bebel, as Engels's literary executor.

I have not shunned this task, but, for the personal reasons already mentioned, I have not found it easy. I openly admit this in order to prevent the reader from reading any uncertainty in the subject-matter into the clumsy and hesitant form of the first chapter. I stand by what I have written with firm conviction. However, I have not always managed to find the precise form and arguments by means of which my thoughts would have gained the clearest expression. In this respect my work is far behind many a work published by others on the same subject. In the last chapter, I have rectified some omissions in the first chapters. Further, as the publication of the work was somewhat delayed, the chapter on cooperatives has undergone some additions in which repetitions could not wholly be avoided.

For the rest, the work may speak for itself. I am not so naive as to expect that it will forthwith convert those who have disagreed with my previous essays; nor am I so foolish as to demand that those who share my point of view in principle should subscribe to everything I have said. In fact, the most doubtful aspect of the work is that it encompasses too much. When I came to speak of the tasks facing us today, I was obliged, unless I wanted to embark on a sea of generalities, to enter into all kinds of detailed questions over which differences of opinion are unavoidable even among those who otherwise think alike. And yet, want of space compelled me to lay stress on certain main points by indicating rather than demonstrating them. However, I am not concerned that others should agree with me on every particular question. My concern, and the main purpose of this work, is to strengthen equally the realistic and the idealistic element in the socialist movement by opposing what remains of the utopian way of thinking in socialist theory.

London, January 1899

Ed. Bernstein

CHAPTER I

The basic tenets of Marxist socialism

(a) The scientific elements of Marxism

With these discoveries socialism became a science. The next thing was to work out all its details and relations.

Engels, *Anti-Dühring*

Today, German Social Democracy accepts as the theoretical basis of its activity the social doctrine which Marx and Engels worked out and called scientific socialism. That is to say that, although Social Democracy, as a fighting party, represents certain interests and tendencies, although it seeks to achieve *goals set by itself*, it does, in the final analysis, determine these goals in accordance with knowledge capable of objective proof, that is, knowledge which refers to, and conforms with, nothing but empirical experience and logic. For what is not capable of such proof is no longer science but rests on subjective impulses, on mere desire or opinion.

In any science, we can distinguish between pure theory and applied theory. The former consists of cognitive principles which are derived from the sum total of the relevant data and which are, therefore, regarded as universally valid. They are the constant element in the theory. An applied science is based on the application of these principles to particular phenomena or to particular cases of practice. The knowledge gained from this application, and put together in propositions, provides the principles of an applied science. These constitute the variable element in the system.

Constant and variable are, however, to be taken only conditionally. Even the principles of pure science are subject to changes which, however, occur mostly in the form of limitations. With the advancement of knowledge, propositions previously regarded as having absolute validity are recognised as conditional and are supplemented by new cognitive principles which, while limiting their validity, simultaneously extend the domain of pure science. Conversely, particular

9

propositions in applied science have continuing validity for certain cases. A principle in agricultural chemistry or electrical technology, insofar as it has been proved true, always remains correct, whenever the preconditions on which it rests are once again satisfied. But the great number of elements that enter into constituting these preconditions and their manifold possibilities of combination produce an infinite variety of such principles and a constant shifting of their importance in relation to one another. Practice creates ever new materials of knowledge and, so to speak, daily changes the picture as a whole, continually letting what were once new acquisitions slip into the category of obsolete methods.

A systematic extraction of the pure science of Marxist socialism from its applied part has not so far been attempted, although there is no lack of important preliminary work for it. Marx's well-known exposition of his conception of history in the preface to *A Contribution to the Critique of Political Economy* and the third part of Friedrich Engels's *Socialism, Utopian and Scientific* should be singled out as the most important statements. In the preface just mentioned, Marx presents the general features of his philosophy of history or society in propositions so concise, definite, and free of all reference to particular forms and phenomena that nowhere else has it been done with equal clarity. No essential thought in Marx's philosophy of history is omitted.

Engels's work is partly a more popular rendering of Marx's principles and partly an extension of them. Reference is made to particular phenomena in the development of modern society, characterised by Marx as bourgeois, and its further path of development is sketched in greater detail, so that in many places one can indeed speak of applied science. Certain of these details can therefore be removed without any damage to the basic theory. But as regards the main principles, the exposition remains sufficiently general to qualify for the pure science of Marxism. This is also warranted, and required, by the fact that Marxism purports to be more than an abstract theory of history. It purports to be also a theory of modern society and its development. If we are making hard-and-fast distinctions, we can indeed classify this part of Marxist theory as applied doctrine, but for Marxism it is an absolutely essential application, without which it would lose nearly all significance as a political science. The general or main propositions of this theory of modern society must therefore be ascribed to the pure doctrine of Marxism. Although the present order of society, with its legal basis in private property and free competition, is a particular case in the history of mankind, it is also a general and enduring fact for the present epoch of culture. Everything that is unconditional in the Marxist characterisation of bourgeois society and its course of development, that is, everything whose validity is free from national or local peculiarities, would accordingly belong in the domain of pure science. But everything which refers to facts and hypotheses which are conditional on a particular time or place, that is, all particular forms of development, would belong to applied science.

It has for some time been fashionable to discredit the more analytical investigations of Marxist theory by calling them scholastic. Such allegations are exceedingly facile and must therefore be treated with the greatest of caution. Conceptual investigation, the separation of the essential from the merely incidental, must ever be undertaken anew if concepts are not to become superficial and deductions ossified into pure dogma. Scholasticism not only furthered conceptual hair-splitting and acted as the handmaiden of orthodoxy; it also, inasmuch as it subjected theological doctrines to conceptual analysis, contributed a great deal to the discomfiture of dogmatism. It undermined the rampart which the teaching of orthodox doctrine raised against free philosophical investigation. The philosophies of Descartes and Spinoza flourished on the ground cleared by scholasticism. There are indeed different kinds of scholasticism: namely, apologetic and critical. It is the latter that has always been a bane to all orthodoxies.

If we distinguish the elements of Marx's system in the fashion mentioned above, we get a criterion for gauging the value of its individual propositions for the system as a whole. With every proposition of the pure science a portion of the foundation would be torn away and a great part of the whole building would be robbed of its support and would be ready to collapse. It is otherwise with the propositions of the applied science. These could be removed without shaking the foundations in the slightest. Indeed, whole series of propositions in the applied science could fall without affecting the other parts. It need only be shown that a mistake was made in the construction of the middle terms. Where no such mistake could be shown, the inevitable conclusion would, of course, be that there was a fault or a gap in the foundation.

However, such a systematic division in all its finer detail lies beyond the purpose of this work, for it is not intended to be an exhaustive exposition and critique of Marx's doctrine. For my purpose it suffices to identify the main parts of what, in my opinion, constitutes the structure of the pure science of Marxism: the above-mentioned programme of *historical materialism*, the general theory of *class conflict* (the seeds of which are already contained in the theory of historical materialism) and the particular theory of the class conflict between bourgeoisie and proletariat; also the *theory of surplus value* together with the theory of the *mode of production of bourgeois society* and, implicit in it, the theory of its developmental tendencies. Like the tenets of applied science, those of the pure science do, of course, vary in their value to the system as a whole.

No one will deny that the most important part in the foundation of Marxism, the basic law which, so to speak, penetrates the whole system, is the particular *theory of history* known as the materialist conception of history. In principle, Marxism stands or falls with this theory; and insofar as it suffers modification, the relationship of the other parts to each other will be affected. Any investigation into the correctness of Marxism must therefore start with the question whether or how far this theory is valid.

(b) The materialist conception of history and historical necessity

We had to emphasise the main principle *vis-à-vis* our adversaries, who denied it, and we had not always the time, the place or the opportunity to give their due to the other elements involved in the interaction.
Friedrich Engels: letter of 1890 reprinted in *Soz. Akademiker*, October 1895

The question of the correctness of the materialist conception of history is a question of the degree of historical necessity. To be a materialist means first of all to assert the necessity of all events. According to the materialist theory, matter moves of necessity in accordance with certain laws; there is therefore no cause without its necessary effect and no event without a material cause. However, since the movement of matter determines the formation of ideas and the directions of the will, these too are necessitated, as are all human events. The materialist is thus a Calvinist without God.[1] If he does not believe in a predestination ordained by a divinity, he does and must believe that from any particular point in time all subsequent events are, through the totality of the given material and the power relations of its parts, determined beforehand.

The application of materialism to the interpretation of history therefore means asserting, from the outset, the necessity of all historical events and developments. For the materialist, the only question is in what way necessity manifests itself in human history, what element of force or what factors of force speak the decisive word, what is the relationship of the various factors of force to one another, and what role in history falls to nature, the economy, legal institutions, and ideas.

Marx's answer, in the place already mentioned, is that he identifies people's current material *forces of production* and *relations of production* as the determining factors. 'The mode of production of material life conditions the general process of social, political, and intellectual life. It is not the consciousness of men that determines their existence, but their social existence that determines their consciousness. At a certain stage of development, the material productive forces of society come into conflict with the existing relations of production or – this merely expresses the same thing in legal terms – with the property relations within the framework of which they have operated hitherto. From forms of development of the productive forces these relations turn into their fetters. Then begins an era of social revolution. The changes in the economic foundation lead sooner or later to the transformation of the whole immense superstructure (the legal and political institutions to which correspond certain forms of social consciousness) . . . No social order is ever destroyed before all the productive forces for which it is sufficient have been developed, and new superior relations of production never replace older ones before the material conditions for their existence have matured within the framework of the old society . . . The bourgeois mode of production is the last antagonistic form of the social process of production . . . but the productive forces developing within bourgeois society create also the material conditions for a solution of this antagonism. The prehistory

[1] This reads like an unacknowledged quotation from Engels, but I can not trace the source.

13

of human society accordingly closes with this social formation' (*A Contribution to the Critique of Political Economy*, preface).

It must first be observed, by way of anticipation, that the concluding sentence and the word 'last' in the preceding sentence are not capable of proof but are hypotheses more or less well grounded. They are, however, not essential to the theory but belong, rather, to the application of it, and they can therefore be passed over here.

Looking at the other sentences, the most striking thing about them, apart from the phrase 'sooner or later' (which indeed hides a good deal), is their apodictic wording. Thus, in the second of the quoted sentences, 'consciousness' and 'existence' are so sharply opposed that we are nearly driven to conclude that human beings are regarded as nothing but the living agents of historical forces whose work they carry out against their knowledge and will. And this is only partly modified in a sentence (omitted here as being immaterial) which stresses the need to distinguish, in social revolutions, between the material revolution in the conditions of production and the 'ideological forms in which men become conscious of this conflict and fight it out'. All in all, the consciousness and will of human beings appear as factors decidedly subordinate to the material movement.

In the preface to the first volume of *Capital*, we come across a sentence which is no less deterministic in its wording. Referring to the 'natural laws' of capitalist production, it says: 'It is a question of these laws themselves, of these tendencies winning their way through and working themselves out with iron necessity.'[2] And yet, just after he has spoken of *law*, this rigid concept is replaced by a more flexible one, that of *tendency*. And then on the next page we find the often-quoted proposition that society can 'shorten and lessen' the birth-pangs of its natural phases of development.

The dependence of men on the relations of production appears much more qualified in the account of historical materialism given by Engels in his polemic against Dühring, a polemic written during the lifetime of Marx and in agreement with him. Here we read that 'the *ultimate causes* of all social transformations and political revolutions' are to be found not in the brains of men but in 'transformations of the mode of production and exchange'.[3] However, '*ultimate* causes' implies attendant causes of another kind, causes of the second and

---

[2] *Capital* I, p. 91.   [3] MECW, vol. XV, p. 254; MEW, vol. XX, p. 249.

third degree, etc., and it is clear that the longer the series of such causes the more limited, both qualitatively and quantitatively, is the determining force of the ultimate causes. The fact of its action remains, but the final shape of things does not depend on it alone. An effect which results from the operation of diverse forces can only be counted on with certainty if all the forces are exactly known and are given their full weight in the calculation. To ignore even a force of lower degree can, as every mathematician knows, result in the greatest of errors.

In his later works – mostly in two letters, one written in 1890, the other in 1894, and both published in the *Sozialistischen Akademiker* of October 1895 – Friedrich Engels limited the determining force of the conditions of production even further. Here, 'legal forms', political, juristic, and philosophical theories, religious ideas or dogmas are enumerated as influences which have an effect on the course of historical conflicts and in many cases '*predominate* in determining their *form*'. 'Thus there are', he says, 'innumerable intersecting forces, an infinite series of parallelograms of forces which give rise to one result – the historical event. This may again itself be viewed as the product of a power which works as a whole unconsciously and without volition. For what each individual wills is obstructed by everyone else, and what emerges is something that no one willed' (letter of 1890).[4] 'Political, juridical, philosophical, religious, literary, artistic, etc., development is based on economic development. But all these react upon one another and also upon the economic basis' (letter of 1895 [*sic*]).[5] One must confess that this sounds somewhat different from the passage from Marx quoted above.

It will, of course, not be maintained that Marx and Engels at any time overlooked the fact that non-economic factors exercise an influence on the course of history. Countless passages from their early writings can be quoted against any such suggestion. But it is a question of *degree* – not whether ideological factors are acknowledged, but what degree of influence, what historical significance, is ascribed to them. And in this regard, it absolutely can not be denied that Marx and Engels originally allowed the non-economic factors a much smaller part in the development of society, a much smaller reactive

[4] Engels to J. Bloch, 21–22. 9. 1890; MESC, p. 499; MEW, vol. XXXVII, p. 464.
[5] Engels to W. Borgius (not Starkenburg, as in MESC), 25 January 1894; MESC, p. 549; MEW, vol. XXXIX, p. 206.

effect on the relations of production, than in their later writings. This is in accordance with the natural course of development of every new theory. A new theory always first appears in sharp apodictic formulation. In order to make itself felt, it must demonstrate the untenability of the old theory, and in this struggle one-sidedness and exaggeration are unavoidable. In the sentence which we placed as a motto at the head of this section, Engels acknowledges this without reservation, and then he goes on to say: 'Unfortunately, however, it happens only too often that people think they have fully understood a new theory and can apply it without more ado from the moment they have assimilated its main principles . . . '[6] Whoever employs the materialist conception of history nowadays is duty bound to use it in its most developed and not in its original form. This means that, in addition to the development and influence of the forces of production and the relations of production, he is duty bound to take full account of the legal and moral concepts, the historical and religious traditions of every epoch, geographical and other natural influences, which include the nature of man himself and his intellectual dispositions.[a] This is to be kept in mind most particularly where it is a matter not just of pure research into earlier historical epochs, but of projecting future developments, where the materialist conception of history is to be a guide to the future.

In contrast to theories which treat human nature as something

---

[a] Needing to oppose the exaggerations of the materialist conception of history – most of which exist, indeed, only in his imagination – Mr Belfort Bax has invented a new conception of history which he calls the *synthetic* conception of history.[7] He has thus replaced a word which tends to encourage exaggeration with a word that is completely devoid of meaning. 'Synthetic' – comprehensive – is a purely formal concept of method, which, however, says absolutely nothing about the standpoint which governs the investigation. As shown above, even the materialist conception of history includes a synthesis of material and ideological forces. But if Bax prefers a meaningless expression to one that is liable to misinterpretation, then he is overtrumped on the other side by G. Plekhanov who, in his *Contributions towards the History of Materialism*, claims for the Marxist conception of history the title 'monistic' (cf. p. 227).[8] Why not rather just 'simplistic'?

[6] Engels to J. Bloch, 21–22. 9. 1890; MESC, p. 500; MEW, vol. XXXVII, p. 465.
[7] Belfort Bax first used the phrase, 'synthetic conception of history', in his controversy with Kautsky. See, for instance, his 'Synthetische contra neu-marxistische Geschichtsauffassung', *NZ*, 15, 1 (1896), 164–71.
[8] Bernstein is no doubt referring to the work better known as *The Development of the Monist View of History*. Georg Plekhanov, *Selected Philosophical Works* (Lawrence & Wishart, 1977), vol. I, pp. 486ff.

given and unchangeable, socialist criticism has quite rightly drawn attention to the great transformations which human nature has undergone in various countries in the course of time, and to the adaptability evinced by human beings of a particular epoch when they are placed in different circumstances. In fact, human nature is very resilient as regards the ability to adapt to new natural circumstances and a new social environment. But there is one thing we must not forget. Where it is a question of large masses of people, as in modern nations with their habits of living which have matured in the course of a development lasting thousands of years, even major changes in the ownership of property are unlikely to produce a rapid transformation of human nature, because economic and property relationships are only a part of the social environment which has a determining effect on human character. Here too a multitude of factors is to be taken into account; and in addition to the modes of production and exchange on which historical materialism lays the main emphasis, there is amongst other things the relation of territorial groupings and agglomerations, that is, the spatial distribution of the population and the transport system – which is indeed determined by the modes of production and exchange but which, once established, itself influences the situation in its own way.

In a letter to Conrad Schmidt dated 27 October 1890, Friedrich Engels showed in striking fashion how from being the products of economic development *social institutions* become *social forces* with an independent movement of their own, which may in their turn react upon the former and can, according to circumstances, help them, hinder them, or turn them into other channels. Taking *state power* as an example, in the first instance, he adds to his own preferred definition of the state as the organ of class rule and repression a very significant reduction of the state to the social *division of labour*.[b] So historical materialism by no means denies the autonomy of political and ideological forces; it denies only that this autonomy is unconditional and shows that, in the end, the development of the economic foundation of social life – the relations of production and the develop-

---

[b] In the *Origin of the Family* it is indeed shown in detail how the social division of labour makes the rise of the state necessary. But later Engels completely neglects this side of the origin of the state and in the end treats the state as merely the organ of political repression, as in *Anti-Dühring*.

ment of classes – exercises the greater influence on the movement of these forces.

But in any case the multiplicity of factors remains, and it is by no means always easy to display the connections between them with such precision that it is possible to determine with certainty where, in any particular case, the strongest impetus for the moment lies. The purely economic causes create, first of all, only a disposition for the reception of certain ideas, but how these then arise and spread and what form they take depends on the participation of a whole range of influences. We do historical materialism more harm than good if, from the outset, we superciliously reject as eclecticism any accentuation of influences other than those of a purely economic nature and any consideration of economic factors other than the techniques of production and their predicted development. Eclecticism – selecting from different explanations and ways of dealing with phenomena – is often only the natural reaction against the doctrinaire desire to derive everything from one thing and to treat everything according to one and the same method. Whenever this desire gets out of hand, eclecticism breaks through again and again with elemental force. It is the rebellion of sober reason against the inbuilt tendency of every doctrine to confine thought in a straitjacket.'

The more that forces other than purely economic ones influence social life, the more the sway of what we call historical necessity is altered. In modern society we must, in this connection, distinguish between two major currents. On the one hand, our understanding of the laws of development, and particularly of economic development, is on the increase. This knowledge is accompanied, partly as its cause but partly also as its effect, by a growing ability to *direct* economic

---

' Naturally, this should not be taken to deny either the tendency of eclecticism to be superficial or the great theoretical and practical value of striving for a unified understanding of things. Without this endeavour there can be no scientific thinking. But life is more comprehensive than any theory, and so strict doctrine must always in the end submit to taking secret loans from eclecticism, that frivolous person who brazenly strolls around the garden of life, and then strict doctrine repays these loans publicly by proclaiming afterwards that it has 'always basically' meant this or that.

> If heart and genius have achieved
> What Locke and Descartes ne'er conceived,
> These gentlemen will promptly prove
> The possibility of th'above.

In the history of the social sciences, a good example of this is provided by the history of the theory and practice of cooperative societies.

development. To the degree that their nature comes to be known, the economic forces of nature, like the physical, cease to be the master of mankind and become its servant. Society is, in theory, more free of economic causation than ever before, and only the conflict of interests among its elements – only the power of private and group interests – prevents the complete translation of this theoretical freedom into practice. But even here the general interest gains increasing strength as against private interest; and to the extent that this is the case, and wherever it is the case, the elemental power of economic forces disappears. Their development is anticipated and is therefore accomplished all the more quickly and easily. Individuals and whole nations thus remove an ever greater part of their life from the influence of a necessity which enforces itself without or against their will.

However, because men pay ever greater attention to economic factors, it can easily seem as if these factors play a greater role today than they did before. This, however, is not the case. The illusion arises only because nowadays the economic motive appears openly on the stage where before it was clothed in modes of social and political domination [*Herrschaftsverhältnisse*] and in all kinds of ideology. Modern society is much richer than earlier societies in ideologies which are not determined by economics or by nature working as an economic force.[4] The sciences, the arts, and a wide range of social relations are nowadays much less dependent on economics than at any other time. Or, to leave no room for misunderstanding, the level of economic development reached today leaves ideological

---

[4] Whoever regards that as paradoxical should remember that it was only in modern society that the most numerous class of the population began to count for anything at all in any ideology which is free in the sense described above. Previously, the rural population and workers were partly legally bound for economic purposes, partly under the influence of ideologies, which reflected the subjection of man to nature. As is well known, the latter is also the main feature of the ideologies (superstitions) of primitive peoples. So when Mr Belfort Bax in his article, 'Synthetic and Materialist Conception of History' (*Sozialistische Monatshefte*, December 1897), says that, while he concedes that in civilisation the economic factor has almost always been decisive, in the prehistoric period it has had little direct influence on speculative thought, that here 'the fundamental laws of human thought and sentiment' have been the determining factor, he turns everything on its head, even where superficial distinctions are concerned. For prehistoric peoples the *natural environment* was *the decisive economic* force and as such had the greatest influence on their thought and sentiment. One of the reasons why Bax's critique of historical materialism misses the mark is that he is ultra-orthodox precisely where the presentation of historical materialism was originally most exaggerated.

and especially ethical factors greater scope for independent activity than was formerly the case. In consequence, the causal connection between technical–economic development and the development of the other social institutions becomes increasingly a mediated one, and thus the natural necessities of the former become ever less decisive for the formation of the latter.

In this way, the 'iron necessity of history' is curtailed; and let me say at once that the consequence of this for Social Democratic practice is not to reduce our socio-political tasks but to *increase* and *qualify* them.

Thus the materialist conception of history as we have it today is different in form from when it was first presented by its originators. They themselves developed it; and they themselves placed limitations on its absolutist signification. Such is, as has been shown, the history of every theory. To retreat from the mature form Engels has given it in his letters to Conrad Schmidt and in those published in the *Sozialistische Akademiker* and to return to the earliest formulations in order to build a 'monistic' interpretation upon them would be a most retrograde step. The earliest formulations are, rather, to be amplified by these letters. The underlying idea of the theory loses nothing of its unity thereby, and the theory itself becomes more scientific. Indeed, only when amplified in this way does it become truly a theory of the scientific treatment of history. In its earliest form it could, in the hands of a Marx, become the instrument of magnificent historical discoveries; but it led even his genius into all kinds of false conclusions.' How much more, then, all those who have neither his genius nor his knowledge at their disposal! As a scientific basis for socialist theory, the materialist conception of history is nowadays valid only in the above-mentioned amplified form; and all applications of it made without, or with insufficient regard for the interaction of material and ideological forces to which it draws attention are to be

' 'It is', says Marx in a much-quoted passage from *Capital*, 'much easier to discover by analysis the earthly kernel of the misty creations of religion than to do the opposite, i.e. to develop from the actual, given relations of life the forms in which these have been apotheosised. The latter method is the only materialist, and therefore the only scientific one' (*Capital* I, 2nd edn, p. 386).[9] In this contrast there is great exaggeration. If one did not already know the apotheosised forms, the kind of development described would lead to all kinds of arbitrary constructions; and if one does know them, then the development depicted is a means of scientific analysis but not a scientific antithesis to analytical elucidation.

[9] *Capital* I, p. 494.

corrected accordingly, whether they are made by the originators of the theory or by others.

The above was already written when I received the October 1898 issue of *Deutschen Worte* containing an article by Wolfgang Heine on 'Paul Barth's Philosophy of History and his Objections to Marxism'. In it Heine defends the Marxist conception of history against the famous Leipzig don's accusation that, since materialism is reduced to technical–economic materialism, the designation 'economic conception of history' would be more appropriate. Against this remark he sets the letters Engels wrote in the 1890s, which we quoted above, and expands upon them with some remarkable observations of his own on the particular proofs of Marxism and on the origin, growth, and efficacy of ideologies. According to him, Marxist theory can concede more to [the influence of] ideology than it has done so far, without thereby forfeiting its conceptual coherence. Indeed, it must make such concessions, if it is to remain a scientific theory capable of giving an adequate account of the facts. It matters little whether Marxist writers have become mindful of the undeniable connection between transmitted ideas and new economic facts, or have emphasised them sufficiently; what is important is whether complete acknowledgment of it can be accommodated within the system of the materialist conception of history.

In principle, this formulation of the question is absolutely right. As always in science, we are, after all, dealing with a *boundary question*. Kautsky makes the same point in his essay, 'What Can the Materialist Conception of History Accomplish?'[10] But we must bear in mind that originally, so far from the question being limited in this way, an almost unlimited determining force was ascribed to the technical–economic factor in history.

Heine believes that in the end the question turns on the *quantitative* relationship of the determining factors, and he adds that it is a judgment of 'more practical than theoretical importance.'

I would suggest that we say 'as much . . . as' rather than 'more . . . than'. But I do share the view that it is a question of very great

---

[10] Karl Kautsky, 'Was will und kann die materialistische Geschichtsauffassung leisten?', *NZ*, 15, 1 (1896), 213–18, 228–38, and 260–71. This was Kautsky's main counterblast to Belfort Bax's 'Die materialistische Geschichtsauffassung', *Die Zeit*, no. 93 (July 1896).

practical importance. It is of very great practical significance to bring propositions formulated on the basis of an excessive emphasis on the technical – economic determining factors in history into line with the known quantitative relationship of other factors. It is not sufficient that practice rectifies theory. If theory is to have any value at all, it must know how to recognise the significance of the rectification.

Finally, the question arises as to how far the materialist conception of history has a claim to its name, if we continue to widen it through the inclusion of other variables in the above-mentioned manner. In fact, according to Engels's explanations, it is not purely materialist, much less purely economic. I do not deny that the name does not completely fit the object. But I seek progress not in making concepts confused but in making them precise; and since, in characterising a theory of history, what matters most of all is to show wherein it differs from other theories, I would, far from taking offence at Barth's title, 'the economic conception of history', consider it, in spite of every-thing, as the most appropriate description of the Marxist theory of history.

Its significance rests on the stress it places on economics. From its recognition and evaluation of economic facts arise its great achievements for the science of history, as does the enrichment which this branch of human knowledge owes to it. An economic conception of history need not mean that only economic forces, only economic motives, are recognised. It need only mean that economics constitute the ever-recurring decisive force, the pivot on which the great move-ments in history turn. To the words 'materialist conception of history' cling all the misunderstandings which are attached to the concept of materialism. Philosophical materialism, or the materialism of the nat-ural sciences, is deterministic. The Marxist conception of history is not. It assigns to the economic basis of national life no unconditional determining influence on the forms which that life takes.

(c) The Marxist doctrine of class conflict and the development of capital

The doctrine of class conflict rests on the foundation of the material-ist conception of history. 'It was seen', wrote Engels in his *Anti-Dühring*, 'that *ᶠ all* past history was the history of class struggles; that

---

ᶠ The fourth edition of the work *Socialism, Utopian and Scientific* adds the following qualifying words: 'with the exception of primitive societies'.

these warring classes of society are always the products of the modes of production and of exchange – in a word, of the *economic* conditions of their time' (3rd edn, p. 12).[11] In modern society, it is the class conflict between the capitalist owners of the means of production and the producers without capital, the wage labourers, which in this respect makes its mark. Marx took the expressions 'bourgeoisie' for the former class and 'proletariat' for the latter from France where, at the time he was working out his theory, they had already become current amongst socialists. This class conflict between bourgeoisie and proletariat is the antagonism in contemporary relations of production transferred to the *human* sphere, namely, the antagonism between the *private* character of the mode of *appropriation* and the *social* character of the mode of *production*. The means of production are the property of individual capitalists, who take for themselves the proceeds of production; production itself, however, has become a *social* process, that is, a production of goods for use made by *many* workers on the basis of a systematic division and organisation of labour. Inherent in, or additional to, this antagonism is another: the systematic division and organisation of labour within the institutions of production (workshops, factories, factory complexes, etc.) stands opposed to the unsystematic disposal of products on the market.

The starting point of the class conflict between capitalists and workers is the conflict of interests which results from the use which the former make of the latter's labour. The investigation of this process of utilisation leads to the theory of *value* and of the production and appropriation of *surplus value*.

It is characteristic of capitalist production and the social order resting on it that, in their economic relationships, men are opposed to one another throughout as buyers and sellers. It recognises in social life no formal legal relations of dependence but only actual ones resulting from purely economic relationships (differences in property, wage relationships, etc). The labourer sells his labour power to the capitalist for a definite period of time and under definite conditions for a definite price, the wage. The capitalist sells the products produced with the help of the worker – that is, the totality of the workers employed by him – in the market at a price which as a rule, and as a condition of the advancement of his enterprise, yields a surplus over and above the amount it cost him to produce them. What, then, is this surplus?

[11] MEWC, vol. XXV, p. 26; MEW, vol. XX, p. 25.

According to Marx, it is the *surplus value* of the labour the worker has performed. The goods are exchanged in the market at a value which is determined by the labour embodied in them, measured according to time. What the capitalist put into production by way of past – we could even say dead – labour in the form of raw materials, auxiliary materials, depreciation of machinery, rent, and other expenses appears again unchanged in the value of the product. It is otherwise with the living labour employed. This cost the capitalist the wage which is exceeded by the proceeds of the labour employed, those proceeds being equivalent to the value of the labour. The labour value is the value of the *quantity* of labour worked into the product; the wage is the price of the labour *power* used in the process of production. The price, or the value of the labour power, is determined by the cost of the worker's subsistence, which corresponds with his historically developed way of life. The difference between the equivalent (the proceeds) of the labour value and the wage is the *surplus value* which it is the natural endeavour of the capitalist to increase as much as possible and, in any case, not to allow to fall.

But competition in the market exerts constant pressure on the prices of commodities, and time and again an increase in sales can be achieved only by reducing the costs of production. The capitalist can achieve this reduction of costs in three ways: by lowering wages, by increasing the hours of work, or by raising the productivity of labour. As there are always definite limits to the first two, his energies are perpetually concentrated on the third. Better organisation and consolidation of labour and improvements in machinery are, in developed capitalist society, the principal means of reducing the costs of production. In all these cases, the consequence is that the *organic composition of capital*, as Marx calls it, is changed. The proportion of capital invested in raw materials, machinery, etc., increases, and the proportion invested in wages decreases; the same quantity of commodities is produced by fewer workers, an increased amount by the old or even by a smaller number of workers. Marx calls the ratio of surplus value to the portion of capital laid out in wages the *rate of surplus value* or of exploitation; the ratio of surplus value to the total capital invested in production he calls the *rate of profit*. It is evident from what has been said that the rate of surplus value can rise while at the same time the rate of profit declines.

We will find that the organic composition of capital will vary

according to the nature of the branch of production. There are enterprises in which a disproportionately large portion of capital is laid
out on machinery, raw materials, etc., and only a relatively small
portion on wages, and others in which wages form the most important
part of the capital outlay. The former represent higher, the latter
lower organic compositions of capital. If the proportional relationship
between wages and the surplus value achieved was the same everywhere, then the rates of profit in the latter branches of production
would necessarily be many times greater than those in the former.
That however is not the case. In fact, in a developed capitalist society
commodities are sold not at their labour value but at the *cost of their
production* which consists of the costs incurred (wages plus the dead
labour used) and an additional charge corresponding to the average
profit on the total production of society or to the rate of profit in that
branch of production in which the organic composition of capital
shows an average ratio of wage capital to capital otherwise employed.
The prices of commodities in different branches of production do
not, therefore, move in the same way in relation to the values of those
commodities. In some, they are permanently far below value and in
others they are permanently above it; only in those branches of production with a medium organic composition of capital do prices
approximate to value. The law of value disappears completely from
the consciousness of producers; it operates only behind their backs,
and it governs the level of the average rate of profit only in the long
term.

The coercive laws of competition and the growing capital wealth
of society tend to produce a steady decline in the rate of profit,
which is delayed but not permanently halted by countervailing forces.
Overproduction of capital goes hand in hand with the creation of a
surplus of workers. Ever greater centralisation spreads throughout
industry, trade, and agriculture; and the expropriation of small capitalists by bigger capitalists becomes increasingly intense. Periodic
crises, brought about by the anarchy in production in conjunction
with underconsumption by the masses, occur with increasing violence
and destructiveness and hasten the process of centralisation and
expropriation by the ruin of innumerable small capitalists. On the
one hand, the collective – cooperative – form of the labour process
becomes general on a steadily growing scale; on the other hand, 'with
the constant decrease in the number of capitalist magnates, who

usurp and monopolise all the advantages of this process of transformation, the mass of misery, oppression, slavery, degradation and exploitation grows; but with this there also grows the revolt of the working class, a class constantly increasing in numbers, and trained, united, and organised by the very mechanism of the capitalist process of production'.[12] Thus the development moves toward a point where the monopoly of capital becomes a fetter upon the mode of production which has flourished alongside it, where the centralisation of the means of production and the socialisation of labour become incompatible with their capitalist integument. This integument is then burst asunder; the expropriators and usurpers are expropriated by the mass of the people; capitalist property is abolished.

This, according to Marx, is the historical tendency of the capitalist mode of production and appropriation. The class which is called upon to carry out the expropriation of the capitalist class and the transformation of capitalist property into public property is the class of wage labourers, the proletariat. For this purpose, the class must be organised as a political party. At a given moment, this class seizes political power and 'turns the means of production in the first instance into state property. But, in doing this, it abolishes itself as proletariat, abolishes all class distinctions and antagonisms, abolishes also the state as state.' The struggle for individual existence with its conflicts and excesses, comes to an end; the state has nothing more to repress and it 'dies out' (Engels, *Socialism, Utopian and Scientific*).[13]

These are, in the briefest possible summary, the most important propositions of that part of Marxist doctrine which is to be included in the pure theory of Marxist socialism. No more, or rather, even less than the materialist theory of history has this part of the theory sprung from the beginning fully formed from the heads of its authors. Even more than in the former case, we can point to a development of the doctrine which, while preserving the main points of view, consists in the modification of propositions originally presented in an apodictic manner. This transformation of the doctrine was in part acknowledged by Marx and Engels themselves. Some of the changes that took place in the course of time in the views of Marx and Engels on various relevant issues are indicated in the preface to *Capital*

[12] *Capital* I, p. 929.
[13] MECW, vol. XXV, p. 267; MEW, vol. XX, p. 261.

(1867), in the preface to the new edition of *The Communist Manifesto* (1872), in the preface and a note to the new edition of *The Poverty of Philosophy* (1884), and in the preface to *The Class Struggles in the French Revolution* (1895). However, not all the changes identified there and elsewhere with regard to particular parts or presuppositions of the theory receive full consideration in its final elaboration. To take just one example. Concerning the revolutionary programme developed in *The Communist Manifesto*, Marx and Engels remark, in the preface to the new edition: 'In view of the gigantic strides of Modern Industry in the last twenty-five years, and of the accompanying improved and extended party organisation of the working class, in view of the practical experience gained, first in the February Revolution, and then, still more, in the Paris Commune, where the proletariat for the first time held political power for two whole months, this programme has in some details become antiquated. One thing especially was proved by the Commune, viz., that "the working class cannot simply lay hold of the ready-made State machinery, and wield it for its own purposes".'[14] That was written in 1872. But five years later, in the polemic against Dühring, it says quite simply: 'The proletariat seizes political power and turns the means of production in the first instance into state property'. (1st edn p. 233; 3rd edn p. 302).[15] And in the new edition of *Revelations concerning the Communist Trial* (1885) Engels reprints the revolutionary programme of 1848 drawn up on the basis of the old conception, as well as the address of the executive of the Communist League which was conceived in the same spirit. On the former he merely remarks laconically that we 'can still learn a lot from it today' and, on the latter, that 'much that is said in it still holds good nowadays' (p. 14).[16] Now, we can refer to the words 'in the first instance', 'a lot', and 'much' and suggest that the propositions are to be understood only conditionally, but this, as we shall see, does not improve matters. Marx and Engels confined themselves partly just to indicating, and partly to establishing only with reference to particular points, the repercussions which acknowledged changes in the facts – and better knowledge of the facts – must have for the shaping and application of the theory. Even so, there is no lack of contradictions in their work. They have

[14] MECW, vol. XXIII, p. 175; MEW, vol. XVIII, p. 96.
[15] MECW, vol. XXV, p. 26; MEW, vol. XX, p. 25.
[16] MESW, vol. II, p. 349; MEW, vol. XXI, p. 216.

27

left to their successors the task of restoring unity to the theory and of establishing unity between theory and practice.

However, this task can be performed only if we give a full and frank account of the gaps and contradictions in the theory. In other words, the *further development and elaboration of Marxist doctrine must begin with criticism of it.* The position nowadays is that one can prove *everything* out of Marx and Engels. This is very convenient for apologists and literary pettyfoggers. But he who has retained just a little bit of theoretical awareness, he for whom the scientific character of socialism is not 'just a showpiece which is taken out of the sideboard on festive occasions but otherwise is not taken into consideration', will, as soon as he becomes aware of these contradictions, feel the need to remove them. The duty of their disciples consists in this, and not in perpetually repeating the words of the masters.

It is in this spirit that the following critique of certain elements of Marxist doctrine will be undertaken. The desire to keep within reasonable bounds a book intended primarily for workers, together with the need to finish it within a few weeks, should explain why an exhaustive treatment of the subject has not even been attempted. At the same time, let it be said once for all that I claim no originality for my critique. Most if not all of what follows has, in substance, already been worked out, or at least suggested, by others. To that extent, the justification of this book is not that it discloses something hitherto unknown but that it acknowledges what has already been disclosed.

But that too has to be done. It was, I believe, Marx himself who once remarked with reference to the fate of theories: 'The Moor's beloved can perish only by the hand of the Moor'.[17] Thus the errors of a doctrine can be considered as overcome only when they are recognised as such by the doctrine's own advocates. Such recognition does not necessarily mean the destruction of the doctrine. It could, rather, turn out that, with the amputation of acknowledged errors, it is – if I may be permitted the use of a Lassallean image – Marx who in the end carries the point against Marx.

---

[17] Not, so far as I can tell, in any of his published works or his correspondence. It is obviously a reference to Shakespeare's *Othello*. In his family circle, Marx's nickname was 'Moor'.

28

CHAPTER 2

Marxism and the Hegelian dialectic

(a) The pitfalls of the Hegelian dialectical method

> In the course of lengthy debates often lasting all night, I infected
> him to his great injury with Hegelianism.
>
> Karl Marx on Proudhon[1]

In their original form, the Marxist conception of history and the
socialist theory which rests upon it were worked out between 1844
and 1847, years when Western and Central Europe were in a state
of great revolutionary ferment. They could be described as the most
radical product of this epoch.

In Germany, this period was the epoch of mounting bourgeois
liberalism. Here, as in other countries, the ideological representation
of the class opposing the establishment far exceeded the practical
requirements of that class. The bourgeoisie – by which I mean the
broad stratum of non-feudal classes standing outside the wage relation – fought against the still semi-feudal state absolutism; its philosophical representation began with absolute rule in order to end with
state rule.

The philosophical current which, in this respect, found its most
radical representative in Max Stirner is known as the radical left wing
of Hegelian philosophy. As Friedrich Engels remarked – like Marx,
he came under its influence for a certain time; they both associated
with the 'Free' at Hippel's wine bar in Berlin – the proponents of
this tendency rejected the Hegelian system, only to fall all the more
under the spell of its dialectic until first the practical struggle against
positive religion (then an important aspect of the political struggle)
and second the influence of Ludwig Feuerbach drove them into an
unreserved acceptance of materialism. However, Marx and Engels
did not remain with Feuerbach's materialism, which was still the

---

[1] MESC, p. 187; MEW, vol. XVI, p. 27.

materialism of the natural sciences, but, influenced by the class war between the bourgeoisie and the working class being waged in France and even more ferociously in England, they developed their theory of historical materialism, using a dialectic stripped of its mystical character.

Engels has stressed with considerable force the role of the dialectical method in the genesis of this theory. Following the example of Hegel, he distinguishes between the metaphysical and the dialectical view of things. He explains the former as that which treats things or their thought-images, their concepts, in isolation as objects fixed and given for all time. The latter, by contrast, regards things in their connections, changes, and transitions, with the result that the two poles of an antagonism, like positive and negative, mutually penetrate one another, all their opposition notwithstanding. However, while Hegel conceives dialectic as the self-development of the concept, with Marx and Engels himself the dialectic of the concept becomes the conscious reflection of the dialectical movement of the real world, and thus the Hegelian dialectic, from standing 'on its head', is once again 'placed upon its feet'.

Thus Engels in his work *Ludwig Feuerbach and the End of Classical Philosophy.*[2]

But placing the dialectic 'upon its feet' is not as simple as that. However things may stand in reality, as soon as we leave the solid ground of empirically verifiable facts and think beyond them, we enter the world of derived concepts, and if we then follow the laws of dialectics, as laid down by Hegel, we will, before we know it, find ourselves once again enmeshed in 'the self-development of the concept'. Herein lies the great scientific danger of the Hegelian logic of contradiction. Its principles may, under certain circumstances, serve very well to clarify the connections and developments of real objects.[a] They may also have been of great use in the formulation

---

[a] Although there too it often obscures rather than illuminates the actual state of affairs. Thus the fact that a change in the quantitative relationships of the components of some object or other changes its characteristics is at best very obliquely and superficially expressed by the principle, 'transformation of quantity into quality'.

It may incidentally be noted that I adopt Engels's definitions of the concepts, metaphysical understanding and dialectical understanding, with the reservation that the qualifying words 'metaphysical' and 'dialectical' in the sense attached to them are valid only for the purposes of this comparison. Otherwise, seeing things metaphysically and

[2] MESW, vol. II, p. 387; MEW, vol. XXI, pp. 292–3.

of scientific problems and have provided the impetus for important discoveries. However, as soon as developments are deductively anticipated on the basis of these principles, the danger of arbitrary construction begins. The more complex the object whose development is in question, the greater this danger becomes. When we are dealing with a fairly simple object, experience and reasoned judgment usually ensure that analogies such as 'the negation of the negation' do not mislead us into inherently improbable deductions about its potential transformations. But the more complex an object is, the greater the number of its elements, the more varied their nature and the more diverse their force relations, the less such principles can tell us about its development because all moderation of judgment is lost from view in proportion that deductions are based upon them.

This is not to say that the Hegelian dialectic has no merit at all. On the contrary, as regards its influence on historiography, F. A. Lange may well have put it most aptly when, in *The Labour Question*, he said that the Hegelian philosophy of history and its basic idea of development through antagonisms and their resolution, 'could almost be called an anthropological discovery'. But Lange immediately laid his finger on the weak point 'almost' when he added that 'as in the life of the individual, so also in history, development through antagonism is accomplished neither as easily and radically nor with the same precision and symmetry as it is in speculative construction' (3rd edn, pp. 248–9).[3] Any Marxist nowadays would agree with this as regards the past; but for the future, even for the very near future, Marxist theory holds that this does not apply. In 1847, *The Communist Manifesto* declared that, given the stage of development reached by the proletariat and the advanced conditions of European civilisation, the bourgeois revolution, on which Germany was embarking, 'will be but the prelude to an immediately following proletarian revolution'.[4]

seeing them as fixed and isolated items are, in my view, two completely different things.

Finally, it should be made clear at this point that it would, of course, never occur to me to criticise Hegel himself or to deny the great services which this distinguished thinker has performed for science. I am only dealing with his dialectic, insofar as it has had an influence on socialist theory.

[3] Bernstein had published an analysis and appreciation of Lange's work as early as 1892 ('Zur Würdigung Friedrich Albert Langes', *NZ*, 10, 2 (1892), 68–78, 101–9, and 132–41). For his intellectual debt to Lange, see Thomas Meyer, *Bernstein's konstruktiver Sozialismus* (Berlin, 1977), pp. 114ff.

[4] MECW, vol. VI, p. 519; MEW, vol. IV, p. 493.

In someone like Marx, who had already devoted serious study to economics, such historical self-deception – and a run-of-the-mill political visionary could hardly do better – would have been incomprehensible if it were not seen as resulting from a remnant of Hegelian contradiction dialectics. To the end of his days Marx, like Engels, never completely got rid of it, but at that particular time of general ferment it was all the more fatal to him. Here we have not just the over-estimation of the prospects of a political action, which can occur in charismatic leaders and has, on occasion, helped them achieve surprising successes, but a purely speculative anticipation of the maturation of an *economic* and *social* development which had hardly shown its first shoots. What was to require generations to accomplish became, when viewed in the light of the philosophy of development in and from antagonisms, the direct result of a *political* upheaval which had first to provide the bourgeois class with free space in which to develop. And when Marx and Engels, a mere two years after writing the *Manifesto*, found it necessary – due to the split in the Communist League – to draw the attention of their opponents in the League to 'the underdeveloped state of the German proletariat' and to protest at 'the aura of sanctity with which the word proletariat is endowed' (*The Communist Trial in Cologne*, p. 21),[5] it was primarily no more than the result of a temporary disillusionment. The same contradiction between actual and postulated maturation of development was to be repeated several times in other forms.

As we are concerned with a point which, in my opinion, has become the most fateful for the doctrine of Marx and Engels, we may be permitted to cite an example drawn from the very recent past.

In a polemical exchange with a Southern German Social Democratic publication, Franz Mehring recently reprinted in the *Leipziger Volkszeitung* a passage from the preface to the second edition of Friedrich Engels's work *On the Housing Question*, where Engels speaks of 'the existence of a certain petty-bourgeois socialism' in German Social Democracy, which can be found 'even in the ranks of the Reichstag group'. Here Engels identifies the petty-bourgeois character of this tendency in the fact that, while it recognises the fundamental views of modern socialism as justified, it postpones their implementation to the distant future, with the consequence that 'for

---

[5] MECW, vol. XI, p. 403; MEW, vol. VIII, p. 413.

the present one has to have recourse to mere social patchwork'. Engels declared this tendency to be quite understandable in Germany, but harmless in view of 'the wonderful common sense' of the German working man.[6] Mehring makes a connection between these statements and the dispute over steamship subventions which had arisen amongst German Social Democrats shortly before the statements were published, and he depicts it as 'the first major controversy over practical politics and proletarian revolutionary tactics in the party'. He adds that what Engels says in the passage in question is what the representatives of the proletarian revolutionary tendency, amongst whom he counts himself, 'think and want': confrontation with what are there called 'petty-bourgeois socialists'.

It can not be denied that Mehring interprets the relevant passage from Engels correctly. That is how Engels saw the situation at the time, in January 1887. And fifteen months previously, he had included in the new edition of *Revelations Concerning the Communist Trial in Cologne* the two circulars which he and Marx had composed in March and June 1850 and which proclaim 'the revolution in permanence' as the policy of the revolutionary proletariat. In the preface he remarked that much that was said there applied also to the imminent 'European upheaval'. The war of 1870–1 was put forward as the most recent convulsion of this kind.[7] And in our century, the period of maturation for European revolutions was fifteen to eighteen years.

That was written in 1885–7. A few years later, a conflict with the so-called Youngsters arose in German Social Democracy. Having simmered for some time, it was brought to the boil in 1890 by the matter of celebrating 1 May by taking a holiday from work. Today nobody would deny that most of the Youngsters honestly believed that they were acting in the spirit of Engels when they opposed the then current 'opportunism' of the parliamentary party. When they attacked the majority of the parliamentary party for being 'petty bourgeois', who was their authority for this, if not Engels? These were, after all, the same people who had constituted the opportunistic majority on the issue of steamship subventions. However, when the then editors of the *Sächsische Arbeiter-Zeitung* finally cited Engels in support of their views, the reply, as Mehring knows, turned out to be of a quite different tenor from that of the passage which he quotes.

[6] MESW, vol. I, pp. 549–50; MEW, vol. XXI, pp. 328–9.
[7] MESW, vol. II, p. 353; MEW, vol. XXI, p. 220.

Engels declared the Youngsters' movement to be merely a 'literary and student revolt', castigated their 'convulsive and distorted Marxism', and declared that their criticisms of the parliamentary party amounted at best to trivialities; the *Sächsische Arbeiter-Zeitung* could hope as long as it liked that the good sense of the German worker would prevail over the addiction to parliamentary success in Social Democracy; he, Engels, would not join them in this hope, and he was not aware of any such majority in the party.[8]

Engels was only following his own convictions in writing this statement, as nobody knows better than the author of these pages. The movement of the 'Youngsters' – which was after all also a movement of workers, and indeed of workers who, under the anti-socialist laws, had belonged to the most active party propagandists – struck him as being a revolt contrived by radicalising intellectuals; and the policy they recommended struck him as so damaging at that particular time that, by comparison, the 'petty-bourgeois' activities in the parliamentary group did indeed appear no more than trivialities.

But, however politically meritorious the 'Reply' published in the *Sozialdemokrat* of 13 September 1890 might have been, it is doubtful whether Engels was wholly justified in shaking the Youngsters from his coat-tails in this fashion. If the European revolution was as close at hand as he had claimed in the preface to the *Revelations* – and by the reckoning he used there, its maturation period had by now been completed – and if the tactics outlined in the circulars were still valid in principle, then the Youngsters were flesh of his flesh and blood of his blood on the main issue. But if not, then the fault lay less with the Youngsters than with the writings tossed into the propaganda campaign in 1885 and 1887 together with the above-mentioned appendices and the ambivalent supplements. However, this ambivalence, so utterly out of character for Engels, was ultimately rooted in the dialectic taken over from Hegel. Its 'yes, no and no, yes' instead of 'yes, yes and no, no', its antagonisms flowing into one another, its transformation of quantity into quality, and all such other dialectical delights, time and again got in the way of a proper assessment of the significance of observed changes. If the original scheme of development constructed by Hegel was to be maintained, then either reality would have to be reinterpreted or all real proportion would have to

[8] 'Antwort an die Redaktion der *Sächsischen Arbeiter-Zeitung*', published in *Der Sozialdemokrat*, 13 September 1890 (MEW, vol. XXII, pp. 68–70).

be ignored in measuring the road to the desired goal. Hence the contradiction: painstaking precision befitting the busy industry of genius in investigating the economic structure of society goes hand in hand with an almost incredible neglect of the most palpable facts; the very same theory that takes the determining influence of economics on power as its starting point concludes with a truly miraculous belief in the creative power of force; and the theoretical elevation of socialism into a science is so frequently 'transformed' into the subordination of any claim to scientific status to a preconceived tendency.

If nothing else, it is surely wholly unscientific to determine the standpoint of a politician or a theorist simply by reference to the view he takes of the speed at which the course of social development proceeds. The identification of the concept 'proletarian' with the idea of direct and immediate resolution of antagonisms amounts to a very impoverished interpretation of this concept. On this view, the crass, the coarse, and the narrow-minded would be 'proletarian'. If belief in the shortly to be expected revolutionary catastrophe is what makes a revolutionary socialist, then it is the putsch-revolutionaries who, more than anyone else, have a right to be so called. In a scientific doctrine there ought to be at least some rational criterion for drawing the line between the visionary dreamer at one end and the petty bourgeois at the other. But there was no question of this; the evaluation remained a matter of pure caprice. Just as things appear smaller as they are viewed from a greater distance, so in practice a remarkable fact generally manifests itself: we find the most 'petty-bourgeois' attitudes, in the sense defined above, among people who actually belong to the working class and who are in the closest contact with the real proletarian movement, whereas people who belong to the bourgeoisie or enjoy bourgeois living conditions, and who either have no contact whatever with the workers' world or who know it only through political meetings inevitably tuned to strike a certain note, positively overflow with revolutionary proletarian sentiment.

In the preface to *The Class Struggles*, written towards the end of his life, Engels acknowledged unreservedly the error which he and Marx had committed in estimating the time which social and political development would take. We can not praise too highly the service he rendered to the socialist movement by this work, which is rightly described as his political testament. There is more in it than lies on

35

the surface. However, the preface was not the place to follow up all the implications of so candid an admission, nor could Engels by any means be expected to undertake the necessary revision of the theory himself. Had he done so, he would without fail have had to come to terms with Hegelian dialectic, if not in so many words, then certainly with the thing itself. It is the treacherous element in Marxist doctrine, the pitfall that lies in the way of any logical consideration of things. Engels either could not or would not transcend it. He drew the consequences of his new awareness only with respect to certain methods and forms of political struggle. However significant what he has to say in this connection may be, it nevertheless covers only some of the questions raised.

It is, for instance, clear that nowadays we must view the political conflicts, on which Marx and Engels have left us monographic studies, from a perspective different from theirs. The self-deceptions they entertained about the course of events mean that their judgment on parties and persons could not be wholly accurate and their policy not always correct, despite the marked realism of their approach. There would be no practical value in correcting them subsequently, were it not for the fact that it is precisely in socialist historiography of recent times that their texts as preserved have played so great a part, and that these early conflicts in particular are constantly cited as examples.

However, what is more important than the revision which modern socialist historiography has to make, according to Engels's preface, is the revision which it implies for the whole conception of the struggle and the tasks of Social Democracy. And this brings us first to a point so far only rarely discussed, namely, the original inner connection between Marxism and Blanquism and the dissolution of this bond.

(b) Marxism and Blanquism

> When the nation has already exhausted its resources; when the country is devoid of commerce and industry; when the workers, demoralised by club politics and factory stoppages, enlist as soldiers in order just to survive ... Then you will know what a revolution is, a revolution evoked by lawyers, accomplished by artists, and led by novelists and poets. Awake from your slumbers, Montagnards, Feuillants, Cordeliers, Muscadins, Fansonists,

and Babouvists. You are not six weeks away from the events I foretell.

Proudhon in *Représentant du Peuple*, 29 April 1848

Various authors have characterised Hegelian philosophy as a reflex of the great French Revolution; and indeed it can, with its antagonistic developments of reason [*Vernunft*], be described as the ideological counterpart of those great conflicts, in which, according to Hegel, 'man took his stand on his head, that is, on thought'.[9] In the Hegelian system, the development of political reason culminated, of course, in the Prussian enlightened police-state of the restoration. However, a year before Hegel's death, the restoration gave way in France to the bourgeois monarchy; a radical impulse once again passed through Europe, which eventually led to increasingly violent attacks on the bourgeois monarchy and on the class whose champion it was: the bourgeoisie. The Empire and the restoration now seemed to the radical representatives of the new movement to be no more than interruptions in the ascending course of development of the great revolution; the bourgeois monarchy had marked a return to the old course, which, in view of the changed social conditions, should henceforth no longer encounter the obstacle which interrupted the course of the French Revolution.

The most radical product of the great French Revolution had been the movement of Babeuf and the Equals. Their traditions were taken over by the secret revolutionary societies which came into being under Louis-Philippe and from which the Blanquist party later emerged. Their programme was the overthrow of the bourgeoisie by the proletariat by means of violent expropriation. In the February Revolution of 1848, the club revolutionaries were called 'Babouvists' and the 'Barbès party' as often as they were called after the man who had in the meantime become their spiritual leader, Auguste Blanqui.

In Germany, Marx and Engels, working on the basis of the radical Hegelian dialectic, arrived at a doctrine very similar to Blanquism. The heirs of the bourgeoisie could only be their most radical counterpart, the proletarians, that intrinsic social product of the bourgeois economy. Following the nowadays unjustly despised socio-critical

[9] G. W. F. Hegel, *The Philosophy of History*, trans. J. Sibree (New York, 1956), p. 447. As Sibree's translation of this passage leaves something to be desired, I have made my own.

37

works of the socialists of the school of Owen, Fourier, and Saint-Simon, they based this on economic-materialistic arguments, but within materialism, by contrast, they argued in Hegelian fashion. The modern proletariat, which for the Saint-Simonians had already played the same role as the peasant had for the school of Rousseau in the previous century, was wholly idealised in their theory, especially as regards its historical potentialities, but also in its abilities and propensities. In this fashion, they arrived, despite their more thorough philosophical training, at the same political position as the Babouvist secret leaguers. Partial revolution is utopian, only the proletarian revolution is still possible, argued Marx in the *Deutsch-französische Jahrbucher* (see the essay, 'Contribution to the Critique of Hegel's Philosophy of Law').[10] This position led directly to Blanquism.

In Germany, Blanquism is viewed only as the theory of secret leagues and the political putsch, as the doctrine of the launching of revolution by a small, purposeful party acting in accordance with well-laid plans. That view, however, stops short at externals and applies, at most, to certain epigones of Blanquism. Blanquism is more like the theory of a method; its method, on the other hand, is merely the outcome, the product of its deeper, underlying political theory. And this is quite simply the theory of the immeasurable creative power of revolutionary political force and its manifestation, revolutionary expropriation. The method is partly a matter of circumstances. Where there is no freedom of association and of the press, secret leagues are obviously appropriate; and where, in a revolutionary upheaval, the country is *de facto* governed by a central political authority, as was the case in France until 1848, a putsch, insofar as only certain experiences were taken into account, was less irrational than the Germans seem to think.[b] To reject putschs does not therefore amount to liberating oneself from Blanquism. Nothing shows this more clearly than the study of the relevant writings by Marx and Engels from the time of the Communist League. Apart from the rejection of putschs, they are permeated throughout with what is, in the last analysis, a Blanquist or Babouvist spirit. In *The Communist*

For the record of Blanquism includes not only failures but also some very significant temporary successes. The proclamations of a republic in 1848 and 1870 were to a high degree due to the intervention of Blanquist social revolutionaries. On the other hand, June 1848 and May 1871 were, in the final analysis, Blanquist failures.

[10] MECW, vol. III, pp. 175ff; MEW, vol. I, pp. 378ff.

Manifesto, it is significant that of all socialist literature only the writings of Babeuf escape criticism; all that is said of them is that, in the great Revolution, they 'expressed the demands of the proletariat', in any case an anachronistic characterisation.[11] The programme of revolutionary action in the *Manifesto* is Blanquist through and through. In *The Class Struggles*, in *The Eighteenth Brumaire*, and particularly in the circular to the Communist League, the Blanquists are presented as *the* proletarian party – 'the really proletarian party' says the circular of June 1850 – a designation in no way based on the social composition of this party but solely on its revolutionary character.[12] The proletarian party of France, in 1848, was the workers grouped around the Luxemburg. The same consideration determines the party position on the warring factions within the Chartist camp.[r] In the account of the course of events in France, in *The Class Struggles* and in *Brumaire*, the masterly analysis of the forces actually at work is interwoven with the already well developed legend of the Blanquists. But nowhere does the Blanquist spirit find such sharp and unconstrained expression as in the circular to the Communist League of March 1850 with its exact instructions as to how the Communists, in the imminent re-eruption of the Revolution, must draw on every possible resource to make this revolution 'permanent'.[13] All theoretical insight into the nature of the modern economy, all knowledge of the current state of the economic development of Germany, which was still far behind that of France at the time – Marx wrote of it then that 'the struggle of the industrial worker against the industrial bourgeois is only a partial fact' – all economic understanding vanishes to nothing before a programme so illusory it could have been set up by any run-of-the-mill club revolutionary. What Marx reproached Willich and Schapper for six months later – that instead of real conditions they made 'mere will into the driving force of the revolution'[14] – was what he and Engels themselves proclaimed at that time.

---

[r] Under 'England' the circular states with a certain satisfaction that the break between the revolutionaries and the moderate group of Chartists was 'essentially expedited by the delegates of the (Communist) League'. It is very doubtful whether the complete defeat of Chartism would have been avoided without that break. But the satisfaction over the happily achieved break is genuinely Blanquist.

[11] MECW, vol. VI, p. 514; MEW, vol. IV, p. 489.
[12] MECW, vol. X, p. 377; MEW, vol. VII, p. 312.
[13] MECW, vol. X, p. 281; MEW, vol. VII, pp. 247–8.
[14] I can not find the source of this reference.

The requirements of modern economic life were totally disregarded, and the relative strengths of classes and their state of development were completely overlooked. Yet proletarian terrorism – which given the state of things in Germany could only manifest itself as such destructively and, therefore, from the first day when it was set to work in the specified fashion *against* bourgeois democracy its effect was inevitably politically and economically reactionary – was extolled as a miraculous force which was to propel the conditions of production to that level of development perceived as the precondition for the socialist transformation of society.

In criticising the circular, we should in fairness remember that it was written in exile and at a time when the passions roused by the victory of the reaction were running at their highest. This natural excitement may well explain certain exaggerations with regard to the imminence of the revolutionary backlash – expectations which, by the way, Marx and Engels very soon abandoned – as well as certain extravagances of presentation, but it can not explain that glaring opposition between programme and reality. This was not the product of a passing mood – to excuse it in this fashion would be to do the authors of the circular an historical injustice – it was the product of an intellectual defect, of a dualism in their theory.

In the modern socialist movement, we can distinguish two main streams which appear at various times in various guises and often in opposition to one another. The one starts from the proposals for reform worked out by socialist thinkers and is in the main aimed at *construction*; the other derives its inspiration from popular revolutionary upheavals and is in the main aimed at *destruction*. According to the possibilities inherent in the conditions of the time, the former appears as *utopian, sectarian, peacefully evolutionary*; the latter as *conspiratorial, demagogic, terroristic*. The closer we get to the present, the more clearly the slogans emerge, on the one side, as emancipation through *economic organisation*, and on the other, as emancipation through *political expropriation*. In earlier centuries, the first tendency was represented for the most part only by isolated thinkers and the latter by occasional popular movements. By the first half of this century, permanently active groups were established on both sides; on the one, the socialist sects as well as all manner of workers' associations, and on the other, revolutionary societies of every kind. There was no lack of attempts to unite them, and the conflicts between them were not always absolute. So when *The Communist Manifesto* claimed that the Fourierists of France reacted against the reformers of the time, and the Owenites of England against the Chartists,[15] that is only completely true of the extremes on either side. The majority of Owenites were entirely in favour of political reform – we need only call to mind men like Lloyd Jones – but they opposed the cult of force as promoted by the more radical Chartists – the 'physical force men' – and withdrew wherever the latter got the upper hand. Similarly with the supporters of Fourier in France.

Marx's theory tried to combine the essentials of both streams. From the revolutionaries it took the conception of the workers' struggle for emancipation as a political class struggle, and from the socialists it took the investigation into the economic and social pre-conditions for the emancipation of the workers. However, this combination was not a solution of the conflict but rather a compromise like the one Engels suggested to the English socialists in *The Condition of the Working Class*: the subordination of the specifically socialist element to the politically radical social-revolutionary element.[16] And whatever further development Marx's theory underwent later, it retained at bottom the character of this compromise, that is, of dualism. It is here we should seek the explanation for the fact that Marxism repeatedly and at frequent intervals appears in a different guise. These are not differences of a kind which, for any fighting party, are produced as changing circumstances require changing tactics; they are differences which appear spontaneously without any compelling external necessity, merely as the product of inner contradictions.

Marxism has superseded Blanquism in just one respect, namely, method. But in another respect, the overestimation of the creative power of revolutionary force for the socialist transformation of modern society, it has never completely freed itself from the Blanquist point of view. The corrections it has introduced – for instance, tighter centralisation of revolutionary power – concern form rather than substance.

In the article from which we took a few sentences as a motto at the head of this chapter, and in which Proudhon, in his own way, predicts the June battle almost to the day, he reproaches the Paris workers who had been influenced in and by the clubs with the fact

[15] MECW, vol. VI, p. 517; MEW, vol. IV, p. 492.
[16] MECW, vol. IV, pp. 524ff; MEW, vol. II, pp. 450ff.

that, as the economic revolution of the nineteenth century is fundamentally different from that of the eighteenth century, the traditions
of 1793, which were incessantly preached to them in the clubs, were
in no way appropriate to the conditions of the time. The Terror of
1793, he explains, in no way threatened the living conditions of the
overwhelming mass of the population. In the year 1848, however, the
reign of terror would see two large classes in collision with one
another. As both were dependent on the circulation of products and
the reciprocity of relations, the collision between them would mean
the ruin of all.

It was expressed with Proudhonistic exaggeration, but considering
the economic structure of France at the time, it hit the nail on the
head.

In France in 1789–94, more than nine-tenths of production and
exchange was limited to local markets; thanks to the low differentiation of the economy in rural areas, the internal national market
played a very subordinate role. So far as the industrial classes were
concerned, the Terror did indeed ruin individuals and occasionally
certain local industries, but however severe it was it affected national
economic life only very indirectly. No section of the classes engaged
in production and commerce was as such threatened by it; the country
was thus able to endure it for a considerable period, and the wounds
which it inflicted on the country were quickly healed. In the year
1848, by contrast, the uncertainty into which the composition of the
provisional government and the emergence and conduct of the seem-
ingly all-powerful clubs threw the business world meant increasing
closures of business enterprises and paralysis of trade and commerce.
Each aggravation of this state of affairs and each day it was prolonged
meant yet further ruin, yet more unemployment, and threatened the
whole business population of the towns, and to some extent also that
of the open countryside, with enormous losses. There could be no
question of a socio-political expropriation of large and small capitalist
heads of production; industry was not sufficiently developed for such
a move, and no organisations which could take their place were available. It would only have been possible to replace one individual with
some other individual, or with a group of individuals, which would
have done nothing to change the social composition of the country
or to improve the condition of the economy. Experienced business
managers would have been replaced by newcomers with all the weak-

nesses of dilettantism. In short, a policy modelled on the Terror of 1793 would have been the most senseless and futile imaginable; and because it was senseless, it was more than merely silly to don the costumes and to revive and surpass the language of 1793. Precisely because a political revolution was in progress, this policy was a crime for which thousands of workers would soon enough have to atone with their lives, and further thousands with their liberty. For all its grotesque exaggerations, the warning of the 'petty-bourgeois' Proudhon therefore evinced a degree of insight and moral courage, in the midst of the Saturnalia of revolutionary bombast, which placed him politically high above the literati, artists, and other bourgeois bohemians who draped themselves in the 'proletarian-revolutionary' mantle and yearned for new Prairials. Almost simultaneously, Marx and Proudhon – the former in *The Class Struggles*, the latter in *The Confessions of a Revolutionary* – described the course of the February Revolution as an historical process in which each major episode represented a defeat for the revolution. However, unlike Proudhon, Marx saw the revolutionary progress precisely in the initiation of the counter-revolution. Only in combat with the latter, he wrote, will the party of overthrow mature into a really revolutionary party.[17] Marx quickly realised that he had deceived himself in estimating the time involved – for here it is a question of revolutionary in the political sense – but he seems never to have recognised fully the error of principle on which this supposition is based, and neither did Engels expose it in his preface to *The Class Struggles*.

Time and again Marx and Engels started by presupposing a revolution which, whatever the changes in its content, would in form follow a course similar to the revolutions of the seventeenth and eighteenth centuries. That is to say, a progressive, radical bourgeois party would first take the helm with the revolutionary workers as a criticising and propelling force behind it. When it had run its course, a yet more radical bourgeois or petty-bourgeois party would probably emerge until the road to the socialist revolution had been completely levelled and the moment had come for the seizure of power by the revolutionary party of the proletariat. Just as this thought finds expression in the circular of March 1850, so it reappears very clearly in 1887 in the preface to *Revelations on the Communist Trial* which says that in

[17] MECW, vol. X, p. 47; MEW, vol. VII, p. 11.

Germany in the next European upheaval, 'petty bourgeois democracy
... *must certainly be the first to come to power*'.[18] The 'certainly' here
was not so much the result of an objective evaluation as an indication
of the course of development considered *necessary* for the successful
rule of Social Democracy. Statements made by Engels orally and in
his letters leave no room for doubt on this point. And indeed, once the
presuppositions are granted, this train of thought is entirely rational.

However, it is precisely the presuppositions that are open to question. All the indications are that, in advanced European countries, a
political revolution which would initially bring a radical bourgeois
party to power is a thing of the past. Modern revolutions have the
tendency to put the most radical of all possible political combinations
at the helm from the very beginning. This was already the case in
France in 1848. The provisional government at that time was the
most radical of the even temporarily possible governments of France.
Even Blanqui realised this, and for that reason, on 26 February, he
vehemently opposed the intention of his followers to disperse the
'treasonable government' and replace it with a genuinely revolutionary one. Likewise, on 15 May, when the revolutionary populace,
having invaded the chamber, proclaimed a government consisting of
him and other revolutionaries and socialists, he made no attempt to
establish himself in the town hall, unlike the 'chivalrous' enthusiast
Barbès, but went quietly home. His political keen-sightedness tri-
umphed over his revolutionary ideology. Just as in 1848, so it went
with the proclamation of the republic in 1870; the Blanquists forced
the proclamation of the republic, but only bourgeois radicals took
part in the government. By contrast, in March 1871, when under the
influence of Blanquist social revolutionaries it came to a rebellion
against the government established by the national assembly, and the
Commune was proclaimed, a different phenomenon emerged: the
bourgeois and petty-bourgeois radicals withdrew, leaving the field
and the political responsibility to the socialists and revolutionaries.

All the indications are that any uprising in the advanced countries
in the near future will take this form. The bourgeois classes in these
countries are no longer in the slightest degree revolutionary, and the
working class is already too powerful to be able to confine itself to
critical opposition after a victorious uprising which it has won for

[18] MESW, vol. II, p. 353; MEW, vol. XXI, p. 220.

itself. Particularly in Germany, the progress of party development up till now means that on the day after a revolution anything but a Social Democratic government would be an impossibility. A purely bourgeois radical government would not last a day, and a compromise government composed of bourgeois democrats and socialists would, for all practical purposes, mean either that a couple of the former were included as decoration in a socialist government or that Social Democracy had surrendered to bourgeois democracy. At a time of revolution, this is surely a most improbable combination.

We may safely assume that considerations of this kind came into play when Engels, in the preface to *The Class Struggles*, extolled universal suffrage and parliamentary activity with unprecedented emphasis as means to the emancipation of the workers and dismissed the idea of seizing political power by revolutionary assaults.[19]

That was a further rejection of Blanquist, albeit modernised Blanquist, ideas. But the question is nonetheless examined exclusively with reference to its importance for Social Democracy as a *political party*. The poor prospect for future uprisings of conscious minorities is demonstrated on the grounds of changed military and strategic conditions; and the participation of the masses, enlightened as to the character of the complete transformation of the social order to be taken in hand, is stressed as an unavoidable precondition for implementing this transformation. However, that covers only the *external means* and the *will*, the *ideology*. The *material* basis of the socialist revolution remains unexamined; the old formula, 'appropriation of the means of production and exchange', reappears unchanged; there is not a single word to indicate that, or whether, anything at all has been altered in the economic preconditions for the transformation of the means of production into state property by means of a great revolutionary act. Only the *how* of *winning* political power is revised; as regards the *possible economic utilisation* of political power, the old doctrine derived from 1793 and 1796 is retained.

Wholly in accordance with this conception, Marx, in 1848 in *The Class Struggles*, had written: 'Public credit and private credit are the economic thermometer by which the intensity of a revolution can be measured. *The more they fall, the more the fervour and generative power of the revolution rise.*'[20] An authentic Hegelian proposition and one

[19] MESW, vol. I, pp. 118ff; MEW, vol. XXII, pp. 509ff.
[20] MECW, vol. X, p. 59; MEW, vol. VII, p. 23.

most illuminating to all minds nourished on a Hegelian diet. However, there is always a point at which ardour ceases to be productive and operates only as a destructive and devastating force. As soon as that point is passed, retrogression rather than progression sets in – the reverse of the original purpose. It is on this that the Blanquist tactic has always foundered in history, even when it was initially victorious. Here, not in the putsch theory, is its weakest point, and it is precisely here that it has never been criticised from the Marxist side.

This is no coincidence. For here criticism of Blanquism would have become self-criticism of Marxism – self-criticism not just of a few superficialities but of very substantial components of its theoretical structure. Above all, as we see here again, of its dialectic. Every time we see the doctrine which proceeds from the economy as the basis of historical development capitulate before the theory which stretches the cult of force to its limits, we find a Hegelian principle. Perhaps only as an analogy, but that makes things worse. The great illusion of Hegelian dialectic is that it is never entirely in the wrong. It squints towards the truth like a will-o'-the-wisp towards the light. It does not contradict itself because, on its own account, everything carries its contradiction within itself. Is it a contradiction to put force in the place so recently occupied by the economy? Oh no it isn't, because force is itself 'an economic power'!

No sensible person will deny the relative correctness of the latter proposition. But if we raise the question as to how and when force as an economic power operates in such a way as to achieve the desired result, then the Hegelian dialectic leaves us in the lurch; then we have to deal with concrete facts and precisely – 'metaphysically' – defined concepts, if we are not to commit the grossest blunders. The logical somersaults of Hegelianism have a shimmer of radicality and wit about them. Like the will-o'-the-wisp, it shows us the prospects ahead in uncertain outline. But as soon as we choose our path in reliance upon it, we invariably land in the swamp. The great things Marx and Engels achieved were achieved not because of Hegelian dialectic but in spite of it. When, on the other hand, they heedlessly passed over the grossest errors of Blanquism, it is primarily the Hegelian element in their own theory that is to blame.

CHAPTER 3

The economic development of modern society

(a) Remarks on the meaning of Marx's theory of value

And from this, incidentally, follows the moral that at times there is a drawback to the popular demand of the workers for 'the full proceeds of labour.'

Engels, *Anti-Dühring*[1]

As we have seen, surplus value is, according to Marx's theory, the pivot of a capitalist society's economy. But to understand surplus value we must first know what value is. Marx's account of the nature and course of development of capitalist society therefore begins with the analysis of value.

According to Marx, the value of commodities in modern society consists in the socially necessary labour expended upon them, measured by time. However, this measure of value necessitates a number of abstractions and reductions. To begin with, pure exchange value must be developed, that is, abstracted from the particular use value of individual commodities. Then, in forming the concept of general or abstract human labour, we must set aside the peculiarities of particular kinds of labour (reducing higher or complex labour to simple or abstract labour). Then, in order to get the socially necessary labour time as the measure of the value of labour, we must set aside differences in the diligence, ability, and equipment of individual workers; and further, when we come to convert value into market value or price, we must set aside the socially necessary labour time required for the particular commodities taken separately. But even the labour value thus derived requires yet another abstraction. In a developed capitalist society, commodities, as has already been mentioned, are sold not at their individual values but at the cost of production, that

[1] MECW, vol. XXV, p. 187; MEW, vol. XX, p. 187.

47

is, the actual cost price, plus an average proportional rate of profit, the level of which is determined by the ratio of the total value of social production to the total wage of the human labour power expended in production, exchange, etc., ground rent having been deducted from the total value of social production and account having been taken of the distribution of capital into industrial, commercial, and bank capital.

So far as individual commodities or categories of commodities are concerned, value is thus bereft of all concrete content and becomes a purely mental construct. But what becomes of 'surplus value' under these circumstances? According to Marx's theory, it consists in the difference between the labour value of products and the payment for the labour *power* expended in their production by the workers. It is therefore clear that, as soon as labour value can claim validity only as an intellectual formula or scientific hypothesis, surplus value becomes all the more a mere formula, a formula which rests on a hypothesis.

As is well known, Friedrich Engels, in an essay posthumously published in *Die Neue Zeit* (1895–6), pointed out a solution to the problem through a historical consideration of the process.[2] According to this essay, the law of value did actually have direct validity, did actually directly govern the exchange of commodities in the period of commodity exchange preceding the capitalist economy. As long as the means of production belong to the producers themselves, be it a matter of natural communities exchanging their surplus product or of self-employed farmers and craftsmen bringing their products to market, it is the labour value of these products about which their price oscillates. But as capital – initially as commercial capital and merchant's capital, then as manufacturing capital, and finally as big industrial capital – inserts itself between the actual producer and the consumer, labour value increasingly vanishes from the surface, and the price of production comes to the fore. The above-mentioned abstractions are intellectual reiterations of processes which have taken place in history and which even today produce after-effects and in fact recur in certain cases and in certain forms. Labour value remains a reality, even if it no longer directly governs the movement of prices.

Engels seeks to demonstrate this in detail from economic history,

[2] 'Wertgesetz und Profitrate', *NZ*, 14, 1 (1895–6), 6–11 and 37–44.

with reference to a passage in the third volume of *Capital*.[3] But however brilliantly he exposes the rise and development of the rate of profit, the article lacks compelling demonstrative force precisely where it deals with the question of value. According to Engels's account, Marx's law of value is supposed to have prevailed generally as an economic law for between five and seven thousand years, from when the exchange of products as commodities began (in Babylonia, Egypt, etc.) until the advent of capitalist production. In the self-same volume of *Die Neue Zeit*, Parvus raised some telling objections to this view by pointing to a number of facts (feudal relationships, undifferentiated agriculture, guild and other monopolies) which hindered the formation of a general exchange value based on the labour time of the producers.[4] It is quite clear that exchange based on labour value cannot be a general rule as long as production for exchange, the utilisation of excess labour, etc., is only a secondary feature of the economic unit, and as long as the circumstances in which the producers take part in the exchange are fundamentally different. The problem of labour constituting exchange value, and thus the problem of value and surplus value, is no clearer at that economic stage than it is today.

But what was more clearly evident at that stage than it is today is the fact of *surplus labour*. When surplus labour was performed in antiquity and in the Middle Ages, there was no deception about it; it was not obscured by any representation of value. When the slave had to produce for exchange, he was a simple surplus labour machine; the serf and the bondsman performed surplus labour in the open form of compulsory service and taxes in kind, for example, tithes. The journeyman attached to a guildmaster could easily see what his work cost his master, and how much he charged his customer for it.[a] This transparency of the relationship between the wage of labour and the price of commodities persists even on the threshold of the capitalist era. Many passages that surprise us in the political-economic

---

[a] Even nowadays surplus labour appears undisguised wherever pre-capitalist methods of industry have survived into modern times. The employee of a small builder who performs a piece of work for a customer knows quite well that his hour's wage is so much less than the price which the master puts in his account for the hour's work done. The same is true for the tailor or gardener, etc., who carries out orders for individual customers.

[3] *Capital* III, pp. 1,037ff.
[4] Pv, 'Der Terminhandel und die Getreidepreise', *NZ*, 14, 1 (1895–6), 718–22.

literature of that time, passages about surplus labour and labour as the sole begetter of wealth, are thus explained. What now appears to us to be the product of profound observation was at the time almost a commonplace. It never occurred to the rich of that epoch to represent their wealth as the fruit of their own labour. At the beginning of the manufacturing period, the increasingly widespread theory of labour as the measure of (exchange) value certainly starts from the conception of labour as the sole begetter of wealth and still thinks of value in very concrete terms; but it does more to confuse than to clarify conceptions of surplus labour. How, on the basis of these conceptions, Adam Smith later represented profit and ground rent as deductions from labour value, how Ricardo further elaborated this idea, and how socialists turned it against the bourgeois economy, we can gather from Marx himself.

However, already in Adam Smith, labour value is conceived as an abstraction from given realities. It is real in the full sense of the term only in 'that early and rude state of society' which precedes the accumulation of capital and the appropriation of land, and also in backward industries. In the capitalist world, by contrast, profit and rent are, for Smith, constituent elements of value in addition to labour, that is wages; and labour value serves him only as a 'concept' to disclose the distribution of the products of labour, that is, the fact of *surplus labour.*[5]

It is, in principle, no different in Marx's system. Marx certainly clings more firmly than Smith to the concept of labour value, which he conceives in a stricter but also more abstract fashion. However, while Marxists, including the present author, believed that a point of fundamental importance for the system was the passionately discussed question as to whether the attribute of 'socially necessary labour time' related only to the *manner* in which the commodities in question were produced or also to the relation between the *quantity* of these goods produced and effective demand, a solution already lay completed in Marx's desk. It gave a quite different complexion to this and other questions, and moved it into a different area and onto a different plane. The value of individual commodities or kinds of commodity now becomes quite secondary, since commodities are sold

---

[5] Adam Smith, *An Inquiry into the Nature and Causes of the Wealth of Nations*, book I, chapter vi. Bernstein seems to have misunderstood Smith's argument. Smith was arguing that profit and rent are component parts of prices, not values.

at their production price – cost of production plus rate of profit. What takes first place is the *value of the total production of society* and the surplus of *this* value over the sum total of the wages of the working class, that is, not the individual but the *entire social surplus value*. What the totality of workers at a given moment produces over and above the portion which they themselves receive constitutes the social surplus value, the surplus value of social production, which individual capitalists share in approximately equal proportion according to the capital they have invested. However, this surplus product is realised only insofar as total production corresponds to total demand, that is, the ability of the market to absorb it. From this point of view, that is, taking *production as a whole*, the value of every single kind of commodity is determined by the labour time which was necessary to produce it under normal conditions of production and in that quantity which the market, that is, the whole community regarded as consumers, can absorb at that time. Now, in reality there is no measure for the total demand at any given time for precisely the commodities under consideration; and so value conceived as above is a purely abstract entity, no less than the marginal utility value of the school of Gossen, Jevons, and Böhm-Bawerk.[6] Both are based on real relations, but both are built up on abstractions.[b]

---

[b] We find an interesting attempt to give labour value a more concrete content, or to transform it into a theoretically measurable quantity, in Leo von Buch's book, *Intensity of Labour, Value, and the Price of Commodities* (Leipzig, Duncker & Humblot, 1896). The author, who was clearly not aware of the third volume of *Capital* when he composed his work, constructs as the measure of the amount of labour value the *marginal intensity* of labour, a product of the relationship of the daily hours worked to the eight-hour day and the relationship of the actual wage to the value of the product of the labour (the rate of exploitation). The shorter the working day and the lower the rate of exploitation, the higher the intensity of labour and hence the labour value of the product. Accordingly, Buch tells us, no exploitation takes place on the basis of labour value. This comes only from the relationship of labour value to the market value of the product, which is the basis of the price, which Buch calls the *assessment value*, rejecting the term exchange value because it is meaningless nowadays where nothing is exchanged.

However strange the theory seems at first glance, it has one point in its favour: because Buch makes a fundamental distinction between labour value and market value, he avoids any conceptual dualism and is able to develop the former in a purer and more rigorous fashion. The only question is whether it was not an anticipation to bring the latter 'value' into the determination of labour value. What Buch wanted to do, namely, to give labour value as opposed to market value a *physiological* basis, could also

[6] H. H. Gossen and W. S. Jevons were (together with C. Menger and L. Walras) responsible for developing the marginal utility theory of value. E. von Böhm-Bawerk extended the theory, but he also used it to combat the growing influence of Marxism.

Such abstractions are, naturally, unavoidable in the treatment of complex phenomena. How far they are admissible depends entirely on the substance and the purpose of the investigation. To begin with, it is just as permissible for Marx to disregard the characteristics of commodities to the point where they are ultimately nothing but embodiments of a quantity of simple human labour as it is for the school of Jevons and Böhm-Bawerk to abstract from commodities all their characteristics except utility. But either abstraction is admissible only for specific purposes of demonstration, and the propositions based upon them are valid only within defined limits.

However, although there is no reliable yardstick for the total demand for any particular kind of commodity at any one time, practical experience shows that within certain periods of time the demand and supply of all commodities approximately equalise themselves. Practical experience further shows that only a part of the community takes an active part in the production and distribution[^c] of commodities, while another part consists of people who enjoy either an unearned income or an income from services not directly connected with production. So, a significantly larger number of people is supported by the labour of those employed in production than is actively engaged in it. Moreover, income statistics show that the strata not engaged in production appropriate a much greater share of the total product than their numerical relationship to the productively active part might suggest. The surplus labour of the latter is an empirical fact demonstrable from *experience* and requiring no deductive proof. *Whether or not Marx's theory of value is correct has no bearing whatsoever on the demonstration of surplus labour. It is in this respect not a demonstrative argument but merely a means of analysis and illustration.*

So if, in the analysis of commodity production, Marx suggests that

be accomplished if he directly included the wage actually paid as a factor in the assessment. However Marx draws attention to this, which the relation of labour value to the wage fundamentally disallows, in the passage in the chapter 'The Labour Process and the Valorization Process', where he says: 'This power (labour power) being of higher value, it expresses itself in labour of a higher sort, and therefore becomes objectified, during an equal amount of time, in proportionally higher values' (vol. 1, 2nd edn, p. 186).[7] Buch's treatise, of which only the first part has appeared and which I will keep in reserve for a more thorough treatment on a suitable occasion, strikes me as being the product of no mean analytical mind and a noteworthy contribution to a problem that has by no means been completely solved.

[^c]: This is preferable to the misleading term 'distribution'.

[7] *Capital* I, p. 305.

individual commodities are sold at their value, he is using a particular case to illustrate the process which, in his own view of the matter, is actually exhibited only by production taken as a whole. The labour time spent on the totality of commodities is, in the sense previously indicated, their social value.*ᵈ* And if even this social value is not fully realised – because depreciation of commodities is constantly occurring due to partial overproduction – it has in principle no bearing on the fact of social surplus value or surplus product. Its quantitative growth will, from time to time, be modified or slowed down, but there is no question of its standing still, much less of a quantitative decrease in any modern state. The surplus product is increasing everywhere; but the ratio of its increase to the increase of wages-capital is, at present, declining in the most advanced countries.

The fact that Marx applies this formula for the value of the totality of commodities to single commodities in itself indicates that, for him, the development of surplus value occurs exclusively in the sphere of production, where it is the industrial wage-labourer who produces it. All other active elements in modern economic life are subsidiary to production and *indirectly* help to *raise* the surplus value when, as for example merchants, bankers, etc. or their staff, they relieve industrial enterprise of work it would otherwise have to do and thus reduce its costs. Wholesale dealers etc. with their employees are merely the transformed and differentiated clerks etc. of the industrialists, and their profits are the transformed and concentrated costs of the latter. The wage-earning employees of these merchants certainly create surplus value for *them*, but no social surplus value. For the profit of their employers together with their own wages is a *deduction* from the surplus value produced by industry. However, this deduction is smaller in proportion than it was before the differentiation of functions under consideration, or than it would be without it. This differentiation only renders possible the development of production on a large scale and

---

ᵈ 'This is in fact the law of value ... that not only is no more labour-time devoted to each individual commodity than is necessary, but out of the total social labour-time only the proportionate quantity needed is devoted to the various types of commodity. *Use-value still remains a condition* ... The social need, that is, *the use-value on the social scale*, here appears decisive for the quota of total social labour-time that falls to the share of the various particular spheres of production' (*Capital* III, 2, pp. 176–7).[8] This sentence alone makes it impossible to dismiss the theory of Gossen and Bohm with a few condescending phrases.

[8] *Capital* III, p. 774.

the acceleration of the turnover of industrial capital. Like the division of labour generally, it increases the productivity of industrial capital, or rather, that of the labour directly employed in industry.

This brief recapitulation of the exposition of mercantile capital (from which, again, banking capital is to be differentiated) and of mercantile profit as set forth in the third volume of *Capital* will suffice. It makes clear the narrow limits within which the labour that creates surplus value is conceived in Marx's system. The mercantile functions mentioned, as well as others not discussed here, are by their nature indispensable to the social life of modern times. Their forms can, and undoubtedly will, be changed; but they themselves will remain, as long as mankind does not dissolve into small self-contained communities, in which they might then be either abolished or reduced to a minimum. However, in the theory of value relevant to contemporary society, the entire outlay for these functions appears as a deduction from surplus value, partly as 'costs' and partly as an integral component of the rate of exploitation.

There is a certain arbitrariness in the evaluation of functions in which we assume, not an actual community, but an artificially constructed and collectively managed community. This is the key to all obscurities in the theory of value. It is to be understood only with the help of this model. We have seen that surplus value can be conceived as a reality only if the economy as a whole is assumed. Marx did not get around to finishing the chapter on classes, which is so important to his theory. In it, it would have been shown with the utmost clarity that labour value is absolutely nothing other than a key, a mental construct like the atom endowed with a soul.' This

---

' We know that we think and we also know pretty well in what way we think. But we will never know how it comes about that we think, how consciousness is formed from external impressions, from the stimulation of the nerves or from changes in the condition and interaction of the atoms of our brain. Attempts have been made to explain it by ascribing to the atom a certain degree of potential consciousness, of animate existence in the sense of the monad theory. But that is a thought construct, an assumption, to which we are forced by our manner of reasoning and our need for a unified conception of the world.

An article in which I drew attention to this fact and remarked that pure materialism is, in the end, idealism gave Georg Plekhanov a welcome opportunity, in *Die Neue Zeit* (no. 44, vol. xvi, part II), to accuse me of ignorance in general and of a complete lack of understanding with regard to the philosophical views of Engels in particular. I will not go into the manner in which the above-named arbitrarily relates my words to things that I did not in any way touch upon. I will only note that his article ends with a report that, one day, Plekhanov asked Engels: 'So do you think old Spinoza was right when

key, employed by the master hand of Marx, led to a disclosure and exposition of the mechanism of capitalist economy, which is more penetrating, logical, and lucid than anything hitherto achieved. However, beyond a certain point it fails to work and has therefore become fatal to nearly every one of Marx's disciples.

The labour theory of value is misleading above all in that it appears again and again as a yardstick for the exploitation of the worker by the capitalist, an error furthered by, amongst other things, the characterisation of the rate of surplus value as the rate of exploitation. It is evident from the foregoing that it fails as such a yardstick, even if one starts from society as a whole and compares the sum total of the wages of labour with the sum total of other income. The theory of value no more provides a criterion for the justice or injustice of the distribution of the produce of labour than does atomic theory for the beauty or ugliness of a piece of sculpture. Nowadays, indeed, we find the best-placed workers, members of the 'labour aristocracy',

---

he said that *thought* and *extent* are nothing but two attributes of one and the same substance?' And Engels replied: 'Of course, old Spinoza was quite right.'[9]

Now, for Spinoza, the substance to which he ascribed these two attributes is God. At least, God as identified with nature, on account of which Spinoza was, already very early on, denounced as having denied God and his philosophy was accused of being atheistical, whereas formally it appears to be pantheistic. This, however, is only disguised atheism for those who maintain the doctrine of a personal God standing apart from nature. Spinoza arrived at the concept of the infinite substance, God, with the usual attributes, and others not precisely specified, by purely speculative means; for him, systematic thought and being were identical. To that extent he concurred with various materialists, but he himself could be called a representative of philosophical materialism only by dint of a completely arbitrary meaning of the word. If we are to mean anything definite at all by materialism, then it must be the doctrine that matter is the ultimate and only ground of things. But Spinoza expressly described his substance, God, as *incorporeal.* Anyone is free to be a Spinozist, but then he is not a materialist.

I know that, in *Ludwig Feuerbach,* Engels gives two definitions of materialism which are different from the above: first, all those who assume nature to be primary are claimed for materialism, and then those who 'sacrifice every idealist crotchet which could not be brought into harmony with the facts conceived in their own and not in a fantastic interconnection'.[10] These definitions give the term materialism so broad a meaning that it forfeits all precision and embraces some very antimaterialistic views. It is manifest again and again, and Plekhanov unwittingly confirms it, that rigid insistence on the term 'materialist' is rooted more in political than in scientific reasons. Whoever does not swear by thinking matter is under suspicion of political heresy; that is the moral of his article. How will I ever survive this anathema?

[9] G. Plekhanov, *Selected Philosophical Works* (Lawrence & Wishart, London, 1976), vol. II, p. 339.
[10] MESW, vol. II, p. 386; MEW, vol. XXI, p. 292.

precisely in those trades with a very high rate of surplus value and the most infamously exploited workers in those with a very low rate.

A scientific basis for socialism or communism can not be built just on the fact that the wage labourer does not receive the full value of the product of his labour. In the preface to *The Poverty of Philosophy*, Engels writes: 'Marx, therefore, never based his communist demands on this, but upon the inevitable collapse of the capitalist mode of production which is daily taking place before our eyes to an ever greater degree.'[11]

Let us see how things stand in this regard.

(b) The distribution of income in modern society

> Accumulation therefore presents itself on the one hand as increasing concentration . . . and on the other hand as repulsion of many individual capitals from one another.
>
> Marx, *Capital*, 4th edn., p. 590

Surplus value is, according to Marx's theory, the *fatum* of capitalists. The capitalist must produce surplus value in order to make a profit, but he can draw surplus value only from living labour. In order to secure the market against his competitors, he must strive to reduce the costs of production and, if he can not lower wages, then he must achieve it by raising the productivity of labour, that is, by improving machinery and saving human labour power. However, in saving human labour power he puts surplus value-producing labour out of commission and thus kills the goose that lays the golden egg. The consequence is a gradually accomplished decrease in the rate of profit which, though temporarily impeded by counteracting circumstances, will always reassert itself. Here is another inner antagonism of the capitalist mode of production. The rate of profit is the incentive for the productive use of capital. If it falls below a certain point, the motive for productive enterprise is weakened, especially as regards new capital which enters the market as an offshoot of the accumulated masses of capital. Capital itself proves to be a barrier to capitalist production. The continued development of production is interrupted. Whilst, on the one hand, every active capital seeks to preserve and

---

[11] Preface to first German edition of Marx's *The Poverty of Philosophy* (London, 1954), p. 11; MEW, vol. XXI, p. 178.

increase its amount of profit by means of feverish productive exertion, on the other hand, stagnation in the expansion of production sets in. This is only the counterpart of the processes which, through relative overproduction, lead to crisis in the market of use-values. Overproduction of commodities simultaneously manifests itself as the overproduction of capital. In the one as in the other, crises bring about a temporary adjustment. Colossal depreciation and destruction of capital take place, and, under the sway of stagnation, a portion of the working class must accept a reduction of wages to below the average, since an increased reserve army of superfluous hands stands at the disposal of capital in the labour market. After a while, the conditions for renewed profitable investment of capital are thus established, and the dance can begin again, but with the inner antagonism described above on a higher level of the scale: greater centralisation of capital, greater concentration of enterprises, increased rate of exploitation.

Now, is all this correct?

Yes and no. It is correct, above all, as a tendency. The forces described exist, and they operate in the given direction. And the processes are also taken from reality. The fall in the rate of profit is a fact, the occurrence of overproduction and crises is a fact, periodic destruction of capital is a fact, the concentration and centralisation of industrial capital is a fact, and the increase in the rate of surplus value is a fact. So far, the account remains, in principle, unshaken. If the picture does not agree with reality, then it is not because anything false has been said but because what is said is incomplete. Factors which have a limiting effect on the antagonisms described are either completely ignored in Marx or are, though dealt with here and there, later abandoned when the established facts are summed up and compared, so that the social effect of the antagonisms appears much stronger and direct than it is in reality.

Thus in the first volume of *Capital* (chapter 23, section 2), Marx speaks of the formation of investors of capital through division ('repulsion of many individual capitals from one another') and remarks that, in consequence of such divisions, the number of capitalists 'grows to a greater or lesser extent' with the accumulation of capital (4th edn, p. 589).[12] However, in his subsequent account, this growth in the number of capitalists is completely ignored, and even

---

[12] *Capital* I, p. 776.

joint-stock companies are dealt with only under the perspective of the concentration and centralisation of capital. So far as the above 'to a greater or lesser extent' is concerned, the case appears to be closed. At the end of the first volume, there is talk only of the 'constant decrease in the number of capitalist magnates',[13] and in this respect the third volume is, in principle, no different. In the treatment of the rate of profit and of mercantile capital, facts are indeed mentioned which point to the splitting up of capital, but without being brought to bear on our point. The reader gets the impression that the number of owners of capital is constantly declining, if not absolutely then relatively to the growth of the working class. In Social Democracy, accordingly, the notion is prevalent, or at least constantly suggests itself, that concentration of industrial entrepreneurs runs parallel with the concentration of wealth.

That is, however, by no means the case. By virtue of its form the joint-stock company tends to be a very significant counterweight to the centralisation of wealth through the centralisation of business enterprises. It permits an extensive division of already concentrated capital and makes it unnecessary for individual magnates to appropriate capital for the purpose of concentrating business enterprises. Although non-socialist economists have used this fact to present social conditions in a falsely favourable light, this is no reason for socialists to conceal it or to explain it away. The point is, rather, to understand the true extent and significance of the fact.

Unfortunately, there is a general lack of statistical evidence for the actual distribution of the original shares, preference shares, etc., of the joint-stock companies which nowadays loom so large, because in most countries they are anonymous (i.e., like other paper money, they can change owners without formalities); whereas in England, where shares registered by name predominate and lists of the shareholders thus established can be inspected by anyone in the State Registry Office, the compilation of more exact statistics of shareholders is a gigantic task on which no one has yet ventured. We can only make a rough estimate of their number on the basis of certain research done on individual companies. Still, in order to show how very deceptive are the ideas advanced on this subject, and how the most modern

[13] Ibid., p. 929.

and crass form of capitalist centralisation, the 'trust', has in fact an effect on the distribution of wealth which is quite different from what it seems to outsiders, I give a few figures, which can be easily verified.

The English Sewing Thread Trust, formed about a year ago, numbers no less than 12,300 shareholders. Of these there were:

6,000 owners of original shares	1,200 marks average capital
4,500 owners of preference shares	3,000 marks average capital
1,800 owners of debentures	6,300 marks average capital

The trust of fine-cotton spinners also had a respectable number of shareholders, namely 5,454:

2,904 owners of original shares	6,000 marks average capital
1,870 owners of preference shares	10,000 marks average capital
680 owners of debentures	26,000 marks average capital

Something similar holds for the Cotton Trust of J. and P. Coates.[f] The shareholders in the Great Manchester Ship Canal amount in round figures to 40,000, those in the large provisions company of T. Lipton to 74,262! A department store recently cited as an example of the concentration of capital, Spiers and Pond in London with a total capital of 26 million marks, has 4,650 shareholders, of whom there are only 550 whose shareholding exceeds 10,000 marks. These are a few examples of the splitting up of wealth in centralised enterprises. Now, obviously, not all shareholders are capitalists to any noteworthy degree, and often one and the same big capitalist appears as a *small* shareholder in all manner of companies. But nevertheless the number of shareholders and their average holding of shares have seen a rapid growth. Altogether the number of shareholders in England is estimated at considerably more than a million, and that does not appear extravagant if one considers that in the year 1896 alone the number of joint-stock companies in the United Kingdom ran to over 21,223 with a paid-up capital of 22,290 million marks, which moreover does not include foreign enterprises not negotiated in England itself, government stocks, etc.[g]

This distribution of national wealth, which in a large number of

---

[f] In all these trusts, the original owners of the combined factories themselves had to take up a portion of the shares. These are not included in the tables given.

[g] At present, English capital invested abroad is estimated at 43 billion marks and its average annual growth at 114 million!

cases we can call the national *surplus product*, is reflected in the figures of the income statistics.

In the United Kingdom in the financial year 1893–4 (the last return I have to hand), the number of persons with estimated incomes of 3,000 marks or more under schedules D and E (incomes from business profits, higher official posts, etc.) amounted to 727,270. To that we must add those assessed on incomes from land and real estate (annuities, ground rent), house rents, and taxable capital investments. These groups together pay almost as much tax as the above-mentioned categories of taxpayers, their taxable income being 6,000 as against 7,000 million marks. That would almost double the number of persons with an income over 3,000 marks.

In the *British Review* of 22 May 1897 there are some figures on the growth of incomes in England from 1851 to 1881. According to these, England numbered roughly 300,000 families with incomes between £150 and £1,000 (the middle and petty bourgeoisie and the top labour aristocracy) in 1851, and roughly 990,000 in 1881. Whilst the population in these thirty years increased in the ratio of 27 to 35, that is, about 30 per cent, the number of these income categories increased in the ratio of 27 to 90, that is, 233.33 per cent. Giffen estimates that there are *one and a half million of these taxpayers* today.[14]

The picture in other countries is not materially different. According to Mulhall, France's 8,000,000 families include 1,770,000 families whose living conditions are big bourgeois or petty bourgeois (average income of 5,200 marks) as against 6,000,000 workers and 160,000 of the very rich.[15] In Prussia in 1854 there were, as readers of Lassalle know; only 440,000 persons with an income of more than 1,000 thaler in a population of 16,300,000. In the year 1894–5, with a total population of nearly 33,000,000, taxes on incomes of over 3,000 marks were paid by 321,296 persons. In 1887–8 the number had risen to 347,328. Whilst the population had doubled, the stratum of better-situated classes had increased more than sevenfold. Even if one makes allowance for the fact that the provinces annexed in 1866 show greater numbers of the well-to-do than Old Prussia and that the prices of many articles of food had risen considerably in the

---

[14] The statistic Bernstein quotes does not occur in Giffen's *Recent Changes in Prices and Incomes Compared* (London, 1888) or in his *The Growth of Capital* (London, 1889).
[15] Michael G. Mulhall, *Dictionary of Statistics* (London, 1899), p. 322.

interval, the ratio of the better-off to the total population increased by at least far more than two to one. If, for instance, we take a later period, we find that in the fourteen years between 1876 and 1890, when the total number of registered taxpayers increased by 20.56 per cent, taxpayers with incomes between 2,000 and 20,000 marks (the well-to-do and the petty bourgeoisie) increased from 442,534 to 582,024, that is, by 31.52 per cent. In the same period the class of actual property owners (incomes of 6,000 marks or more) grew from 66,319 to 109,095 [sic], that is, by 58.47 per cent. Five-sixths of this increase, namely 33,226 out of 38,776, fall in the middle stratum of incomes between 6,000 and 20,000 marks. Conditions are precisely the same in the most industrialised state of Germany, namely *Saxony*. There, between 1879 and 1890, the number of incomes between 1,600 and 3,300 marks rose from 62,140 to 91,124, and that of incomes between 3,300 and 9,600 marks from 24,414 to 38,841.[h] Similarly with the other individual German states. Of course, not all recipients of higher incomes are 'property-owners', but we can see to how great an extent this is the case from the fact that, in 1895–6 in Prussia, 1,152,332 persons with a taxable nett *property* of more than 6,000 marks were drawn into the supplementary tax bracket. Over half of them, namely 598,063, paid tax on a nett property of more than 20,000 marks, and 385,000 on one of more than 32,000 marks.

It is thus quite wrong to suppose that the present development shows a relative or indeed absolute decrease in the number of property-owners. The number of property-owners increases, not 'to a greater or lesser extent', but simply to a *greater* extent, that is absolutely *and* relatively. If the activity and the prospects of Social Democracy depended on a decrease in the number of property-owners, then it might indeed 'go to sleep'. But the contrary is the case. *The prospects of socialism depend not on the decrease but on the increase of social wealth.* Socialism, or the socialist movement of modern times, has already outlived many superstitions; it will also outlive the superstition

---

[h] From 1890 to 1892, this latter class rose by a further 2,400, namely, to 39,266. As for the former class, I do not have the absolute figures for 1892. It is only to be noted that between 1879 and 1892 the number of incomes between 800 and 3,300 marks (better-placed workers and petty bourgeois) in Saxony rose from 227,839 to 439,948, i.e. from 20.94 per cent to 30.48 per cent of those liable to pay tax. It should be mentioned that the figures pertaining to Prussia and Saxony are taken partly from *The Dictionary of the Political Sciences* and partly from Schonberg's *Handbook*.

that its future depends on the concentration of property or, if one prefers, on the absorption of surplus value by a diminishing group of capitalist mammoths.' Whether the social surplus product is monopolised by 10,000 persons or is shared among half a million people in graduated amounts, is essentially a matter of complete indifference to the nine or ten million heads of families who are the losers in this transaction. Their struggle for a more just distribution, or for an arrangement which would include a more just distribution, is not on that account less justifiable and necessary. On the contrary. It might cost less surplus labour to keep a few thousand privileged persons in luxury than half a million or more in unjust prosperity.

If society were constituted, or if it had developed, in the manner socialist theory has hitherto supposed, then indeed it would be only a short space of time before the economic collapse occurred. But that, as we can see, is precisely not the case. Far from social differentiation being simplified compared with earlier times, it has become to a high degree gradated and differentiated both in respect of incomes and work. And if we did not have the fact empirically demonstrated before us by income statistics and occupational statistics, then it could be shown in a purely deductive way as the necessary consequence of modern economy.

What characterises the modern mode of production above all else is the great increase in the productivity of labour. The effect is an equally big *increase in production* – the mass production of *goods for use*. Where is this wealth? Or to direct the question at the heart of the matter, where is the *surplus product* which the industrial wage labourers produce above and beyond what they consume within the boundaries set by their wages? If 'capitalist magnates' had ten times as large stomachs as popular satire attributes to them and kept ten times as many servants as they actually do, their consumption would be only a feather in the scales against the size of the annual national product – for we recall that large-scale capitalist production is above all *mass*-production. It will be said that they export the surplus. Good,

---

' With regard to statistics for top incomes, by the way, socialist literature usually overlooks the fact that a very large percentage of such incomes accrues to *legal* persons, i.e. corporate bodies of every kind (joint-stock companies etc.). Thus, in Saxony in the year 1892, of the 11,138 persons liable to pay tax and with incomes of more than 9,600 marks 5,594 were legal persons, and the higher you go the more the latter predominate. Of those with incomes of more than 300,000 marks, 23 were natural persons and 33 were legal persons.

but, in the end, the foreign customer himself pays only in commodities. In world trade the circulation of coined money plays a diminishing role. The richer a country is in capital, the greater is its import of commodities, for the countries to which it lends money can as a rule pay interest only in the form of commodities.[j] Where, then, is the quantity of commodities which the magnates and their servants do not consume? If the commodities do not in one way or another go to the proletarians, they must be snapped up by other classes. The only alternatives which the continued increase in production allows are: either a progressive relative diminution in the number of capitalists and an increase in the prosperity of the proletariat, or a numerous middle class. Crises and unproductive expenditure on armies etc. consume a lot, but even so they have, in recent years, absorbed only a fraction of the total surplus product. If the working class were to wait until 'capital' had removed the middle classes from this world, then it really could take a long nap. Capital expropriates these classes in one form and then, time and again, brings them back to life in another. It is not 'capital' but the working class itself that has the task of absorbing the parasitical elements of the economy.

The fact that the wealth of modern nations is, in increasing volume, wealth in movable consumer goods has provided Manchesterist authors with support for embellishing present conditions in all kinds of ways. In its time, this has caused nearly all socialists to go to the opposite extreme and to regard as social wealth only fixed wealth *sub specie* capital, which is gradually personified into a mystical entity. Even the clearest minds lose their sound judgment the moment this notion of 'capital' heaves into view. Marx once remarked of the liberal economist J. B. Say that he sets himself up as a judge of crises because he knows that a commodity is a product.[16] Nowadays many believe that they have said everything there is to say about social wealth when they point to the specific form of enterprise capital.

As for the proposition in my letter to the Stuttgart Conference, that the increase of social wealth is accompanied not by a shrinking number of capitalist magnates but by a growing number of capitalists of all degrees, a leading article in the New York *Volkszeitung* taxes

---

[j] England gets its outstanding interest paid in the form of surplus imports to the value of 2 billion marks, the greater part of which are articles of mass consumption.

[16] *Capital* I, p. 210.

me with its being false, at least so far as America is concerned, for the census of the United States proves that production there is dominated by a number of concerns which is shrinking relatively to its total size. What a refutation! The critic believes he can demolish my assertion about the general *class structure* by pointing to the structure of *industrial enterprises*. It is as if someone were to say that the number of proletarians was shrinking in modern society because where the individual worker formerly stood the trade union stands today.

Of course, the explanation will then be added that this combination of enterprises is the main point; whether a new class of idlers is developed among shareholders is neither here nor there.

First of all, that is an opinion and not a refutation of the fact being stressed. So far as social analysis is concerned, the one fact is just as important as the other. It can, from a certain point of view, be the less important. But that is not the question. The question is whether or not it is true. I am really not completely unaware of the concentration of enterprises; in fact I mentioned it in a subsequent sentence. I state two facts, and the critic thinks that he can show that one of them is false merely by declaring the other to be important. I hope I can succeed in laying the ghost that clouded the vision of him and others like him.

At the Stuttgart Conference itself, Karl Kautsky also referred to my above-mentioned remark and objected that, if it were true that capitalists were increasing and not the propertyless, then capitalism was gaining strength and we socialists would never reach our goal at all.[17] But what Marx said is still true: the growth of capital means the growth of the proletariat.

This is the same confusion, but less crude and from a different angle. I had nowhere said that the proletarians did not increase. When I stressed the increase in capitalists of all degrees, I was speaking of people, not of entrepreneurs. But Kautsky evidently remained hooked on the concept, 'capital', and concluded that a relative increase of capitalists must mean a relative diminution of the proletariat, which, however, would contradict our theory. And he cites Marx's view, quoted above, against me.

Now, I have already touched upon a proposition of Marx's which

---

[17] Tudor and Tudor, p. 295.

suggests something different from the one Kautsky cites. Kautsky's mistake consists in identifying capital with capitalists or property owners. However, I would also like to draw Kautsky's attention to something else which weakens his objection. And that is what Marx calls the *organic* development of capital.[18] If the composition of capital changes in such a fashion that constant capital increases and variable capital decreases, then, in the enterprises concerned, the absolute increase of capital means a relative decrease in the proletariat. However, according to Marx, that is precisely the characteristic form of modern development. Applied to the capitalist economy as a whole, this does in fact mean: absolute increase of capital, relative decrease in the proletariat. The workers who have become redundant through the change in the organic composition of capital find work again each time only to the extent that *new* capital is introduced into the market to provide them with employment. My view is in harmony with Marx's theory precisely at the point which Kautsky questions. The consequence of Marx's reasoning is that, if the number of workers is to increase, then capital must increase proportionally even faster. I think Kautsky will grant that without further ado.

So far, the only question is whether the increased capital is capitalist property merely *qua* enterprise *stock* or also as *shares* in an enterprise.

If not, Mr Smith, the worthy master fitter, who carries on his trade with six journeymen and a few apprentices, would be a capitalist, but Mr Brown, a man of private means with several hundred thousand marks in his coffers, or his son-in-law, Mr Jones, the engineer, who has a larger number of shares received as dowry (not all shareholders are idle), would be propertyless. The absurdity of such a classification is obvious. Property is property, whether fixed or movable. A share is not only capital, it is capital in its most perfect, one could say its most sublime, form. It is the title to a share in the surplus product of the national or the world economy free from all gross contact with the demeaning aspects of business activity – dynamic capital, if you like. And if they each and all lived only as idle *rentiers*, the increasing platoons – nowadays we could speak of battalions – of shareholders, by their mere existence, the manner of their consumption, and the number of their social retainers, represent a force with a powerful

---

[18] Bernstein is probably referring to chapter 13 of *Capital* III. See particularly pp. 318–19.

influence on the economic life of society. The share restores those interim stages in the social scale which, as heads of production, had been obliterated from industry by the concentration of businesses.

However, there is also something to be said about this concentration. Let us look at it more closely.

(c) Occupational classes in the production and distribution of social wealth

England, the very country in Europe that is considered the most advanced in terms of capitalist development, lacks general statistics for the types of trade in industry. Such statistics exist only for certain branches of production which come under the Factory Act and for particular localities.

According to the Factory Inspector's report for 1896, the factories and workshops under the Factory Act employed a total of 4,398,983 persons. According to the census of 1891, that is not quite half the persons designated as employed in industry. The number in the census, omitting the transport industry, is 9,025,902. Of the remaining 4,626,919 persons, we can reckon a fourth to a third as tradesmen in the branches of production referred to, and in some medium-sized and large businesses which do not come under the Factory Act. That leaves, in round numbers, *3 million* employees and small masters in very small businesses. The 4 million workers under the Factory Act were distributed among a total of 160,948 factories and workshops, which yields an average of 27 to 28 per establishment.[k] If we separate factories from workshops, we get 76,279 factories with 3,743,418 workers and 81,669 workshops with 655,565 workers, on average 49 workers per factory and 8 workers per registered workshop. The average number of 49 workers to a factory already shows what a closer examination of the tables in the report confirms, that at least two-thirds of the businesses registered as factories belong to the category of medium-sized businesses of 6 to 50 workers, which leaves at most 20,000 to 25,000 businesses of 50 workers or more, which may represent altogether about 3 million workers. At best three-quarters of the 1,171,990 persons employed

---

[k] The particulars of 1,931 registered factories and 5,624 workshops had not come in when the report was drawn up. They would have further diminished the number of workers per enterprise.

in transport can be regarded as belonging to large companies. If we add these to the foregoing categories, we get a total of between 3.5 and 4 million workers and assistants in large companies, as against 5.5 million in medium and small businesses. The 'workshop of the world' is, therefore, still far from having fallen prey to large-scale industry to anything like the degree that is often supposed. Rather, industrial enterprises show the greatest diversity, even in the British Empire, and no major class is disappearing from the scale.[1]

If we compare the above figures with the *German industrial statistics* for 1895, we find that the latter show, on the whole, the same picture as the English. Large-scale industry occupied nearly the same position in relation to production in Germany in 1895 as in England in 1891. In Prussia in 1895, 38 per cent of industrial workers belonged

---

[1] German workers who have emigrated to England have repeatedly expressed their astonishment to me at the fragmentation of businesses they have encountered in the wood, metal, etc., manufacturing industries of this country. The present figures in the cotton industry show only a moderate increase in the concentration of establishments since the time when Karl Marx wrote. The table shows a comparison with the last figures given by Marx.

	1868	Change	%
Factories	2,549	2,538	−0.43
Power looms	379,329	615,714	+62
Spindles	32,000,014	44,504,816	+39
Workers	401,064	528,795	+32
Workers per factory	156	208	+33

This is not an exceptionally high concentration for a 22-year period in an industry as subject to technological revolution as this one is. Furthermore the number of power looms increased by 62 per cent, but the number of spindles grew only slightly faster than the workers employed. Of these, from 1870 onwards, the number of adult male workers showed a greater increase than women and children (see *Capital* I, 4th edn. p. 400 and *Statistical Abstract for the United Kingdom from 1878 to 1892.*) There was even less concentration in the other branches of the textile industry. Thus, from 1870 to 1890, the number of wool and worsted factories increased from 2,459 to 2,546, and the number of workers employed in them increased from 234,687 to 297,053, i.e. from 95 workers per factory to 117. Here, in contrast to the cotton industry, the number of spindles increased much faster than the number of looms, which, with 112,794 to 129,222, showed an increase which lagged behind the increase in workers employed, so that we can speak of concentration only in the spinning mills.

The factory inspectors' report for 1896 puts the number of factories in the whole textile industry of Great Britain at 9,891, which belonged to 7,900 enterprises and employed 1,077,687 workers, as against 3,968 factories in 1870 with 718,051 workers – a consolidation from 120.3 workers per enterprise to 136.4.

to large-scale industry. In Prussia and in the rest of Germany, the creation of large-scale industry has been accomplished with extraordinary speed. While various branches of industry (including the textile industry) still lag behind England, others (machines and tools) have on average reached the English position, and some have overtaken it (the chemical and glass industries, certain branches of the printing trade, and probably also electrical engineering). Nevertheless, the great mass of persons employed in industry, also in Germany, are to be found in small and medium-sized businesses. Of the 10.25 million persons employed in industry in 1895, something more than 3 million were in large companies, 2.5 million in medium-sized companies (6 to 50 persons), and 4.75 in small ones. *Master craftsmen* still numbered 1.25 million. In five trades their number, as against 1895 [*sic*], had risen both absolutely and relatively (to the increase in population), in nine it had risen only absolutely, and in eleven it had declined absolutely and relatively."

In *France*, industry still lags behind agriculture in size; according to the census of 17 April 1894, it represented only 25.9 per cent of the population, whereas agriculture represented nearly twice as much, namely, 47.3 per cent. The ratio is similar in *Austria* where agriculture accounts for 55.9 per cent of the population and industry accounts for 25.8 per cent. In France there were 1 million self-employed in industry as against 3.3 million employees, and in Austria there were 600,000 self-employed as against 2.25 million workers and day labourers. Here too the relationship is very much the same. Both countries boast a range of highly developed industries (textiles, mining, construction, etc.) which, in terms of size, are a match for the most advanced countries but which are only a partial phenomenon in the national economy.

Switzerland, with 127,000 self-employed, has 400,000 workers in industry. *The United States of America*, which the above-mentioned contributor to the New York *Volkszeitung* says is the most developed capitalist country in the world, had, according to the census of 1890, a relatively high average of workers per establishment, namely, 3.5 million workers in 355,415 industrial enterprises, that is, 10:1. But, as in England, this excludes cottage industries and very small businesses. If one takes the figures of the Prussian industrial statistics

---

" See R. Calwer, 'The Development of Handicraft', *Die Neue Zeit*, xv, 2, p. 597.

from the top downwards, one gets almost exactly the same average as that of the American census. And if we look more closely at the industries surveyed by the census in the *Statistical Abstract* of the United States, we encounter a great number of branches of manufacturing with an average of five or fewer workers per establishment. Thus, on the very first page, we have 910 manufacturers of agricultural implements with 30,723 workers, 35 munition factories with 1,993 workers, 251 factories making artificial feathers and flowers with 3,638 workers, 59 factories making artificial limbs with 154 workers, and 581 sail-cloth and awning factories with 2,873 workers.

If the relentless advance of technology and the centralisation of businesses in an increasing number of branches of industry is a fact the significance of which even obdurate reactionaries can hardly ignore nowadays, it is a no-less-well-established fact that in a whole range of branches of industry small and medium-sized businesses prove to be quite capable of surviving alongside large companies. Also, there is in industry no pattern of development that holds equally for all branches. Companies which are completely mechanised remain as small or medium-sized businesses, while branches of the arts and crafts, which were thought to be safe for small businesses, are, all of a sudden, irretrievably lost to big business. The same holds for cottage industries and small workshops. For a long time, in the canton of Zurich, domestic weaving in the silk industry declined. However, between 1891 and 1897 domestic weavers increased from 24,708 to 27,800, while the workers and employees in the mechanised weaving-mills increased only from 11,840 to 14,550. Whether this increase in domestic weavers is to be welcomed as an economic phenomenon is another matter. Our first concern here is simply to establish the fact and nothing else.

A number of circumstances allow the continuation and renewal of small and medium-sized businesses. They can be divided into three groups.

First, a number of industries or branches of industry are nearly as well suited for small or medium businesses as they are for a large company, and the advantages which the latter has over the former are not so significant that they can outweigh the peculiar advantages of the smaller domestic establishment. As is well known, this is the case with, amongst others, various branches of wood, leather, and metal work. Alternatively a division of labour occurs in which large-

69

scale industry does half or three-quarters of the work, which is then finished for the market by smaller enterprises.

Second, in many cases the manner in which the product must be made available to the consumer favours its being made in a smaller establishment, as is most evidently the case with bakeries. If it were only a matter of technology, baking would have been monopolised by big industry long ago, for the many bread factories yielding a good profit show that they can be carried on with good results. But in spite of them and the pastry factories (which are also gradually winning a market), or side by side with them, the small and medium-sized bakeries are holding their own thanks to the advantage which direct access to the consumer gives them. Insofar as they only have to deal with capitalist enterprises, master bakers have nothing to fear for some time to come. Their increase since 1882 has certainly not kept step with the increase in population, but it is still worth mentioning (77,609 as against 74,283).

But bakery is only an extreme example. The same holds for a whole range of trades which combine production with the provision of services. The trades of farrier and wheelwright are cases in point. The American census shows 28,000 farrier and wheelwright businesses with a total of 50,867 persons, of whom just one-half are self-employed. The German occupational statistics show 62,722 blacksmiths and farriers, and it will certainly be a long while before the advent of motor vehicles driven by steam etc. kills them off only to bring new small workshops into being, as everyone knows the bicycle has done. The same holds for tailors, shoemakers, saddlers, carpenters, carpetmakers, watchmakers, etc., where dealing with customers (and, in varying degree, repair-work) and shop-keeping will keep independent entities alive – of which indeed many, though by no means all, provide only proletarian incomes.

Last but not least, large-scale industry itself breeds smaller and medium-sized businesses, partly by mass-production and the consequent reduction in the cost of the materials needed for work (ancillary materials, half-manufactured goods, etc.), partly by the disposal of capital on the one hand and the 'liberation' of workers on the other. In large and small amounts new capital is forever coming onto the market in search of investment, and the market's receptivity for new goods steadily increases with the growth in social wealth. Here shareholders, mentioned earlier, play no small part. The market could not, in fact, survive on the handful of millionaires, even if the 'hand' had a few thousand fingers. However the hundreds of thousands of rich and well-to-do people do have something to say in the matter. Almost all the luxury goods for these classes are manufactured from scratch, or in many cases finished, by small and medium-sized enterprises; and they can well be capitalist enterprises, especially if the materials they work up are expensive or if they use costly machinery (manufacture of jewellery, work in fine metals, art printing). It is only later that the large company, insofar as it does not itself take over the article in question, 'democratises' one or other new luxury by reducing the cost of the materials.

Overall, then, despite continuing changes in the grouping of industries and the internal organisation of companies, it looks today not as though large companies are constantly absorbing small and medium-sized companies but as though they are simply growing *alongside* them. Only the very small businesses decline both absolutely and relatively. But, as far as small and medium-sized businesses are concerned, they too increase, as is apparent from the figures given in table 1.

Table 1. *Number of employees in German companies, 1882 and 1895*

	1882	1895	Increase (%)
Small companies (1–5 persons)	2,457,950	3,056,318	24.3
Small/medium companies (6–10)	500,097	833,409	66.6
Larger/medium companies (11–50)	891,623	1,620,848	81.8

However, in the same period, the population increased by only 13.5 per cent.

So although, in the period in question, big business enlarged its workforce at an even greater rate – by 88.7 per cent – it was only in isolated cases that this meant the absorption of small companies. In fact, in many cases no competition at all – or no increased competition – takes place between large and small businesses (consider large engineering and bridge-building works). The example of the textile industry, which our literature is wont to mention, is in many respects misleading. The increase in productivity achieved by the spinning-jenny as compared with the old spindle has been repeated only occasionally. A lot of large companies are superior to small and medium-sized companies, not in the productivity of the labour employed, but simply in the size of the enterprise (ship-building), and they leave the sphere of activity of the latter completely, or largely, untouched. Anyone who hears that, in the year 1895, Prussia saw nearly double as many workers employed in big business as in 1882, that in 1882 they represented only 28.4 per cent of the total industrial work-force whereas in 1895 they represented 38 per cent, may be easily persuaded that small business will soon be a thing of the past and that it has ceased to play any role in the economy. But the figures quoted show that the rapid growth and expansion of big business represents only one side of economic development.

As in industry, so in *trade*. Despite the efflorescence of large department stores, medium and small trading companies are also holding their own. There is, of course, no question of denying the parasitical element in trade, for instance, in connection with the so-called carrying trade. Yet it must be observed that, even here, there has been much exaggeration. Large-scale production and the steady rise in international commerce put ever larger quantities of commodities on the market which must, in some way or another, be brought to the consumer. There is no denying that this could be done more cheaply and efficiently than through the present carrying trade. However, so long as this does not happen, the carrying trade will survive. And just as it is illusory to expect large-scale industry to reduce small and medium-sized companies to an insignificant remnant in the foreseeable future, so it is utopian to expect capitalist department stores to absorb small and medium-sized shops to any degree worth mentioning. They harm individual businesses, and here and there they occasionally sow confusion among all the small traders. But after a while the latter nonetheless find a way of competing with the large stores and of using all the advantages which local connections give them. New specialisations and combinations of companies are developed, and also new forms and methods of carrying on business. At present, the capitalist department store is much more a product of the great increase in the *wealth of commodities* than an instrument for the destruction of the parasitical retail trade. It has had more effect in shaking the latter out of its routine and breaking it of certain monopolistic habits than in exterminating it. The number of retail enterprises is steadily growing. In England, between 1875 and 1886,

72

Table 2. *Number of persons employed in trade and commerce in Prussia in 1885 and 1895 (excluding the railways and the post office)*

Number of employees	1885	1895	Increase (%)
2 and fewer	411,509	467,656	13.6
3 to 5	176,867	342,112	93.4
6 to 50	157,328	303,078	92.6
51 and more	25,619	62,056	142.2
Total	771,323	1,174,902	

it grew from 295,000 to 366,000. The number of persons engaged in trade rose even more. As, on this matter, the English statistics of 1891 were compiled according to different principles from those of 1881," we will take the figures from the Prussian statistics given in table 2.

The increase is proportionately the largest in the big companies, but these represent not much more than 5 per cent of the total. It is not the large companies that provide the small businesses with the most murderous competition; the latter do their best to provide it among themselves. But in proportion only a few of them are killed off. And the scale of companies remains structurally undamaged. The small medium-sized businesses show the greatest increase.

Finally, when we come to *agriculture*, we meet with a movement throughout Europe and partly also in America, which nowadays contradicts everything which socialist theory has hitherto assumed with regard to the relationship between the sizes of business enterprises. Where trade and industry showed only a slower upward movement in large-scale enterprises than had been assumed, agriculture shows either a *standstill* or an actual *decline* in the size of enterprises.

First of all, as regards *Germany*, the business census of 1895 shows the proportionately largest increase, as compared with the census of 1882, in the group of *medium-sized peasant holdings* (5 to 20 hectares), namely, nearly 8 per cent; and the growth in the total area they occupied is even greater, namely about 9 per cent. The small peasant holdings next below them (2 to 5 hectares) show the next largest

---

" So far as we can tell from them, they show an increase of more than 50 per cent in the last decade.

Table 3. *1895 business census figures giving the size of agricultural holdings in Germany*

Kind of holding	Number	Cultivated area	Total area
Very small (up to 2 hectares)	3,236,367	1,808,444	2,415,414
Small (1–5 hectares)	1,016,318	3,285,984	4,142,071
Medium-sized (5–20 hectares)	998,804	9,721,875	12,537,660
Large (20–100 hectares)	281,767	9,869,837	13,157,201
Very large (100+ hectares)	25,061	7,831,801	11,031,896

increase: 3.5 per cent growth in enterprises and an 8 per cent increase in total area. Very small holdings (under 2 hectares) increased by 5.8 per cent and their total area by 12 per cent, but the part of this total area used for agricultural purposes shows a decrease of nearly 1 per cent. The already partly capitalistic large farming operations (20 to 100 hectares) show an increase of not quite 1 per cent, which is wholly accounted for by forestry enterprises, and large holdings (more than 100 hectares) show an increase of not quite 0.33 per cent, for which the same holds.

The figures in question for 1895 are shown in table 3.

Over two-thirds of the total area fall under the three categories of peasant holding; about a quarter come under large enterprises. In Prussia, the proportion of peasant holdings is even more favourable; there they occupy *nearly three-quarters* of the agricultural area, 22,875,000 hectares out of 32,591,000.

If we turn from Prussia to neighbouring Holland, we find that the large holdings have actually decreased, and the medium-sized small peasant holdings have *trebled* (see table).[o]

In Belgium, according to Vandervelde,[p] landed property as well as the cultivation of the land has undergone continuous decentralisation. The last general statistics show an increase in the number of *land-owners* from 201,226 in the year 1846 to 293,524 in the year 1880, and an increase of *tenants* from 371,320 to 616,872. In 1880, the total cultivated area of Belgium amounted to not quite 2 million hectares, of which more than a third was worked by its owners. The

[o] See M. H. Vliegen, 'The Agricultural Programme of Dutch Social Democracy', *Die Neue Zeit*, xvii, 1, pp. 75ff.
[p] 'Agricultural Socialism in Belgium', *Die Neue Zeit*, xv, 1, p. 752.

Table 4. *Changes in size of holdings in Holland, 1884–93*

Size of holding	Holdings		Increase decrease	%
	1884	1893		
1–5 hectares	66,842	77,767	+10,925	+16.2
5–10 hectares	31,552	94,199	+62,647	+198.5
10–50 hectares	48,278	51,940	+3,662	+7.6
Over 50 hectares	3,554	3,510	−44	−1.2

Table 5. *Agricultural enterprises in France, 1882*

Size of holding	Holdings	Total area (hectares)
Under 1 hectare	2,167,767	1,083,833
1–10 hectares	2,635,030	11,366,274
10–40 hectares	727,088	14,845,650
40–100 hectares	113,285 ⎤	
100–200 hectares	20,644 ⎥	22,266,104
200–500 hectares	7,942 ⎥	
over 500 hectares	217 ⎦	
	5,672,003 [*sic*]	48,478,028 [*sic*]

allotment economy in Belgium reminds one of Chinese agrarian conditions.

In the year 1882, France had the agricultural enterprises shown in table 5.

Of the holdings between 40 and 100 hectares there are in round numbers 14 million hectares, and of those over 200 hectares there are about 8 million, so that, on the whole, large holdings represented between a fifth and a sixth of the cultivated area. The small, medium, and large peasant holdings cover almost three-quarters of French soil. Between 1862 and 1882 holdings of 5 to 10 hectares had increased by 24 per cent, and holdings of 10 to 40 hectares had increased by 14.28 per cent. The agricultural statistics of 1892 show an increase in the total number of holdings of 30,000, but a decrease of 33,000 in the last-named categories, which suggests a further subdividing of agricultural enterprises.

But what is the situation in *England*, the classic land of large-scale land ownership and capitalist agriculture? We know the lists of mammoth landlords which from time to time appear in the press as an illustration of the concentration of land ownership in England, and we know the passage in *Capital* where Marx says that John Bright's assertion that 150 landlords own half the soil of England, and twelve own half the soil of Scotland, has never been refuted (*Capital* I, 4th edn, p. 615).[19] Now, although the land in England is monopolistically centralised, it is not so to the extent that John Bright believed. According to Brodrick's *English Land and English Landlords*, roughly 14 million out of the 33 million acres of land in England and Wales listed in the Domesday Book were the property of 1,704 owners with 3,000 acres (1,200 hectares) each or more. The remaining 19 million acres were divided among 150,000 owners of one acre or more, and among a large number of owners of smaller plots. For the whole of the United Kingdom in 1892, Mulhall estimated the number of owners of 10 acres or more to be 176,520 (altogether ten-elevenths of the area).[20] Now, how is this land cultivated? Here are the figures for 1885 and 1895 for Great Britain (England, Wales, and Scotland, but without Ireland), translated into hectares for the sake of a more convenient comparison of the sizes of holdings, insofar as it is a question of classification (table 6).[q]

Here too, there is a decrease in the large and very large holdings and an increase in the small and medium-sized ones.

However, the trade figures tell us nothing about the area under

Table 6. *Size of agricultural holdings in Great Britain (excluding Ireland), 1885–95*

Holdings	1885	1895	Difference
2–20 hectares	232,955	235,481	+2,526
20–40 hectares	64,715	66,625	+1,910
40–120 hectares	79,573	81,245	+1,672
120–200 hectares	13,875	13,568	−307
Over 200 hectares	5,489	5,219	−270

[q] According to the ratio of 1 acre = 4,000 square metres, which is not quite exact but will serve for the purpose of comparison. The figures are taken from the *Blue Book on Agricultural Holdings*.

[19] *Capital* I, p. 804.
[20] Mulhall, *Dictionary of Statistics*.

Table 7. *Sizes of holdings in Great Britain in 1895*

Size of holding	Acres at 40 ares	Percentage of total area
Under 2 hectares[r]	366,792	1.13
2–5 hectares	1,667,647	5.12
5–20 hectares	2,864,976	8.79
20–40 hectares	4,885,203	15.00
40–120 hectares	13,875,914	42.59
120–200 hectares	5,113,945	15.70
200–400 hectares	3,001,184	9.21
over 400 hectares	801,852	2.46
	32,577,643 [*sic*]	100

cultivation. Let us therefore supplement them with the figures for the total area listed under the various classes of holding. They paint a positively amazing picture (see table 7).

According to this, just 27 to 28 per cent of agricultural land in Great Britain is in large holdings, and only 2.46 per cent is in very large holdings. On the other hand, more than 66 per cent is in medium-sized and large holdings. In Great Britain, the proportion of such holdings (in which, to be sure, the large capitalist farm predominates) is greater than it is, on average, in Germany. Even in England itself, holdings of between 5 and 120 hectares comprise 64 per cent of the area cultivated, and only about 13 per cent of the area is in holdings of more than 200 hectares. In Wales, apart from very small holdings, 92 per cent are farms of between 2 and 100 hectares, and in Scotland the figure is 72 per cent.

Of the cultivated area, 61,014 holdings with 4.6 million acres of land were cultivated by their owners, 19,607 holdings were cultivated partly by their owners and partly by tenants, and 439,405 by tenants only. It is well known that in *Ireland* the small peasant and the small tenant completely outweigh the rest. The same holds for *Italy*.

All of this leaves no doubt that in the whole of Western Europe, as well as in the eastern states of the American union, the small and medium-sized agricultural holding is everywhere on the increase, and the large and very large holding is on the decrease. There is no doubt

---

[r] To which 579,133 plots of less than 4,000 square metres must be added.

that the medium-sized holdings are often of a pronounced capitalist type. The concentration of enterprises in agriculture does not take the form of individual enterprises annexing ever greater areas of land, as observed by Marx (*Capital* I, 4th edn, p. 643, note)[21]; it takes the form, quite simply, of intensified cultivation, changes to methods that require more labour per unit of land or to modified ways of rearing cattle. It is well known that this is to a large extent (not altogether) the result of agricultural competition by overseas and east European agrarian states or territories. And furthermore, the latter will, for a good while yet, be in a position to supply the European market with corn and other products of the soil at such cheap prices that no major dislocation in the factors of development is to be expected from this direction.

So, although the tables of income statistics for the advanced industrial countries do, in part, register the mobility, and thus the volatility and uncertainty, of capital in the modern economy, and although a growing proportion of the incomes or wealth they record is paper value which a strong puff of wind could, in fact, easily blow away, yet this range of incomes stands in no fundamental opposition to the gradation of economic units in industry, trade, and agriculture. The scale of incomes and the scale of businesses display a fairly pronounced parallelism in their structure, especially where the middle ranks are concerned. Nowhere do we see them on the wane; rather, we see them undergoing considerable expansion almost everywhere. What is removed from above in one place they supplement from below in another, and what drops down out of their ranks over there is made good over here from above. If the collapse of modern society depends on the disappearance of the middle ranks between the apex and the base of the social pyramid, if it depends on the absorption of these middle ranks by the extremes above and below them, then its realisation is no nearer in England, France, and Germany today than at any earlier time in the nineteenth century.

However, a building can appear outwardly as sound as ever and yet be decayed if the stones themselves or significant layers of stones have decayed. The soundness of a business company proves its worth in times of crisis; it remains therefore, for us to investigate what the position is with regard to the economic crises which are peculiar to

---

[21] *Capital* I, p. 831.

the modern order of production and what manifestations and repercussions we can expect from them in the near future.

(d) Crises and the ability of the modern economy to adapt

The fact that the movement of capitalist society is full of contradictions impresses itself most strikingly on the practical bourgeois in the changes of the periodic cycle through which modern industry passes, the summit of which is the general crisis.

Marx, preface to second edition of *Capital*[22]

The controversy over the economic crises of the modern social organism, their causes and their cure, has been scarcely less heated than that over the pathological crises, that is, the ailments, of the human body. Those who like to make comparisons will easily find points of comparison for parallels between the different kinds of theory which have been posited with regard to both sets of phenomena. For instance, the partisans of the extreme economic liberalism associated with J. B. Say, who regarded trade crises as being simply the economic organism's self-healing process,[23] can be seen as the closest soul-mates of the adherents of so-called natural homeopathy. And the various theories which recommend medical intervention in human illnesses according to various principles (symptomatic medical treatment, constitutional treatment, etc.) can be compared with the various social theories which regard as appropriate all sorts of state intervention into the causes and manifestations of economic crises. If, however, we go on to examine more closely the representatives of the systems on both sides, we shall make the remarkable discovery that there is very little consistency indeed in the ideas which ingenious psychologists of history attribute to the human race, and that an extensive belief in approved medical practitioners and their art can very easily be combined with rigid economic Manchesterism, and *vice versa*.

---

[22] Ibid., p. 103.
[23] Jean-Baptiste Say, *Traité d'économie politique* (Paris, 1803). Say argued that commodities create their own demand, and that demand creates its own supply, and he concluded that general crises of overproduction are therefore impossible, though there may be temporary local dislocations.

In socialist circles, the most popular explanation of economic crises is that they are caused by under-consumption. Friedrich Engels, however, has on several occasions taken sharp exception to this view. Most bluntly perhaps in the third section of the third chapter of his polemic against Dühring, where he says that the under-consumption of the masses is indeed 'also a prerequisite condition of crises', but that it tells us just as little about why crises exist today as about why they did not exist before.[24] As an example, Engels refers to the conditions in the English cotton industry in the year 1877 [sic] and declares that, in view of these, it is a bit thick 'to explain the complete stagnation in the yarn and cloth markets by the underconsumption of the English masses and not by the overproduction carried on by the English cotton-mill owners' (3rd edn, pp. 308–9).[*] But Marx himself also occasionally spoke out very sharply against the derivation of crises from underconsumption. 'It is a pure tautology', he says in the second volume of *Capital*, 'to say that crises are provoked by a lack of effective demand or effective consumption.'[25] If the attempt is made to give this tautology the semblance of greater profundity by saying that the working class receives too small a share of its own product, and that the evil would therefore be remedied if it received a larger share, we need only note that 'crises are always prepared by a period in which wages generally rise, and the working class actually does receive a greater share in the part of the annual product destined for consumption'.[26] It thus appears that capitalist production 'involves certain conditions independent of people's good or bad intentions, which permit the relative prosperity of the working class only temporarily, and moreover always as a harbinger of crisis' (ibid., pp. 406–7). To which Engels adds in a footnote: 'This should be noted by prospective supporters of Rodbertus's theory of crises.'

A passage in the second part of the third volume of *Capital* stands in apparent contradiction to all these statements. For there Marx says

---

[*] In a footnote, Engels remarks: 'The underconsumption explanation of crises originated with Sismondi, and in his exposition it still had a certain meaning.'[27] Rodbertus took it from Sismondi and Dühring copied it from Rodbertus. Engels polemicises in a similar fashion against Rodbertus's theory of crises in the preface to *The Poverty of Philosophy*.[28]

[24] MECW, vol. XXV, p. 272; MEW, vol. XX, p. 266.
[25] *Capital* II, p. 486.
[26] Ibid., p. 487.
[27] MECW, vol. XXV, p. 273; MEW, vol. XX, p. 267.
[28] Karl Marx, *The Poverty of Philosophy* (Lawrence & Wishart, 1956), pp. 7–11.

about crises that: 'The ultimate reason for all real crises always remains the poverty and restricted consumption of the masses, in the face of the drive of capitalist production to develop the productive forces as if only the absolute consumption capacity of society set a limit to them.'[29] That is not very different from Rodbertus's theory of crises, for he too regards crises as being caused not simply by underconsumption by the masses but by this in conjunction with the rising productivity of labour. However, in the passage from Marx cited above, underconsumption by the masses is emphasised, even in opposition to the anarchy of production – disparities in various branches of production and price changes that temporarily cause a general stagnation – as the ultimate reason for all *true* crises.

Insofar as there is a real difference of view between this and the view expressed in the above-cited passage from the second volume, the explanation must be sought in the very different times in which the two statements were made. There is an interval of no less than thirteen to fourteen years between them, and the passage from the third volume of *Capital* is the earlier one. It was written in 1864 or 1865, whereas the passage from the second volume was certainly written later than 1878 (on this, see Engels's remarks in the preface to the second volume of *Capital*). Generally speaking, the second volume contains the latest and ripest fruits of Marx's research.

In another passage in this second volume, a passage already written in 1870, the periodic character of crises – the approximately ten-year cycle of production – is connected with the time it takes for fixed capital (laid out in machinery, etc.) to turn over. The development of capitalist production has the tendency, on the one hand, to expand the value and extend the life-span of fixed capital, and on the other, to diminish this life by constantly revolutionising the means of production. Hence the 'moral depreciation' of this portion of fixed capital before it is 'physically spent'. 'The result is that the cycle of related turnovers, extending over a number of years, within which the capital is confined by its fixed component, *is one of the material foundations for the periodic cycle* in which business passes through successive periods of stagnation, moderate activity, overexcitement and crisis' (vol. II, p. 164).[30] The periods for which capital is invested certainly differ greatly, and do not coincide in time. But a crisis is always the

---

[29] *Capital* III, p. 615.   [30] *Capital* II, p. 250.

81

starting point for a large volume of new investment. If we consider society as a whole, it is therefore also 'more or less a new material basis for the next turnover cycle' (p. 165).[31] This thought is taken up again in the same volume where the reproduction of capital is dealt with (i.e. the process of the constant renewal of capital for the purposes of production and consumption on a social basis), and there it is shown how, even with reproduction remaining at the same level and with the productivity of labour unchanged, the differences in the life-span of fixed capital which occur from time to time (if, e.g., more constituent components of fixed capital decay in one year than in the previous year) must result in crises of production. Foreign trade can indeed help, but insofar as it does not just replace elements (and their value), it 'only shifts the contradictions to a broader sphere, and gives them a wider orbit'.[32] A communist society could prevent such disturbances by perpetual relative overproduction, which is 'equivalent to control by the society over the objective means of its own reproduction'. Within capitalist society, however, it is an anarchic element. This example of disturbances merely through the differences in life-spans of fixed capital is striking. 'A disproportionate production of fixed and circulating capital is a factor much favoured by the economists in their explanation of crises. It is something new to them that a disproportion of this kind can and must arise from the mere *maintenance* of the fixed capital; that it can and must arise on the assumption of an ideal normal production, with simple reproduction of the social capital already functioning' (ibid., p. 468).[33] In the chapter on 'Accumulation and Reproduction on an Expanded Scale', overproduction and crises are mentioned only incidentally as the self-evident results of possibilities of combination which are connected with the process depicted. Yet here again the concept of 'overproduction' is very energetically maintained. 'Thus,' he says on page 499, 'if Fullarton, for example, does not want to recognise overproduction in the customary sense, but does recognise the overproduction of capital, in particular of money capital, this proves once again how utterly unable even the best bourgeois economists are to understand the mechanism of their system.'[34] And on page 524 it is shown that if, as can occasionally happen even with capitalist accumulation, the constant part of the portion of capital destined for the production of

[31] Ibid., p. 264.   [32] Ibid., pp. 544–5.
[33] Ibid., p. 545.   [34] Ibid., p. 574.

the means of consumption is greater than the wages capital plus the surplus value of the portion of capital destined for the production of the means of production, this would be overproduction in the first sphere and 'could only be balanced out by a major crash'.[35]

In the third volume, Engels on several occasions applies the idea developed above – that the expansion of the market extends the contradictions of the capitalist economy into wider spheres and thus heightens them – to more recent phenomena. The notes on page 97 in the first part of this volume and on page 27 in the second part are particularly noteworthy. In the latter note, which recapitulates and completes what is said in the former, the colossal expansion of the means of communication experienced since the time Marx wrote – which has genuinely established the world market for the first time – the entry of ever fresh industrial countries into competition with England, and the unlimited extension of the sphere of investment for surplus European capital are designated as factors by which '*most of the former breeding-grounds of crises and occasions for crisis formation have been abolished or severely weakened*'. But after characterising cartels and trusts as means for limiting competition in the home market and the protective duties with which the non-English world surrounds itself as 'the weapons for the final general industrial campaign to decide supremacy on the world market', he concludes: 'And so each of the elements that counteracts a repetition of the old crises, conceals within it the nucleus of a far more violent future crisis.' Engels raises the question whether the industrial cycle, which in the infancy of world trade (1815 to 1847) was about five years long and, from 1847 to 1867, took ten years, has not undergone a new extension, and whether we do not find ourselves 'in the preparatory phase of a new world crash of unheard-of severity'. However, he also leaves open the alternative that the acute form of the periodic process with its former ten-year cycle 'seems to have given way to a more chronic and drawn-out alternation, affecting the various industrial countries at different times, between a relatively short and weak improvement in trade and a relatively long and indecisive depression'.[36]

The time that has elapsed since this was written has left the question unanswered. No signs of a worldwide economic crash of unprecedented violence have been detected, nor can the improvement of

[35] Ibid., p. 596.   [36] *Capital* III, p. 620.

trade between crises be characterised as particularly short-lived. Rather, a third question arises – which, incidentally, was already partly contained in the previous one – namely, (1) whether the enormous geographical expansion of the world market in conjunction with the extraordinary reduction in the time required for transport and the transmission of news have not so increased the possibilities of *levelling out* disturbances, and (2) whether the enormously increased wealth of the European industrial states in conjunction with the elasticity of the modern credit system and the rise of industrial cartels have not so diminished the *reactive force* of local or individual disturbances on the general state of business that, at least for some time, general trade crises similar to the earlier ones are to be regarded as unlikely.

This question, which I raised in an article on the socialist theory of collapse, has met with various kinds of opposition.[37] Amongst others, it has caused Dr Rosa Luxemburg to read me a lecture, in a series of articles published in the *Leipziger Volkszeitung* in September 1898, on the nature of credit and on the capacity of capitalism to

---

[ˈ] The articles bear the title, 'Social Reform or Revolution'[38] However, Miss Luxemburg does not pose the question in the way that, up till now, it has normally been posed in Social Democracy, namely, as a question of alternative roads to the realisation of socialism. Rather, she puts them [the alternative roads] in contrast to one another so that only one of them – on her view of revolution – can lead to the goal. According to her, the wall between capitalist and socialist society will not be breached by 'the development of social reforms and of democracy', but will, on the contrary be made 'stronger and higher'.[39] Therefore, if Social Democracy does not want to make its own work harder, it must strive to impede social reforms and the extension of democratic institutions wherever possible. The essay which ends with this conclusion begins appropriately with the remark that the propositions put forward by me (and by Dr Conrad Schmidt) on the development towards socialism are 'upside-down reflections of the external world'. 'A theory of the introduction of socialism by social reform, in the era of Stumm-Posadowsky?' she declaims. 'Of trade-union control over production, after the defeat of the English engineers? Of a Social Democratic majority in parliament, after constitutional revision in Saxony and attacks on universal suffrage for Reichstag elections?'[40] She seems to be of the opinion that one has to present historical theories not in conformity with the sum of the observed phenomena of the whole epoch and the whole area covered by the advanced countries but on the basis of temporary reactionary convulsions in this or that individual country; not on the basis of the balance-sheet of the total achievements hitherto of the workers' movement but with a view to the outcome of a particular conflict. This is to argue in the same way as the man who declared vaccinations to be useless because they did not protect him against falling out of trees.

---

[37] Tudor and Tudor, pp. 165–6.   [38] Tudor and Tudor, p. 269.
[39] Ibid., p. 540–2.   [40] Tudor and Tudor, p. 257.

adapt.[41] As these articles, which have also appeared in other socialist papers, are true examples of false dialectics, but handled at the same time with great talent, it seems to me to be appropriate to examine them here.'

Miss Luxemburg maintains that credit, far from working against crises, is the means by which they are brought to a head. To begin with, it enables capitalist production to expand without measure, it accelerates the exchange of goods and the cycle of the process of production, and it is, in this fashion, the means by which the contradiction between production and consumption is brought to the fore as often as possible. It enables the capitalist to dispose of the capital of others and thus to engage in reckless speculation. But if a recession sets in, its contraction intensifies the crisis. Its function is to banish the residue of stability from all capitalist conditions and to make all capitalist forces elastic, relative, and sensitive to the highest degree.

Now, all that is not exactly new to anyone who knows a little about socialist literature in general and about Marxist socialism in particular. The only question is whether it correctly describes the present facts of the case, or whether there is not another side to the picture. According to the laws of dialectic, to which Miss Luxemburg is so fond of giving play, it must certainly be the case. But even without referring back to these laws, one could say that a thing like credit, capable of so many forms, must operate in different ways under different conditions. Marx, furthermore, by no means treats credit as if it were merely a destructive agent. Amongst other things, he assigns it the function of constituting 'the form of transition towards a new mode of production', and, with regard to this, he expressly emphasises 'the dual character of the credit system'.[42] Miss Luxemburg knows the passage in question very well; she even repeats the passage from it where Marx speaks of the mixed character – 'half swindler, half prophet' – of the principal spokesmen for credit (John Law, Isaac Pereire, etc.). But she refers exclusively to the destructive side of the credit system and says not a word about its productive and creative capacity, which Marx expressly brings into play. Why this amputation, why this strange silence with regard to the 'dual character'? The brilliant dialectical fireworks by means of which the power of the credit system as a means of adaptation is presented as

---

[41] Ibid., pp. 249ff. [42] *Capital* III, p. 572.

a one-day wonder is dissolved into smoke and mist as soon as one looks more closely at this other side which Miss Luxemburg glides over so coyly.

Besides, the individual propositions of her demonstration will not bear close scrutiny. Credit, she tells us, 'aggravates the contradiction between the mode of production and the mode of exchange by stretching production to the maximum while paralysing exchange at the slightest pretext'.[43] A very witty observation; but the pity of it is that the sentence can be turned around any way one wants without its becoming incorrect. Transpose the two nouns in the second part, and the sentence is just as correct as it was before. Or one could say that credit abolishes the antagonism between the mode of production and the mode of exchange in that it periodically levels out the disparities between production and exchange, and one would still be right. 'Credit', we are further told, 'aggravates the contradiction between property relationships and the relationships of production by forcibly expropriating large numbers of small capitalists and concentrating vast productive forces in the hands of a few.'[44] This proposition contains just as much truth as does its precise opposite. We are only expressing a fact frequently attested in reality when we say that credit abolishes the contradiction between property relationships and the relationships of production in that, by uniting many small capitalists, it transforms vast productive forces into collective property. As we have seen in the section on the distribution of income, this is quite obviously the case with joint-stock companies in their simple and their advanced forms. If Miss Luxemburg wishes to counter this by appealing to Marx who, in the section referred to, yet again attributes to the credit system a growing tendency to limit the number of the few who exploit social wealth, then it must be replied that no empirical proof of this assertion is provided by Marx. Nor could it be, for Marx often refers to facts which contradict it – for instance when, in chapter 22 of volume III, he deals with the tendency of the rate of interest to fall, he refers to the growing number of *rentiers* in England, as established by Ramsay (*Capital* III, part 1, p. 428).[45] But though Marx is repeatedly liable to confuse legal and physical persons (for that, after all is what underlies this assumption), it does not cloud his perception of the positive economic potential of credit. This is

---

[43] Tudor and Tudor, p. 254.   [44] *Capital* III, p. 484.   [45] Ibid., pp. 571–2

86

most clearly apparent where he speaks of workers' cooperatives, the most characteristic type of which is, for him, still the old producers' cooperative – he calls it the cooperative factory – and of this he says that it reproduces all the defects of the existing system, and must reproduce them. But nevertheless, he continues, it positively abolishes the antagonism existing in the capitalist factory. If it is the offspring of the factory system based on capitalist production, it is equally the offspring of the *credit system* resting on the same basis, without which, Marx tells us, they would not have been able to develop, and it '*presents the means for the gradual extension of cooperative enterprises on a more or less national scale*' (*Capital* III, part 1, p. 428).[46] Here we have the reversal of Luxemburg's dictum in superlative form.

That the credit system makes speculation easier is an experience centuries old; and it is also a hoary experience that speculation does not stop production when the form and constitution of the latter are sufficiently developed for its operation. However, for its part speculation depends on the relationship between known circumstances and unknown circumstances. The more the latter predominate, the more will speculation flourish; the more it is pushed back by the former, the more the ground is cut from under its feet. Therefore the most frantic outbursts of commercial speculation occur *at the dawn of the capitalist era*, and speculation usually celebrates its wildest orgies in countries where capitalist development is still young. In the domain of industry, speculation flourishes most luxuriantly in *new* branches of production. In modern industry, the older a branch of production is – except for the manufacture of goods exclusively for the fashion trade – the more does the speculative element cease to play a decisive role in it. The conditions and movements of the market are more exactly observed and are taken into account with greater certainty.

Nevertheless, this certainty is always only relative, because competition and technological advance preclude absolute control of the market. Overproduction is to a certain extent unavoidable. However, overproduction in individual industries does not mean general crises. In order to produce a general crisis, the industries in question would either have to be of such importance as consumers of the manufac-

[46] Ibid.

tures of other industries that if they came to a halt, so would the others, and so on; or they would, by means of the money market, that is, through a general paralysis of credit, have to deprive the others of the wherewithal to continue production. However, it is evident that the greater the wealth of a country and the more developed its credit system – not to be confused with heightened business activity on credit – the less is the likelihood of any such consequence. For here the possibilities of adjustment multiply in growing measure. In a passage, which I cannot find at the moment, Marx once said – and the correctness of his claim is supported by a mass of evidence – that the contractions in the centre of the money market are much more quickly overcome than at various points on the periphery. And Marx had in view a money market which was much more restricted, even in England, than it is today. Thus he still tells us *Capital* III part 2, p. 18) that, with the expansion of the market, credit is extended and thus the element of speculation must become more and more dominant in business.[47] However, the revolution in the means of communication achieved since then has, in this regard, more than neutralised the effects of great distances." Crises in the money market may not have been banished from the world, but at least, as far as we are concerned, contractions of the money market caused by business enterprises far apart from each other and hard to control are significantly reduced.

The relationship of financial crises to trade and business crises is not yet so fully explained that, in any particular concrete case in which the two coincide, we can say with certainty that it was the trade crisis, that is, overproduction, that directly caused the financial crisis. In most cases, indeed, it was clearly not actual overproduction but overspeculation that paralysed the money market and thus depressed

---

" Engels calculates that, thanks to the Suez Canal, cargo steamers, etc., America and India have been brought nearer to the industrial countries of Europe by 70 to 90 per cent, and he adds that 'the two major foci of crisis between 1825 and 1857 . . . have lost in this way a good deal of their explosive potential' (*Capital* III, part 1, p. 45).[48] On p. 395 of the same volume, Engels maintains that certain speculative activities connected with credit fraud, which Marx characterises as factors of crisis in the money market, have been brought to an end by the overseas telegraph.[49] Engels's corrective parenthesis on p. 56 of the second part of volume III is also worth noting for its judgment on the development of the credit system.

[47] Ibid., p. 612.   [48] *Capital* III, p. 164.   [49] Ibid., p. 537.

business as a whole. This follows from the details which, in the third volume of *Capital*, Marx gives from the official investigations into the crises of 1847 and 1857,[50] and it is confirmed by the facts which Professor Herkner adduces in connection with these and other crises in his sketch of the history of trade crises in *The Dictionary of Political Sciences*. From the facts cited by Herkner, Dr Luxemburg draws the inference that the crises we have had so far were not at all the right crises but were only *infantile ailments* of the capitalist economy, the symptoms, not of a contraction, but of a *widening* of the domain of the capitalist economy, that 'we have not yet reached the stage of full capitalist maturity presupposed in Marx's model of periodic crisis formation'. According to her we find ourselves 'at a stage in which crises are no longer a symptom of the rise of capitalism and not yet a symptom of its demise'. This time will only come when the world market is fully developed and can not be enlarged any further by sudden expansions. Then the conflict between the forces of production and the limits of exchange must become ever sharper and more turbulent.[51]

Against this it must be observed that the crisis-model in Marx, or for Marx, depicted not the future but the present, and the expectation was only that, in the future, it would recur in ever harsher forms and with ever greater severity. In denying that the model has the significance Marx imputed to it for the whole epoch which has just gone by and in presenting it as a deduction which did not yet correspond with reality, but which was the logical construction of an anticipated event based on the existence of certain elements in an embryonic state, Miss Luxemburg questions Marx's prognosis of future social development, insofar as this prognosis depends on the theory of crises. For if it was not yet valid for the time in which it was formulated, and if it has not been confirmed by practice in the time between then and now, to what more distant point in the future can the model be represented as relevant? Referring it to the time when the world market is fully developed is a theoretical flight into the world to come.

It is absolutely impossible to know when the world market will be fully developed. Miss Luxemburg is, surely, not ignorant of the fact that there is not only an extensive but also an *intensive* expansion of

---

[50] Ibid., pp. 249.   [51] Ibid.

89

the world market and that nowadays the latter is of much greater importance than the former.

In the trade statistics of the major industrial countries, exports to countries with long-established populations play by far the greatest role. To the whole of Australasia (all the Australian colonies, New Zealand, etc.) England exports less, in terms of value, than it does to a single country, France; and to the whole of British North America (Canada, British Columbia, etc.) it exports less than it does to Russia alone; and to both these colonial territories together, which are indeed of a respectable age, it exports less than it does to Germany. England's foreign trade with all its colonies, including the whole of the immense Indian Empire, amounts to not quite a third of its trade with the rest of the world, and as for the colonial acquisitions of the last twenty years, the exports thither have been ridiculously small.[*] The extension of the world market takes place much too slowly to provide a sufficient outlet for the actual increase in production, were it not for the fact that the countries already involved offered it an ever larger market. No a priori limit can be set for this intensive expansion of the world market, which takes place at the same time as its spatial extension. If the general crisis is an immanent law of capitalist production, then it must establish itself as true now or in the near future. Otherwise the proof of its inevitability hovers in the air of abstract speculation.

We have seen that, compared with earlier times, credit nowadays is subject not to more but to fewer of the contractions that lead to a general paralysis of production and is to that extent becoming less of a factor in the creation of crises. But insofar as it tends to promote overproduction hothouse-fashion, this is increasingly countered within various countries – and even on an international level here and there – by the manufacturers' association which seeks to regulate production as a cartel, syndicate, or trust. Without embarking on

---

[*] Here are some of the figures for 1895. Of total exports, 75.6 per cent went abroad – nine-tenths of it to the old countries – and 24.4 per cent went to British colonies. Measured by value, the amounts exported (including transit goods) were: to British North America 6.6 million pounds sterling, to Russia 10.7, to Australasia 19.3, to France 20.3, to Germany 32.7, to the whole of British East and West Africa 2.4, i.e. not even 1 per cent of the total exported, which amounted to 285.8 million. In 1895, exports to all British possessions were about 64.8 per cent higher than in the year 1860, and to other countries they were 77.2 per cent higher (see *Constitutional Yearbook* of 1897).

prophecies as to their ultimate vitality and effectiveness, I have acknowledged their ability to influence the relationship between productive activity and market conditions in such a way that the danger of crises is diminished.[52] Miss Luxemburg refutes this as well.

First, she denies that associations of manufacturers could become general. The final aim and effect of such associations are to increase their share of the total amount of profit gained in the commodity market by eliminating competition within a particular branch of industry. However, one branch of industry can achieve this only at the expense of another, and the organisation could not possibly, therefore, become general. 'If they were extended to all branches of industry, they would cancel each other out.'[53]

This proof is identical, down to the last hair, to the long-since-exploded proof of the uselessness of trade unions. Indeed, its support is immeasurably more fragile than that of the wages fund theory of blessed memory.[54] It is the unproven, unprovable, or rather demonstrably false assumption, that in the commodity market there is always only a fixed amount of profit to be distributed. It assumes, amongst other things, that prices are determined independently of changes in the cost of production. But even given a fixed price and, furthermore, a fixed technological basis of production, the amount of profit in one branch of industry can be increased without thereby diminishing the profit of another, namely, by reducing unnecessary costs, eliminating unfair competition, better organisation of production, and the like. It is obvious that an association of manufacturers is an effective means to this end. The problem of the division of profits is the last obstacle of all which stands in the way of manufacturers' associations becoming universal.

According to Dr Luxemburg, another point that speaks against the ability of cartels to check the anarchy of production is that they seek to achieve their purpose – stopping the fall in the rate of profit – by leaving fallow a portion of the accumulated capital, thus doing precisely what, in another form, crises achieve. The remedy resembles the disease as one drop of water resembles another. A part of the capital which has been socialised by the organisation is converted back into private capital, each portion tries its luck off its own bat, and 'the employers' organisations inevitably burst like bubbles and

[52] Ibid., p. 165.   [53] Ibid., p. 254.   [54] Ibid., p. 255.

make way once more for free competition, in an intensified form'.[55]

This assumes, in the first place, that the surgical removal of a gangrenous limb resembles the destruction of that limb by gangrene 'as one drop of water resembles another', because in both cases the limb is lost. The devastation of capital by an elemental event, which is what crises are, and the laying off of capital by an industrial organisation are two very different things, because the one means only a temporary stoppage whereas the other means direct destruction. However, it is nowhere written that capital which is superfluous in one branch of production can be employed, or must seek employment, only in that same branch of production. For a change, this assumes that the number of branches of production is fixed for all time, which again is contradicted by reality.

Miss Luxemburg's final objection fares somewhat better. She argues that cartels are unsuitable for controlling the anarchy of production because, as a rule, the entrepreneurs in a cartel achieve their high rate of profit on the home market by using the capital the home market can not employ in order to produce goods for export at a much lower rate of profit. The consequence: increased anarchy on the world market, the opposite of the result intended.[56]

'As a rule', this manoeuvre only works where the cartel is covered by a protective tariff which makes it impossible for foreign countries to pay it back in the same coin. In the sugar industry, to which Miss Luxemburg refers as an illustration of her thesis, it is the intensified form of protective tariff, the export premium, which has brought about the delights described. But it is worth noting that the agitation against this beneficial arrangement is much stronger in the countries which rejoice in it than it is in the country which dispenses with it and whose sugar production is exposed, without protection, to competition from countries blessed with export premiums and sugar cartels, namely England. And the English know why perfectly well. This premiumed competition has undoubtedly done severe damage to the English refiners – though by no means to the degree often supposed, for the English refiner of course also gets his raw material, raw sugar, with the export premium removed. Whereas in the year 1864 only 424,000 tons of sugar were refined in England, 623,000 tons were refined in 1894, and 632,000 tons in 1896. In the meantime, produc-

---

[55] Ibid.   [56] Ibid., pp. 254–6.

tion had indeed reached an even higher figure (it was 824,000 in 1884), but though this level could not be maintained, the sugar-related industries (confectionery, jams, preserved fruit, etc.) achieved an impetus which outweighed this relative decline tenfold. From 1881 to 1891 the number of persons employed in England's sugar refineries suffered no decline whatsoever, while those employed in the confectionery industry alone nearly doubled." To this must be added the rapidly growing manufacture of jams and marmalade, which have become popular articles of consumption, employing thousands upon thousands of workers. Had the continental sugar manufacturers wiped out the whole of England's refining industry by means of the sugar premium and similar manoeuvres, which however is not the case, then the loss of job opportunities for some 5,000 workers would have been balanced by a gain of at least eight times that number of job opportunities. This does not take into account the impetus which cheap sugar has given to the cultivation of soft fruit in England. Besides, it is said that premiumed beet-sugar has ruined the planters of cane-sugar in the British colonies, and there is no lack of cries of distress from the West Indian planters. But this worthy class of persons bears a distressing resemblance to those desperate agriculturalists who under any circumstances would be ruined by the mathematics of the case. In fact, England imports more cane sugar from its possessions today than it used to (from 2,300,000 hundredweight in the year 1890, the imports of cane sugar from the British possessions rose to 3,100,000 hundredweight in the year 1896); it is just that other colonies have overtaken the West Indies. In 1882, exactly two-thirds of the total export from British possessions fell to the share of the West Indies; in 1896, it was less than half. The profits of the planters have certainly deteriorated, but that is not quite the

" *The relevant figures from the census are:*

	Persons employed		
	1881	1891	Difference
Sugar refineries			
Men	4,285	4,682	+317 [*sic*]
Women	122	238	+116
Confectionery industry			
Men	14,305	20,291	+5986
Women	15,285	34,788	+19,503

same thing as ruin, unless heavy indebtedness previously incurred is involved.

However, we are concerned neither with denying the harmful effects of current simple and compounded protectionist policies, nor with issuing an apology for industrialists' associations. It never entered my head to maintain that cartels etc. are the last word in economic development and are capable of removing permanently the antagonisms of modern economic life. On the contrary, I am convinced that where in modern industrial states cartels and trusts are supported and strengthened by protective tariffs they must, in fact, become crisis factors in the industry concerned – and also for the 'protected' country itself, if not initially then in any case ultimately. The only question is how long the people concerned will be content with this arrangement. Protective tariffs are not a product of the economy but an intervention in the economy by political authorities seeking to bring about economic effects. The industrial cartel as such is a very different animal. Even when nurtured hothouse-fashion by protective tariffs, it has grown out of the soil of the economy itself and is a characteristic means of adjusting production to the movements of the market. There is no question that at the same time it is, or can become, a means for monopolistic exploitation. But neither is there any question that, in its first capacity, it represents an enhancement of all previous remedies for overproduction. With much less risk than an individual enterprise, it can temporarily limit production in times of a glut on the market. What is better, it is also in a position to take steps against unfair competition from abroad. To deny this is to deny the superiority of organisation over anarchic competition. But that is what we do when we deny in principle that cartels can have a modifying effect on the nature and frequency of crises. How *far* they can do so is for the present a matter of pure conjecture, for we do not yet have sufficient experience to reach any definite conclusion. And in these circumstances, there are even fewer fixed points of reference for the predetermination of future *general* crises, as Marx and Engels originally envisaged them, as aggravated repetitions of the crises of 1825, 1836, 1847, 1857, and 1873. The very fact that for many years socialists believed that an increasing *contraction* of the industrial cycle was the natural consequence of the increasing concentration of capital – a spiral development – but that Friedrich Engels in 1894 felt obliged to ask whether we were not facing a new *extension* of the cycle, in other words the precise opposite of the previous assumption, serves as a warning against the abstract inference that these crises *must* repeat themselves in the old form.[x]

The history of individual industries shows that their crises by no means always coincide with the so-called general crises. Whoever reads what Marx says about the history of the English cotton industry in volume I and volume III of *Capital* (I, chapter 13 and III, chapter 6) will find it established, and recent history confirms it, that this and other major branches of industry go through phases of buoyant business activity and stagnation which have no profound effect on most of the other industries.[57] As we have seen, Marx believed he could establish that the need for an accelerated renewal of fixed capital (instruments of production, etc.) provided a material foundation for periodic crises,[y] and it is absolutely correct that this is an important element in the formation of crises. But it is not correct, or it is no longer correct, that these periods of renewal occur at the same time in the various industries. And thus a further factor of the great general crisis is eliminated.

All that remains is the point that productive capacity in modern society is much greater than the actual demand for products as determined by buying power, that millions live in inadequate housing and are inadequately clothed and fed, despite the fact that there are abundant means available to provide adequate housing, clothing, and food; that out of this incongruity, overproduction takes place again and again in different branches of production, so that either certain articles are in fact produced in greater quantity than can be used – for example, more yarn than the existing weaving mills can work up – or certain articles are produced not indeed in greater quantity than can be used but in greater quantity than can be bought; that in

---

[x] Here we are, of course, speaking only of the *economic* basis of crises. Crises resulting from political events (wars or serious threats of war) or from very widespread crop failure – local failures no longer have any effect in this respect – are of course always possible, as was already remarked in my article on the theory of collapse.[58]

[y] The use of the word 'material' in the passage mentioned (vol. II, p. 164) is not without interest in judging how Marx understood this concept. According to the usual present definition of the concept, the explanation of crises by underconsumption would be just as materialistic as basing them on changes in the process of production, e.g. tools.

[57] *Capital* I, pp. 587ff and III, pp. 219ff. In neither place does Marx quite make the point which Bernstein ascribes to him.

[58] Tudor and Tudor, p. 166.

consequence of this, great irregularities occur in the employment of workers, which makes their condition extremely insecure, reduces them again and again to humiliating dependence, and brings forth overwork in one place and unemployment in another; and that of the means used nowadays to combat the most extreme manifestations of this evil, cartels of capitalist entrepreneurs represent monopolistic associations against the workers on the one hand and against the public at large on the other, and they tend to wage war over people's heads, and at their expense, with similar monopolies in other industries and other countries or, by international or inter-industrial agreements, to adjust production and prices arbitrarily to suit their own need for profit. In effect, the capitalist means of defence against crises bear within themselves the seeds of a new and more onerous *bondage* for the working class, as well as the seeds of production privileges which are a more acute form of the old guild privileges. From the standpoint of the workers, it seems to me to be much more important at present to keep in mind the potentialities of cartels and trusts than to prophesy their 'impotency'. Whether in the long run they are able to achieve their prime objective, the prevention of crises, is in itself a minor question for the working class. But it becomes a very significant question as soon as expectations of any kind as regards the movement for the liberation of the working class are linked to the general crisis. For then the idea that cartels can do nothing to prevent crises can be the cause of fatal neglect.

The short sketch we gave in the introduction to this chapter of the Marx–Engels explanations of economic crises will suffice, in conjunction with the pertinent facts adduced, to show that the question of crises is a problem that cannot be solved categorically with a few tried and trusty slogans. We can only establish what elements in the modern economy promote crises and what forces impede them. It is impossible to decide a priori the ultimate relation of these forces to one another, or their development. Unless unforeseen *external* events bring about a general crisis – and as we have said, that can happen any day – there is no compelling reason to conclude, on purely economic grounds, that such a crisis is imminent. Local and partial recessions are unavoidable. Thanks to the present organisation and expansion of the world market, and thanks particularly to the great *expansion in food production*, a general stagnation is not unavoidable. The expansion of food production is of particular importance for our problem. Perhaps nothing has contributed so much to the mitigation of business crises, or to the prevention of their increase, as the fall in rents and food prices.

CHAPTER 4

The tasks and opportunities of Social Democracy

(a) The political and economic prerequisites of socialism

If we asked a number of people of any class or party to give a brief definition of socialism, most of them would be in some difficulty. Those who do not simply toss off some phrase they have heard must first be clear as to whether they are characterising a state of affairs or a movement, a perception or a goal. If we consult the literature of socialism itself, we will find very different accounts of the concept depending on whether they fall into one or other of the categories indicated above. They will vary from its derivation from legal ideas (equality, justice) to its succinct characterisation as social science and its identification with the class struggle of the workers in modern society and the explanation that socialism means cooperative economics. In some cases, fundamentally different conceptions provide the basis for this variety of explanations, but for the most part they are simply the result of seeing or representing one and the same thing from different points of view.

In any case, the most precise characterisation of socialism will be the one that takes the idea of cooperation as its starting point, because this idea expresses simultaneously an economic and a legal relationship. It takes no long-winded demonstration to show that the legal side is just as important as the economic side. Quite apart from the question whether, and in what sense, law is a primary or secondary factor in the life of a society, its law at any one time undoubtedly gives the most concentrated depiction of its character. We identify forms of society not according to their technological or economic foundations but according to the basic principle of their legal institutions. We do indeed speak of an age of stone, bronze, machinery, electricity, etc., but we speak of a feudal, capitalist, bourgeois, etc., order of society. This fits in with the characterisation of socialism as

98

a movement towards, or the state of, a cooperative order of society. It is in this sense – which, indeed, also accords with the etymology of the word (*socius* = associate) – that the term is used in what follows.

Now, what are the preconditions for the realisation of socialism? Historical materialism finds them first of all in the modern development of production. The spread of capitalist big business in industry and agriculture provides a lasting and steadily growing material basis for the drive towards a socialist transformation of society. In these enterprises, production is already socially organised; only the management is by individuals, and the profit is appropriated by individuals, not on the basis of their work, but on the basis of their share of the capital. At work the worker is separated from the ownership of his instruments of production; he is in the dependent condition of a wage-earner, from which he does not escape as long as he lives; and the burden is increased by the uncertainty connected with this dependence on his employer together with the fluctuations in the state of trade, which is the consequence of the anarchy of production. Like production itself, the living-conditions of the producers also tend towards the socialisation and the cooperative organisation of work. As soon as this development is sufficiently advanced, the realisation of socialism becomes an imperative necessity for the further development of society. To bring it about is the task of the proletariat organised as a class party which, for this purpose, must seize political power.

So, as the first precondition of the general realisation of socialism we have a certain level of capitalist development and, as the second, we have the exercise of political power by the class party of the workers, Social Democracy. In the transitional period, the form in which this power is exercised is, according to Marx, the dictatorship of the proletariat.[1]

As regards the first precondition, it has already been shown in the chapter on classes of establishment in production and distribution that although big business does in fact predominate in industry nowadays it, together with the businesses dependent upon it, represents at most half of the population engaged in production, even in a country as advanced as Prussia. We get the same picture if we take the

---

[1] See, for instance, *The Class Struggles in France*, MECW, vol. X, p. 127; MEW, vol. VII, pp. 89–90. Also Engels's 'Introduction' to *The Civil War in France*, MESW, vol. I, p. 485; MEW, vol. XXII, p. 199.

figures for Germany as a whole, and it is not much different in England, the most industrialised country in Europe. In other foreign countries, with the possible exception of Belgium, the relation of big business to small and medium-sized businesses is much less favourable. In agriculture, however, we invariably find small and medium holdings, not only in a significant proportional preponderance over large holdings, but also well placed to strengthen their position. In trade and commerce, the relation of the groups of businesses is similar.

It is true that the picture given by the overall figures of company statistics is subject to many qualifications when the individual sections are examined more closely. This is a point I myself have already made in my article on the theory of collapse, after I had expressly referred, in earlier articles of the series *Problems of Socialism*, to the fact that the number of employees in a company is no sure indication of the extent to which it is capitalist in nature.[2] The objections which, in the *Sächsische Arbeiter-Zeitung*,[3] Parvus has raised against the use I made, in the passage referred to, of the total figures for groups of companies said essentially nothing that I had not already stated on many occasions myself, and they are quite irrelevant to the question of the likelihood of an imminent economic collapse, which is what we are concerned with here.[a] It may be that some of the hundreds

[a] I will not dwell on Parvus's misinterpretations of my remarks, nor on the grotesque comparisons (cab drivers vs railways, etc.) with which he sought to ridicule my reference to the relative strength of small and medium-sized businesses. They are in the first instance irritating, coming as they do from a man I had believed to be capable of better things, but they are not worth serious refutation.

However, for the reasons set forth in the text, I can not see how the facts which Heinrich Cunow adduces against me in his utterly appropriate article on the theory of collapse have any bearing on my thesis.[4] He will accept that what he says about banking and commercial agencies was not unknown to me when he learns that I was myself employed for many years in the banking business and that I also know from experience about the wholesale trade. And as regards subsidiary and branch companies, I have myself written, in an earlier article in the series *Problems of Socialism*: 'In practice, subsidiary companies which perhaps operate with a great deal of constant and very little variable capital and employ expensive machines and few workers are listed in the statistics of the Reich as small factories or even small workshops, whereas in fact they belong to the factory-size companies . . . We may take it to be well established that the workshop and the small factory appear much more prominent in the trade statistics than they are in reality' (*Die Neue Zeit*, xv, 1, p. 308). And as for agriculture: 'The area can be quite small and still serve as the basis for a completely capitalist business. Statistics which

[2] Tudor and Tudor, pp. 161ff.   [3] Ibid., pp. 179ff.
[4] Cunow, 'Zur Zusammenbruchstheorie'.

of thousands of small businesses are capitalist in nature and that others are completely or partly dependent on capitalist big businesses, but this can make only a slight difference to the overall picture provided by the statistics for business enterprises. It can not disprove the great and growing diversity of enterprises and the differentiated structure of industry. If we strike a quarter or even a half of all small businesses in Germany off the list as being dependants of medium and large businesses, there remain in industry alone a million businesses, from giant capitalist enterprises down in ever-broadening circles to the hundreds of thousands of small handicraft enterprises. The latter do indeed, from time to time, pay tribute to the process of concentration but they do not, for that reason, show any sign of disappearing from the scene. In addition to the figures given on this subject in the second section of our third chapter, let us cite from the statistics of the German *building trade* the fact that from 1882 to 1895 the number of self-employed increased from 146,175 to 177,012 and the number of employees from 580,121 to 777,705. This does indeed signify a modest increase in dependants per enterprise (from 3.97 to 4.37) but it does certainly not signify a reduction in handicraft enterprises.[b]

It follows that insofar as the centralised form of enterprise is a precondition for the socialisation of production and distribution, it is only partially met, even in the most advanced countries of Europe. So if, in the near future, the German state wanted to expropriate all enterprises employing, say, twenty persons or more, whether for complete state management or for sub-contracting, there would still be hundreds of thousands of enterprises in trade and industry, with *more than 4 million workers*, to be carried on under private management. In agriculture, if all holdings of more than 20 hectares were nationalised – which no one dreams of doing – *more than 5 million* privately managed holdings would remain with a total of nearly 9 million workers. We can form an idea of the magnitude of the task

rely on the area of the establishment say less and less about their economic character' (ibid., p. 380). Similarly in my article on 'The Theory of Collapse' on p. 552, xvi, 1, with regard to the figures for trade and commerce.

[b] See Schmoele, *Social Democratic Trade Unions in Germany*, part two, volume I, pp. 1 ff. where also the dark side of small enterprises in the building trade is exhibited.[5]

[5] Josef Schmoele, *Die Sozialdemokratischen Gewerkschaften in Deutschland seit dem Erlasse des Sozialisten-Gesetzes* (Jena, 1896).

which would be borne by the state, or the states, on taking over the larger enterprises if we bear in mind that we are talking about several hundred thousand enterprises in trade and industry with 5 to 6 million employees and, in agriculture, more than 300,000 enterprises with 5 million workers. Imagine the huge resources of judgment, expertise, and managerial talent which a government or national assembly must have at its command to be equal to even just the direction or economic control of such a gigantic organism!

At this point, our attention will perhaps be drawn to the large number of intelligentsia produced by modern society, who would gladly offer their services in a period of transition. I have no doubt whatsoever as to the energy and good-will of this social group; indeed, I drew attention to it nearly eighteen years ago.[6] But it is precisely in this *embarras de richesses* that the danger lies, and what the malice of the enemy can not accomplish is easily achieved by the benevolence of our growing army of good friends. Even in normal times, benevolence is a dubious customer.

But let us set this question aside for a while and underline the fact that the material precondition for the socialisation of production and distribution, the advanced centralisation of industry, is only partly achieved.

The second precondition is, according to Marx's doctrine, the seizure of political power by the proletariat. This seizure can be thought of in various ways: by the path of parliamentary struggle through exploitation of the franchise and the use of all other legal ways and means, or by the use of force by means of revolution.[c]

It is well known that, until quite late in their lives, Marx and Engels considered the latter path as inevitable nearly everywhere, and even today various adherents of Marx's doctrine believe it to be unavoidable. It is also often held to be the shorter way.[d]

---

[c] Here and in what follows, 'revolution' is used exclusively in the *political* sense of the term, as being synonymous with a *rising* or *extra-legal force*. On the other hand, the term *social transformation* will be used for fundamental change in the social order. This leaves open the question as to the way in which it is achieved. The purpose of making this distinction is to eliminate all misunderstandings and ambiguities.

[d] 'But is there anyone to whom it is not obvious that once the workers have come to power and achieved absolute control of administration and legislation in the large cities, where they constitute the overwhelming majority, the economic revolution would be only a question of months, nay, perhaps of weeks?' (Jules Guesde, 'The Eighteenth of March (1871) in the Provinces', *Zukunft* of 1877, p. 87).

[6] In his 'Klippen', *Der Sozialdemokrat*, 12 April 1890.

This view derives its plausibility primarily from the idea that the working class is the most numerous and (being propertyless) the most active social class. Once in possession of power, it would not rest until it had replaced the foundations of the existing system with such arrangements as would make the restoration of that system impossible.

It has already been mentioned that, in formulating their theory of the dictatorship of the proletariat, Marx and Engels had in mind the Terror in the French Revolution as a typical example. Further, in *Anti-Dühring*, Engels described St Simon's discovery in 1802 that the Reign of Terror was to be understood as the rule of the propertyless masses as a stroke of genius.[7] That is probably an exaggeration, but however highly one rates this discovery, the outcome of the rule of the propertyless fares no better in St Simon than it does in Schiller, nowadays decried as a 'philistine'.[8] The propertyless of 1793 were only capable of fighting the battles of others. They could

'But we declare: Give us governmental power for half a year, and capitalism would be relegated to history.' (Parvus in *Sächsische Arbeiter-Zeitung*, 6 March 1898.)

The latter proposition comes at the end of an article in which, amongst other things, it is shown that even after the social revolutionary government has taken the regulation of the total production in hand, the replacement of commodity trade by an artificially contrived system of exchange is not feasible. In other words, Parvus, who has given serious attention to economics, understands on the one hand that 'the trade in commodities has permeated so deeply all conditions of social life that it can not be replaced by an artificially contrived system of exchange', and in spite of this conviction, which has long been mine (it was already hinted at in the article on 'The Social and Political Significance of Space and Number', but was to have been treated more thoroughly in a later article in the series *Problems of Socialism*),[9] he imagines that a social revolutionary government could, with the present structure of industry, 'regulate' the whole of production and, in half a year, exterminate root and branch the capitalist system that has grown up out of the production of commodities with which it is so intimately bound up. It is evident that an enthusiasm for the use of force can turn otherwise well-informed people into political juveniles.

[7] MECW, vol. XXV, p. 246; MEW, vol. XX, p. 241. The reference is to Saint-Simon's *Lettres d'un habitant de Genève à ses contemporains.*

[8] Possibly a reference to Engels's remark: 'The superstition that philosophical idealism is pivoted round a belief in ethical, that is, social, ideals, arose outside philosophy, among the German Philistines, who learned by heart from Schiller's poems the few morsels of philosophical culture they needed', *Feuerbach and the End of Classical German Philosophy*, MESW, vol. II, p. 376; MEW, vol. XXI, p. 281.

[9] Parvus's article is the last in a series of three entitled 'Soziale Revolution und Sozialismus'. It is difficult to tell precisely which passage in 'The Social and Political Significance of Space and Number' contains the 'hint' mentioned by Bernstein. (Tudor and Tudor, pp. 83ff.)

only 'rule' as long as the Terror lasted. When it had exhausted itself, as it was bound to do, their rule came to an abrupt end. According to the view of Marx and Engels, the modern proletariat would not be exposed to this danger. But what is the modern proletariat?

If it includes all those without property, all who derive no income from property or from a privileged position, then it does certainly constitute the absolute majority of the population of the advanced countries. But this 'proletariat' is a mixture of extraordinarily varied elements, of social groups which are even more differentiated than was 'the people' of 1789. As long as present property relations persist, they do indeed have more common or, at least, similar interests than antagonistic ones; but they would quickly become aware of the different natures of their needs and interests as soon as the present propertied and ruling groups are removed or deprived of their position.

I have previously remarked that modern wage-earners are not the homogeneous mass uniformly devoid of property, family, etc., as predicted in *The Communist Manifesto*, that it is precisely in the most advanced manufacturing industries that a whole hierarchy of differentiated workers is to be found, and that among these there is only a tenuous feeling of solidarity.[10] In the article already mentioned, H. Cunow sees this remark as confirming the fact that, even when speaking in general terms, I have English conditions particularly in mind. In Germany and in the other civilised countries on the Continent, the better-placed worker is not isolated from the revolutionary movement as he is in England. In contrast to England, the best-paid workers stand in the forefront of the class struggle. English caste feeling is not a consequence of present social differentiation but an after-effect of the earlier system of crafts and guilds and of the older trade-union movement which was modelled on them.[11]

Again, I must reply to Cunow that he is telling me nothing new – indeed, nothing new that is correct and nothing new that is incorrect (i.e. he tells me nothing that has not already occurred to me). His concluding remarks, for instance, are incorrect. The theory which links the English trade unions with the guilds rests on very shaky foundations. It overlooks the fact that the guilds in England were expropriated already in the Reformation, except in London, and that it is precisely in London that the trade-union movement has never

[10] Tudor and Tudor, pp. 235–41.
[11] Heinrich Cunow, 'Zur Zusammenbruchstheorie', *NZ*, 17, 1 (1898–9).

managed to gather particular momentum, a state of affairs for which the guilds, which still exist there, bear very little responsibility. If certain guild-like features are to be found in the English trade-union movement, it is not so much a legacy from the old guild system – which, indeed, existed much longer in Germany than in England – as one of the chief products of Anglo-Saxon *freedom*, of the fact that the English worker was never under the thumb of a police-state, not even at the time of the suppression of the right of association. The sense of individuality or, to speak like Stirner for once, the sense of *own-ness* is developed in freedom. It does not rule out acceptance of what is different in nature or what belongs to the common interest, but, when it is one-sided, it easily becomes the cause of a certain edginess which appears hard and narrow-minded. I certainly do not want to wrong the German workers, and I fully appreciate the idealism which, for example, moved the Hamburg workers for decades to make sacrifices for the common cause and for the proletarian struggle for freedom, sacrifices unequalled in the labour movement. But so far as I can tell from my knowledge of the German labour movement and from the opportunities I have had of following it, the effects of the differentiation of trades described above have made themselves felt even there. Special circumstances, such as the dominance of the political movement, the artificial suppression of the trade unions, and the fact that on the whole the differences in wages and hours of work are generally less in Germany than in England, prevent their manifesting themselves in a particularly striking fashion. But any one who observes the organisations of the German trade-union movement with any attention will find enough facts to confirm what I have said. I refrain from citing well-known examples, although I have many to hand, including some from my own active experience in Germany. I confine myself to the following remarks.

The trade unions do not create the phenomenon, they only bring it into prominence as an unavoidable result of actual differences. It is unavoidable that substantive differences in manner of work and level of income ultimately produce different ways and requirements of life. The precision-tool maker and the coalminer, the skilled house-decorator and the porter, the sculptor or modeller and the stoker, lead as a rule very different kinds of life and have very different kinds of wants. Where the struggle to maintain their living standards does not bring them into conflict, the fact that they are all wage-earners can eliminate these differences from their awareness, and the consciousness that they are engaged in a common struggle against capital may produce a lively mutual sympathy. Such sympathy is not wanting even in England; the most aristocratic of aristocratic trade unionists have often enough extended such sympathy to less-well-situated workers, as many of them are good democrats politically, even if they are not socialists.' But there is a great difference between this political or socio-political sympathy and the economic solidarity which stronger political and economic pressure may neutralise but which, as this pressure diminishes, will ultimately make itself felt in one way or another. It is a big mistake to suppose that, in principle, England is an exception here. In another form, the same phenomenon is evident in France; the same goes for Switzerland, the United States, and, as I have said, to a certain degree Germany as well.

But even if we suppose that there is no such differentiation among industrial workers, or that it exercises no influence on the way they think, the fact is that industrial workers are everywhere a minority of the population. In Germany, there are 7 million, including workers in cottage industries, out of 19 million income earners. And then we have the technical etc. civil service, the shop employees, and the agricultural labourers.

In all these occupational categories the differentiation is even more pronounced. There is no clearer evidence for this than the grim history of the movement to organise them into unionised interest groups. On the whole, nothing is more misleading than to infer a real similarity in conditions from a formal similarity of situation. Formally, the commercial clerk stands in the same relationship to his boss as the industrial wage-labourer stands to his work-master and yet – apart from a section of the lower ranks in large companies – he will feel socially much closer to his boss than the wage-labourer does to his, although the difference in incomes is often much greater. In the countryside, on the other hand, the way of life and the work of master and man are, on small farms, much too similar to allow room for class conflict in the sense of the urban worker's struggle, and on most large farms the division of labour or differentiation is

---

' In the English socialist movement, just as elsewhere, the better paid, that is the educated workers of higher intellectual endowment, provide the elite troops. Very few so-called unskilled workers are found in the members' meetings of the socialist societies.

too great and the personnel is proportionately too small. There is, therefore, little developed sense of solidarity to be found between a foreman, a day-labourer, and a cowherd. That leaves us, at most, with the large farms; but, as we have seen, they consistently constitute only a minority of agricultural enterprises and, furthermore, they display many basic differences in the labour relations between the entrepreneurs and the various groups of personnel. It simply will not do to equate the social aspirations of the 5 or 6 million agricultural employees, which the German occupational statistics record after subtracting the top personnel (managers, etc.) with those of the industrial workers. Only a very small number can be assumed, or expected, to have a serious inclination for, and understanding of, aspirations which go beyond the mere improvement of their conditions of work. For by far the greatest number of them, the socialisation of agricultural production can be no more than an empty word. For the immediate future, their main aspiration is to own their own land.

However, the proposition that industrial workers yearn for socialist production is also, for the most part, an assumption rather than an established fact. The increase in socialist votes in public elections does indeed imply a steadily growing support for socialist aspirations, but no one would maintain that all votes cast for socialists come from socialists. And even if we regard the non-socialist and non-proletarian electors who vote for Social Democrats as compensating for those adult socialist workers who do not yet have the right to vote, then we have in Germany, where Social Democracy is stronger than in any other country, only 2,100,000 socialist voters out of 4,500,000 adult industrial workers, to which half a million adult male employees in trade and commerce should be added. At present, more than half of the industrial workers of Germany are either indifferent to Social Democracy, or regard it with incomprehension, or view it with hostility.

Moreover, the socialist vote expresses primarily a vague demand rather than a definite *intention*. A very small percentage of workers takes an active part in working for the socialist emancipation. The trade-union movement in Germany is making gratifying progress. Nevertheless, at the end of 1897, it numbered about 420,000 organised workers in trades the workforce of which amounted to 6,165,735 persons (see *Korrespondenzblatt der Generalkommission der*

Gewerkschaften Deutschlands, 1 and 8 August 1898). Even if we include about 80,000 members of Hirsch's unions,[12] it still amounts to only a ratio of one organised to eleven unorganised workers in the trades in question.^f After subtracting those who are also members of trade unions, the number of politically active workers in Germany is fairly estimated at 20,000; and if we assume an equal number of workers excluded from participation in political or trade union activity by factors outside their control, then we get a total of about 900,000 workers who show by their actions a significant active interest in their own emancipation. They represent 40 per cent of those who vote for Social Democracy. However, of the 5.5 million votes cast for non-socialist candidates, we can reckon that a quarter to a third are conscious, *class*-conscious opponents of Social Democracy, which gives us nearly double the head-count.

I know full well that the demonstrative force of assertions such as the foregoing is very relative; for instance, the importance of the spatial distribution and the socio-political significance of groups is completely ignored. However, we are only attempting to get a more-or-less satisfactory criterion for evaluating the quantitative relationships between those elements which are assumed by the theory to be so ordered as to produce more than merely occasional and indefinite implications for socialism. What, for instance, can we say about the tables of social forces presented in accordance with utterly superficial criteria, with which Parvus thought he could trump me in his seventh article?[13] It is as if the large numerical superiority of the propertyless over property owners, which he cites, was an altogether new historical fact unknown to anyone. And yet we find socialist newspapers declaring the imminence of the social revolution as a conclusion from the contrast between the fifteen million strong 'proletarian army', as calculated by Parvus, and the 1,600,000 'capitalist army' (plus 3 million small farmers and artisans 'ruined by capital' but not yet sunk into

---

^f Nevertheless, already in five trades more than a third of the workers were organised, namely: printers 61.8, sculptors 55.5, dockers 38, coppersmiths 33.6 and shoemakers 31.7 per cent of those employed. They were followed by lithographers at 21.8 and porcelain workers at 21 per cent of those employed.

[12] A reference to the Hirsch-Duncker trade associations launched in 1868 by the German Progressive Party in response to the growth of the Lassallean unions. They were politically Liberal.

[13] 'Die Klassengliederung des Deutschen Reichs', *Sächsische Arbeiter-Zeitung*, 22 February 1898.

the proletariat, and 820,000 individuals independent of capital). The truly oriental composure with which Parvus enlists in the 'proletarian army' the 5,600,000 agricultural employees from the occupational statistics is exceeded only by the boldness with which he claims that there are 2 million 'proletarians in trade'.[f] Even if we assumed that all these elements would greet with joy a revolution which brought the socialists to the helm, we would be very little nearer a solution to the main problem.

There can surely be no dispute that an immediate takeover of the total production and distribution of products by the state is out of the question. The state could not even take over the bulk of the medium-sized and large businesses. The local authorities, further-more, could be of little help as intermediaries. They could at most take those companies into common ownership which produce goods or services locally, and for the immediate locality, and even then they would have their work cut out for them. But is it plausible that those enterprises which up till now supply the market at large could all be municipalised at a stroke?

Let us take just an industrial town of medium size, say, Augsburg, Barmen, Dortmund, Hanau, Mannheim, etc. No one would be so foolish as to suppose that, in a political crisis or on some other occasion, the local authorities there could take over the management of all the factories and trading companies in those places and run them with success. They would either have to leave them in the hands of their former proprietors or, if they wanted to expropriate them absolutely, they would have to hand over the companies to workers' cooperatives on some sort of leasing arrangement.

In all such cases, the question resolves itself practically into the question of *the economic potentiality of cooperatives.*

[f] The figures in the occupational statistics for trade and commerce are:

Self-employed and company directors	843,556
Commercial personnel	261,907
Commissioners, servants, drivers, etc.	1,233,045
Total	2,338,508

Besides, Parvus's table is not unprecedented. In Höchberg's *Zukunft* of 1877, C. A. Schramm reckoned, on the basis of the recently published results of the Prussian occupational statistics for 1876, that there was a 'socialist contingent' of 85 per cent of the population in Prussia, 4.6 million possible supporters of socialism as against 992,000 class enemies (*Zukunft*, pp. 186ff). However, Schramm did not draw the same bold conclusion as Parvus.

(b) The effectiveness of economic cooperatives

In Marxist literature, the question of the effectiveness of cooperatives has hitherto been treated in a very cursory fashion. Setting aside the literature of the 1860s and a few of Kautsky's essays, we find little about cooperatives, apart from very general and mostly negative observations.

The reasons for this neglect are not far to seek.

First, Marxist practice is predominantly political and is directed at the seizure of political power, and moreover, as a matter of principle, almost the only significance it attaches to the trade-union movement is as a direct form of the class struggle of the workers. As for cooperatives, Marx was driven to the view that on a small scale they are fruitless and, furthermore, have at most a very limited experimental value. Only through the community as a whole could something be got off the ground. This is the general tenor of Marx's comments on workers' associations in *The Eighteenth Brumaire.*[h] Later, he somewhat modified his view of cooperatives, as is evidenced in *inter alia* the resolutions on cooperatives proposed by the General Council at the Geneva and Lausanne Congresses of the International[14] as well as the passage apparently originating from Marx, or at least approved by him, in G. Eccarius's *A Worker's Refutation*, where the same significance is attached to cooperatives as harbingers of the future as to the guilds in Rome and the early Middle Ages[15] and further, the passage already alluded to in the third volume of *Capital*, which, written at the same time as the above resolutions and Eccarius's work, emphasises the significance of cooperatives as forms of transition to socialist production.[16] However, the letter on the draft of the Gotha Programme (1875) sounds once again much more sceptical

---

[h] 'In part it [the proletariat] throws itself into doctrinaire experiments, exchange banks, and workers' associations, hence into a movement in which it renounces the revolutionising of the old world by means of the latter's own great, combined resources'. (*The Eighteenth Brumaire*, 1st edn, p.8).[17]

[14] The Geneva Congress took place in 1866 and the Lausanne Congress in 1867. For Marx's view of cooperatives on these occasions, see 'Instructions for the Delegates', MECW, vol. XX, p. 190; MEW, vol. XVI, pp. 195–6.

[15] J. George Eccarius, *Eines Arbeiters Widerlegung der national-ökonomischen Lehren John Stuart Mills* (Berlin, 1869), p. 76.

[16] *Capital* III, p. 572.

[17] MECW, vol. XI, p. 110; MEW, vol. VIII, p. 122.

about cooperatives,[18] and, from the middle of the 1870s onward, this scepticism prevails everywhere in Marxist socialist literature.

This can be regarded as being partly an effect of the reaction which set in after the Paris Commune and which gave the whole labour movement a new character with an almost exclusively political orientation. But it is also the result of the unhappy experiences which people everywhere had with cooperatives. The high-flown expectations which the progress of the English cooperative movement had aroused were not fulfilled. For all socialists of the 1860s, real cooperatives were cooperatives for production, and consumers' associations were at best part of the bargain. But the opinion which Engels expressed in his essays on the housing question prevailed: namely, that if consumers' associations became universal the consequence would certainly be a reduction in wages (*The Housing Question*, new edn, pp. 34–5).[19] The resolution drawn up by Marx for the Geneva Congress states:

> We recommend workers to embark on cooperative production rather than cooperative stores. The latter touch only the surface of the present economic system, the former strikes at its foundations . . . To prevent cooperative societies from degenerating into ordinary bourgeois limited liability partnerships, all workers employed by them, whether shareholders or not, should receive the same dividend. As a purely temporary measure, it might be appropriate that the shareholders receive a modest amount of interest.

However, it was precisely the producers' cooperatives founded in the 1860s that failed nearly everywhere. They were either forced into liquidation, or they dwindled into being small businesses which, if they did not employ workers for a wage in just the same way as other firms, were in a state of sickly decline. On the other hand, consumers' associations were, or appeared to be, really nothing more than retail outlets. No wonder that in socialist circles people increasingly turned their backs on the cooperative movement. The reaction was strongest in Germany, where in any case people's minds were still preoccupied with the conflict between Lassalle and Schulze-Delitzsch.[20] The

[18] MECW, vol. XXIV, pp. 93–4; MEW, vol. XIX, p. 27.

[19] MECW, vol. XXIII, pp. 345–6; MEW, vol. XVIII, p. 241.

[20] See Schulze-Delitzsch's *Capitel zu einem deutschen Arbeiter-Katechismus* (Berlin, 1863) and Lassalle's reply, *Herr Bastiat-Schulze von Delitzsch, der ökonomische Julian, oder Capital und Arbeit* (Berlin, 1863).

strong tendency towards excessive state socialism which, in the mid 1870s, was supported by a large part of German Social Democracy (by no means only the Lassalleans), and which often contrasted oddly with the radicalism of the party, was largely due to the misfortunes experienced with the cooperatives. Bankrupt self-help cooperatives were now remarked upon only with satisfaction. In the Gotha Programme, and indeed already in its draft form, the demand for producers' cooperatives with state aid was formulated in a way that rendered it impossible to implement. In his letter on the Programme, the criticism which Marx levelled at the relevant paragraphs was aimed more at the manner of expression than at the basic train of thought.[21] Marx did not know that the 'Marat of Berlin', Hasselmann, whom he held mainly responsible for the paragraphs in question, was a dyed-in-wool Blanquist. Just like Marx, Hasselmann would have described the workers in the 'atelier' patronised by Buchez as reactionaries.[22]

Two circumstances are responsible for the fact that there is no penetrating critique of cooperatives in Marx. The first is that, when he wrote, there was not sufficient experience of the different forms of cooperative to provide a basis for formulating a judgment. The exchange marts which belonged to an earlier period had proved absolute failures. But, second, Marx did not approach the cooperatives with that theoretical impartiality which would have allowed his theoretical perceptiveness to penetrate further than that of the average socialist for whom evidence such as that provided by cooperatives of workers and master craftsmen was sufficient. On this matter, his great analytical powers were hampered by the preconceived doctrine, or formula, of expropriation – if I may so express myself. Cooperatives were acceptable to him only in that form in which they represented the most direct opposition to capitalist enterprise. Hence the recommendation to workers that they go in for producers' cooperatives because these attack the existing economic system 'at its foundations'. That is entirely in the spirit of the dialectic, and it

---

[21] MECW, vol. XXIV, pp. 93–4; MEW, vol. XIX, p. 27.

[22] When the republican government established *ateliers nationaux* in 1848, Buchez was president of the National Assembly. Louis Blanc wanted the state to provide workers in the various trades with capital to set up their own independent cooperative workshops, a scheme with which Buchez had some sympathy. However, the *ateliers* the government in fact established were simply a form of unemployment relief. Workers were given unskilled work on various public projects for a minimum wage.

is formally in accordance with the social theory which takes as its starting point the idea that production is, in the last instance, the factor which determines the form of society. It is also, apparently, in accordance with the view which perceives in the antagonism between labour already socialised and private appropriation the fundamental contradiction pressing for a solution in the modern mode of production. The producers' cooperative appears as the practical solution to this antagonism within the framework of private enterprise. Thinking along these lines, Marx argued that, although the cooperative in which 'the associated workers are their own capitalist' necessarily reproduced all the faults of the present system, it did nonetheless 'positively' abolish the antagonism between capital and labour and thus proved that the capitalist entrepreneur was superfluous.[23] Yet experience has since taught us that industrial producers' cooperatives constituted in just that way were not, and are not, in a position to provide such a proof; that it is the most ill-fated form of cooperative labour; and that Proudhon was in fact quite right when, with reference to it, he maintained against Louis Blanc that the association is 'not an economic force'.[i]

Social Democratic critique has hitherto simply ascribed the economic failure of the pure producers' cooperatives to their lack of capital, credit, and markets, and has explained the decay of those cooperatives which have not actually failed economically by reference to the corrupting influence of the capitalistic or individualistic world around them. This is all to the point, as far as it goes, but it does not exhaust the question. It is an established fact that a large number of cooperatives that suffered financial failure did have sufficient working capital and had no greater marketing difficulties than the average enterprise. If producers' associations of the kind depicted had been an economic force superior to, or even equal to, capitalist enterprise, then they should at least have maintained themselves in the same condition and indeed flourished, as did many private enterprises launched with exceedingly modest means; and they would not

---

[i] If Proudhon appears sometimes to oppose and sometimes to support association, this contradiction is explained by his having at one time quite a different form of association in mind than at another. He denies to the essentially monopolistic cooperative what he grants to the mutualistic cooperative, that is, to the association operating a system of reciprocity. However, his critique is full of exaggerations and is more intuitive than scientific.

[23] *Capital* III, pp. 511 and 572.

have succumbed so miserably to the psychological influence of the capitalist world around them, as they have done time and again. The history of those producers' cooperatives which have not suffered financial collapse speaks almost more loudly against this form of 'republican factory' than does that of those that went bankrupt. For it tells us that, in such cases, further development always entails exclusiveness and privilege. Far from undermining the foundations of the present economic system, they stand as proof of its relative strength.

On the other hand, the consumers' cooperatives, which socialists in the 1860s regarded with such scorn, have in the course of time really proved to be an economic force, an efficient organism capable of a high degree of development. Compared with the lamentable figures found in the statistics for the pure producers' cooperatives, the figures for the workers' consumers' cooperatives look like the budget of a world empire as against that of a small country town. And the *workshops* established and operated for such consumers' cooperatives have already produced more than a hundred times the quantity of goods made by pure, or nearly pure, producers' cooperatives.[j]

The deeper reasons for the economic as well as the psychological failure of the pure producers' cooperatives have been admirably set

---

[j] The figures for the latter kind of producers' cooperative are extremely difficult to ascertain, because the official statistics of cooperative production do not distinguish between them and the much-more-numerous and larger workers' joint-stock production companies. According to the returns of the British Board of Trade in 1897, the value of the year's production of those cooperatives which returned a report to the Board was, in marks:

Consumer cooperatives in their own workshops	122,014,600
Milling cooperatives	25,288,040
Irish dairies	7,164,940
Cooperatives for the purposes of production	32,518,800

The milling cooperatives, nine in number, had 6,373 members, and in 1895–6 (I do not have the relevant statement for 1897) they employed 404 persons; the Irish dairies and the cooperatives for the purposes of production, a total of 214 associations, had 32,133 shareholders and, in 1895–6, they employed 7,635 persons. It would be a very generous estimate to suppose that about one-twentieth of the cooperatives could be designated as cooperatives in which the associated workers are their own capitalists.

Against this, the registered British working men's consumer cooperatives had, in the year 1897:

Members	1,468,955
Capital (in marks)	408,174,860
Sales	1,132,649,000
Profits	128,048,560

forth by Mrs Webb in her work on the British cooperative movement
(published under her maiden name, Potter), although she does, perhaps, occasionally exaggerate. For Mrs Webb, as for the great majority of English cooperative members, cooperatives owned by their
employees are not socialist or democratic but '*individualist*' in character.[24] We may take exception to this use of the word, but the line of
thought is quite correct. Such cooperatives are not in fact socialist,
as incidentally Rodbertus had already shown.[25] It is precisely where
the workers are the sole owners that a cooperative is constitutionally
in contradiction with itself. Such an arrangement implies equality on
the workshop floor; it implies full democracy; it implies a republic.
However, as soon as such a cooperative has reached a certain size,
which can be quite modest relatively speaking, equality breaks down
because a differentiation of functions and therefore subordination
becomes necessary. If equality is given up, the cornerstone of the
building is removed, the other stones soon follow, disintegration sets
in, and the cooperative is transformed into an ordinary business
enterprise. On the other hand, if equality is maintained, further
expansion becomes impossible, and the cooperative retains its dimin-
utive size. That is the alternative facing all pure producers'
cooperatives; caught in this dilemma they have all either atrophied
or perished. So far from being the appropriate method of putting
capitalists out of business in the context of modern large-scale production, they are, rather, a return to pre-capitalist production. So
much is this the case that the few instances of relatively successful
producers' cooperatives are found in the handicraft trades; and most
of these are not in England, where the spirit of large-scale industry
prevails among the workers, but in stoutly 'petty-bourgeois' France.
Students of national psychology like to depict England as the country
where the people seek equality in freedom, and France as the one
where they seek freedom in equality. The history of the French producers' cooperatives does indeed contain many pages describing how,
with touching devotion, the greatest sacrifices were made in order to
maintain formal equality. But there is not a single instance of a pure

---

[24] Beatrice Potter, *The Co-operative Movement in Great Britain* (London, 1891). Within the
cooperative movement, cooperatives owned by employees were known as 'individualist'.
Miss Potter contrasts them with the democratic administration of consumers' cooperatives.

[25] I can not trace the source of this reference.

producers' cooperative in modern large-scale industry, although the latter is, for all that, widely enough established in France.

In his book, *The Housing Cooperative* (Leipzig, Duncker & Humblot), Dr Franz Oppenheimer has won the distinction of substantially extending and deepening the investigations of Mrs Potter-Webb. The first chapters offer, in a very clearly arranged classification, an analysis of the different forms of cooperative, which, in certain respects, can scarcely be bettered as far as critical acumen is concerned. Oppenheimer introduces into the classification of cooperatives the distinction in principle between associations for *buying* and associations for *selling*. In our view, he overestimates its significance in certain respects, but the distinction must, on balance, be regarded as very fruitful. It is the basis on which a truly scientific explanation of the financial and psychological failure of the pure producers' cooperatives is possible – an explanation in which personal faults, lack of capital, etc., are finally and definitely relegated to second place as contingent factors which explain the exception but not the rule. Only to the extent that the cooperative is essentially an association of purchasers do both its general aims and its particular interests make its expansion desirable. However, the more the cooperative is an association of *sellers*, and the more it is devoted to the sale of industrial products manufactured by itself (the case of agricultural cooperatives is different), the greater is the internal conflict. As the cooperative grows, so do its difficulties. The risks become greater, market competition becomes more severe; obtaining credit also becomes more difficult, as does the struggle for the rate of profit, that is, the individual's share in the general mass of profit. Once again, therefore, the association is forced to be exclusive. Its interest in profit conflicts not only with the interest of the consumer but also with that of all other sellers. On the other hand, an association of purchasers essentially benefits from growth; its interest in profit, although contrary to that of the seller, agrees with that of all other purchasers. It strives to push the rate of profit down, to make goods cheaper – an endeavour shared by all purchasers as such as well as by the community as a whole.

Out of this difference in the economic nature of the two kinds of cooperative arises the difference in management so clearly set forth by Mrs Potter-Webb: the essentially *democratic* character of all genuine purchasers' associations, and the tendency towards *oligarchy* characteristic of all genuine sellers' associations.[26] At this point, it should be noted that Oppenheimer makes a logical distinction in assigning to sellers' associations those consumers' associations which pay dividends only to a limited number of shareholders. Only the consumers' association which gives all purchasers a proportionally equal share in the proceeds is a genuine purchasers' cooperative.[k]

The differentiation of cooperatives into associations for purchase and associations for sale is of value to the theory of the nature of cooperatives precisely where it touches on socialist theory. Whoever objects to the terms 'purchase' and 'sale' as being too specially tailored for capitalist commodity production can replace them with the concepts of provision and alienation; but he will only realise all the more clearly how much greater significance the former has for society than the latter. The provision of goods is the fundamental general interest. In this regard, all the members of society are in principle associates. Everyone consumes, but not everyone produces. Even the best producers' cooperative, as long as it is only an association for purchase or sale, will always be in latent opposition to the community; it will have a special interest opposed to that of the community. Society would have the same differences with a producers' cooperative engaged in any branch of production or public service on its own account as it does with a capitalist enterprise, and it

---

[k] For that reason, Oppenheimer regards the distinction between buying and selling cooperatives as better than the hitherto customary one between production and distribution cooperatives, because the latter starts from an altogether incorrect definition. It is quite wrong to describe bringing an object to the market, or to the buyer, as an unproductive act; it is just as good a '*producer*' (a production) as the manufacture of one object (a product) from another (raw material). Distribution, however, means simply 'dividing up', and the use of this word for that other function is the cause of very serious conceptual confusion.

This is also our opinion, and the use of different expressions for functions as different as delivery and distribution is certainly much to be recommended. On the other hand, including the functions of manufacture and delivery in the same concept, 'production', would only cause further confusion. The fact that in practice there are cases where it is extremely difficult to separate or distinguish them is no reason not to distinguish between the concepts. Nuances are to be found everywhere. The tendency lurking behind the separation, i.e. to characterise only factory work as being productive, can be dealt with in other ways.

[26] Potter, *The Co-operative Movement*, p. 157. Bernstein is simplifying Miss Potter's case. She does indeed stress the democratic character of consumers' associations, but she describes producers' cooperatives as exhibiting 'an amazing variety of aristocratic, plutocratic, and monarchical constitutions which defy scientific classification'.

117

depends entirely on the circumstances whether it would be easier to come to an understanding with it.

But to return to the point which initially led us to digress into the field of the theory of cooperatives, it has been sufficiently demonstrated that it is quite erroneous to assume that the modern factory of itself generates a greater disposition for cooperative work. Take any history of the cooperative movement you please, and you will find that the self-governing cooperative factory always appears as an unsolvable problem in that where everything else goes tolerably well it disintegrates through lack of *discipline*. It is as with republicanism and the modern centralised state. The larger the state, the greater the problem of republican administration. Similarly, republican organisation in the workshop becomes an increasingly difficult problem as the enterprise becomes larger and more complicated. For exceptional purposes, it might be appropriate for people themselves to name their immediate leaders and to have the right to remove them. But given the tasks which the management of a factory entails, where daily and hourly prosaic decisions liable to cause friction have to be made, it is simply impossible that the manager should be the employee of those he manages and that he should be dependent for his position on their favour and bad temper. Such a state of affairs has always proved to be untenable in the long run, and it has led to a change in the forms of the cooperative factory. In short, the technological evolution of the factory has produced *bodies* for collective production; it has not in equal measure brought *souls* any nearer to collective management. The desire to bring an enterprise under cooperative management with the attendant responsibilities and risks stands in inverse ratio to its size. But the difficulties grow at an increasing rate as the enterprise grows.

Consider the matter in concrete terms. Take any large modern industrial enterprise, a large engineering works, a power station, a chemical factory, or a modern combined publishing company. All these and similar large industrial enterprises can indeed be managed quite well *for* cooperatives to which all the employees may belong, but they are completely unsuited for cooperative management by the employees themselves. There would be no end to the friction between the different departments and the very differently constituted categories of employee. Cunow's contention that there is only a very moderate feeling of solidarity between groups of workers differentiated by level of education, style of life, etc. would then be demonstrated in the clearest possible way.[27] What one usually understands by cooperative labour is only a misleading transference of the very simple forms of collective work carried out by groups, gangs, etc., of *undifferentiated* workers and which is fundamentally only contract work by groups.[1]

Only a way of thinking which depends entirely on superficial indications can therefore suppose that the elimination of capitalist property or properties would be the most important step in the transformation of capitalist enterprises into a viable socialist system. It really is not as simple as that. These enterprises are very complex organisms, and the elimination of the hub from which all the other organs radiate would, if not accompanied by a total organisational transformation, mean their immediate destruction.

What society itself can not manage, whether at the national or the local government level, it would be wise to leave to the enterprise itself to handle, especially in troubled times. The apparently more radical action would very soon prove to be also the most inefficient. Viable cooperatives can not be conjured up by magic or established by fiat; they must *grow*. However, where the soil is prepared for them they do indeed grow.

At present, the British cooperatives already possess the 100 million thaler, and more, which Lassalle considered sufficient as *state credit* for carrying out his association scheme[28] (see the figures quoted on p. 114). This may be only a small fraction of Britain's national wealth; subtracting the capital invested abroad and capital that is counted twice, it amounts to only one four-hundredth of the nation's capital. But it by no means exhausts the British worker's capital power. And, furthermore, it is steadily growing. It has nearly doubled in the ten years from 1887 to 1897, and it has grown faster than the number of members. The membership rose from 851,211 to 1,468,955; their property rose from £11,500,000 to £20,400,000. Recently, the *pro-*

---

[1] 'The thing was not easy. People like the cotton workers do not easily accept the equality which is demanded for the successful conduct of a cooperative' (sketch of the history of the Burnley Self Help Association in *Co-operative Workshops in Great Britain*, p. 20).

[27] Cunow, 'Zur Zusammenbruchstheorie'.

[28] Lassalle first advocated workers' cooperatives with state credit in his *Offenes Antwortschreiben*. The 'famous 100 million' was mentioned in a speech delivered in 1863 and published in his *Arbeiterlesebuch. Ferdinand Lassalles Gesamtwerke*, 10 vols. (Leipzig, 1899–1909), vol. I.

duction of the cooperatives has increased even faster. In the year 1894, its value only amounted to a total of 99 million marks, but in 1897 it was nearly double the amount, namely, 187 million marks. Of this, nearly two-thirds came from purchasers' associations, while the remaining third came from all kinds of cooperatives, of which a large part were, or are, merely modified purchasers' associations or cooperatives producing for them. In the three years from 1894 to 1897, the consumers' or purchasers' associations had more than doubled their own output. Its value rose from 52 to 122 million marks.

These are such astonishing figures that when one reads them one is forced to ask: where are the limits to this growth? Enthusiasts for the cooperative system have reckoned that, if the British cooperatives accumulated their profits instead of distributing them, they would, in some twenty years' time, be in a position to buy all the land in the country with all the houses and factories. This is, of course, a calculation in the manner of that fanciful reckoning of compound interest on the celebrated penny invested in year one. It forgets that there is such a thing as ground rent, and it assumes an increase of growth which is a physical impossibility. It overlooks the fact that the very poorest classes are virtually inaccessible to consumers' cooperatives, or that these classes can be brought into such cooperatives only very gradually. It overlooks the fact that, in the countryside, a cooperative society has only a very limited sphere of operation, that it can indeed reduce the costs of the middleman but it can not eliminate them. Opportunities will therefore always arise for the private entrepreneur to adjust to changed circumstances and, at a certain point in time, a slowing down in the growth of a cooperative becomes an almost mathematical certainty. Above all, however, it forgets, or does not consider, that without a distribution of dividends a cooperative society would invariably grind to a halt, that for large classes of the population it is precisely the dividend, that apple of sin execrated by doctrinaire supporters of the cooperative system, which is the main attraction of a cooperative society. It is often maintained nowadays that the dividend of a cooperative society is no indication of the greater cheapness of its goods, that on average a retailer sells most goods just as cheaply as a cooperative society so that the dividend only represents the sum of small, unnoticed rises in the price of certain articles. This may be a gross exaggeration, but nevertheless it is not altogether unfounded.

The workers' cooperative society is just as much a kind of savings bank as a means of combating the exploitation which the parasitical middleman represents for the working classes.''' But as many people do not have a very deep-seated impulse to save, they prefer the convenience of buying at the nearest shop to the toil and trouble of going further afield for the sake of a dividend. This is, incidentally, one of the factors that has made the spread of cooperative societies very difficult – and still makes it difficult – precisely in England. The English worker is by no means particularly inclined to save. Altogether, it would be quite wrong to say that, from the start, England provided particularly favourable soil for cooperative societies. Quite the contrary. The settled habits of the working class and the great expansion of urban areas which the cottage system entails completely outweigh the advantage of better wages. What has been achieved in England is primarily the fruit of hard, unflinching organisational work.

And it is work which was, and is, well worth the trouble. Even if cooperative societies achieved nothing more than to reduce the rate of profit in the retail trade, thus cutting the ground from under their own feet, they would have performed a very useful service for the nation's economy. And there can be no doubt that this has been the tendency. Here is an instrument by means of which the working class can commandeer a considerable portion of the social wealth which would otherwise serve to increase and thus strengthen the propertied classes, and this without direct destruction of life and without recourse to the use of force which, as we have seen, is no simple matter.

The statistics for cooperatives show the sorts of sums that are involved. In 1897, from a total capital of 367 million marks and a sales total of 803 million marks the 1,483 workers' cooperatives in England realised a total profit of 123 million marks." That makes a profit rate of 15.25 per cent on goods sold and 33.50 per cent on

---

''' Naturally, the word parasitical applies to the trade itself and not to the persons engaged in it. If we wanted to apply it to the latter, then we would also have to describe very many so-called 'productive' workers as parasites, because what they produce is useless, or worse, to the community.

The activity of the middleman is parasitical mainly because the increase in the number of middlemen beyond a certain limit has the effect not of lowering prices through competition but of *increasing* prices.

" We are here disregarding both the large purchasing cooperatives which let the consumers' associations have their goods at a very moderate mark-up.

capital employed. Something similar holds for the bakers' co-operatives which are essentially also just consumers' cooperatives.*

From a capital of 5 million marks and sales of 8.5 million marks they realised a profit of 1.2 million marks, a profit rate of 14 per cent on sales and 24 per cent on the capital employed. The flour-milling cooperatives, for which the same holds as for the bakers, realised on average a profit of 14 per cent on capital.

The average rate of profit for producers' cooperatives which do not produce food is very different. Here, 120 cooperatives with a total capital of 14.5 million and sales of 24 million realised a gain of 770,000 marks; that means 3.25 per cent profit on sales and 5 per cent on capital.

If these figures could be regarded as typical for the relationship of the profit rates in industry and in the retail trade, then the proposition that the worker is exploited as a producer rather than as a consumer would seem to be of very limited validity. And, in fact, it does indeed express only a qualified truth. This stems from the fact that the theory of value, on which it rests, abstracts completely from the retail trade. Furthermore, it assumes unrestricted free trade in the commodity 'labour power' so that any reduction in its costs of production (i.e. of the labourer's means of subsistence etc.) also leads to a reduction in its price – the wage. Nowadays this free trade in labour power has already, for a large proportion of workers, been significantly curtailed by trade-union protection, labour legislation, and the pressure of public opinion. And finally it assumes that the worker has no hold on those to whom the entrepreneur must give a share of the surplus product, notably the landowners, a supposition which is already being overtaken by events. For instance, as long as workers confront the employers unorganised and excluded from the legislative process, it is correct that questions such as taxing the value of land are more matters of controversy among property-owners than matters in which workers have an interest.* However, as this precondition disappears, there is a growing awareness that lowering the ground rent leads to

---

* They had 230 associations with 7,778 individuals as shareholders and employed altogether 1,196 persons, a fact which betrays the features of a purchasing cooperative. Bakeries administered by the general consumers' associations themselves are not included.

* However, I only concede the 'more', since even then the matter would not be without material interest for the workers.

an increase not in the profit on capital but in the minimum standard of living. Conversely, the unchecked continuance and further development of ground rent would in the long run nullify most of the gains made by trade unions, cooperatives, etc., in raising the living standard of the working man.

But this is by the way. We can take it as proven that cooperative societies have by now shown themselves to be a significant economic force, and though other countries still lag behind England in this field, cooperatives have taken firm root in Germany, France, Belgium, etc., and are gaining ground. I refrain from giving the figures because the fact itself is well known, and endless figures are wearisome. Legislative chicanery can, of course, hinder the spread of cooperative societies and the full development of their potentialities; and, furthermore, their success is dependent on a certain level of economic development. But here we are primarily concerned with showing what cooperatives can accomplish. And if it is neither necessary nor possible for cooperatives as we know them today to take over all the production and distribution of goods, and if, on the other side, the ever-widening domain of public services provided by state and local government limits their activity, there is nevertheless on the whole a large enough field open to them to justify great expectations, without lapsing into the afore-mentioned cooperative utopianism. Since, in not much more than fifty years, the movement launched with £28 by the Rochdale weavers developed into a movement which now commands a capital of 20 million pounds, it would take a brave man to predict how close we are to the time when this growth reaches its limit and what forms of the movement still slumber in the hidden depths of time.

Many socialists have little sympathy for cooperative societies because they are too 'bourgeois'. There are salaried officials and workmen employed for wages; profits are made, interest is paid, and disputes occur about the level of dividend. Certainly, if we consider just the form of things, a state school, for instance, is a much more socialist institution than a cooperative society. But the development of public services has its limits, and it takes time; meanwhile, the cooperative society is the most easily accessible form of association for the working class, precisely because it is so 'bourgeois'. Just as it is utopian to imagine that society could leap feet first into an organisation and way of life diametrically opposed to what prevails at present,

123

so it is, or was, utopian to want to start off with the most difficult form of cooperative organisation.

I still remember the feeling of theoretical compassion with which, in 1881, I listened to my friend Louis Bertrand from Brussels as he began to speak at the Thur Conference on the subject of cooperatives. How could an otherwise intelligent person expect anything to come from such an expedient? Then, in 1883, when I got to know the 'Genter Vooruit', the bakery at any rate made sense to me and I saw that in the end it did no harm to sell some linen, footwear, etc., on the side. However, as the leaders of the 'Vooruit' talked to me about their plans, I thought: you poor fellows! you are going to ruin yourselves. They did not ruin themselves but worked quietly, with clear vision, and along the path of least resistance, and they built up a form of cooperative society appropriate to the conditions in their country. It has proved to be of the greatest value to the Belgian labour movement and has provided the solid core around which the hitherto disparate elements of this movement could crystallise.

Whether or not the potentialities are fully realised depends entirely on how one tackles the problem.

In short, cooperative production will be a reality, though probably not in the forms imagined by the first theorists of the cooperative movement. At present, it is still the most difficult way to actualise the idea of cooperation. It has already been mentioned that the English cooperatives command more than the 100 million thaler which Lassalle required for his cooperative plan. And were it merely a question of finance, pecuniary resources other than those available at present would be at their disposal. The friendly societies and the trade unions no longer know where to invest their accumulated funds. (The latter are now asking the government to allow them to invest their funds in savings banks where they receive a better rate of interest than the government pays capitalists.) But it is not exactly, or not only, a question of financial resources. Nor is it a question of building new factories for a market already saturated. There is no lack of opportunities to buy established and well equipped factories at a reasonable price. It is primarily a question of *organisation* and *management*, and here there is still much to be desired.

'Is it, in the first place, capital that we need?' we read in the

Cooperative News, the main organ of the British cooperatives; and the author of the article answers the question with a decided negative. 'As it appears, we have at present at our disposal some £10,000,000, which are only waiting to be employed in a cooperative way, and a further £10,000,000 could doubtless be quickly procured if we were fully in a position to apply it usefully in our movement. Do not let us, therefore, conceal the fact – for it is a fact – that even at the present hour in the cooperative world there is a greater need of more intelligence and capacity than of more money. How many among us would buy nothing that was not made and finished under cooperative conditions, if it were possible to live up to this ideal? How many of us have not again and again attempted to use goods made by cooperators without being perfectly satisfied?' (*Cooperative News*, 3 December 1898).

In other words, financial means alone will not solve the problem of cooperative work. Quite apart from other preconditions, it requires its own organisations and its own management, and neither can be improvised. Both must be carefully chosen and tested. It is therefore more than doubtful whether a time in which feelings are inflamed and passions excited, as in a revolution, can in any way be conducive to the solution of this problem, which has already proved to be so difficult in ordinary times. Common sense suggests that precisely the opposite must be the case.

Even the workshops of those English bulk-purchasing cooperatives which have sufficient resources and command an adequate market often need quite a long time before their products can compete with those of private industry, as the reports and debates at their annual general meetings make clear.

However, the increasing figures for their own production have also shown that the problem can be solved. Even various producers' cooperatives have managed to solve the problem, in their own way. The low rate of profit, which we recorded above, does not apply to all. If, however, we survey them one by one, we find that, with very few exceptions, those producers' cooperatives did best which were financed by trade unions or consumers' associations, not primarily for the profit of the employees but for that of a larger membership to which the employees belonged or could belong if they wished – a form which, for all that, comes close to the socialist way of thinking.

125

Table 8. *Rate of profit of workers–shareholders' cooperatives, 1896*

Type of company	Number of share-holders	Number of workers	Share capital (Marks)	Loan capital (Marks)	Profit Amount Marks	Profit Rate %
Fustian (moleskin) weaving-mill, Hebden Bridge	797	294	528,340	129,420	96,580	14.70
Hearth-rug factory, Dudley	71	70	40,800	31,360	23,100	32.00
Shoe-factory, Kettering	651	(210?)	97,800	75,720	40,020	23.00
Clothing factory, Kettering	487	(50?)	79,160	35,660	28,240	24.6
Shoe factory, Leicester	1,070	–	197,580	286,680	49,680	10.25
Metalworking factory, Walsall	87	190	52,280	48,260	22,080	9.24 [sic]
Jersey factory, Leicester	660	(250?)	360,160	246,540	56,040	22.00 [sic]

Table 8 gives some relevant figures, taken from the 1897 report of the workers-shareholders' cooperatives. They apply to the financial year 1896.

All these factories do, of course, pay wages at trade-union rates and keep to the normal working day. The shoe-factory in Kettering has an eight-hour day. It is still expanding and is now building a new wing to its factory, which comes up to the most modern standards. It is worth noting that in almost all cases the number of shareholders includes a large number of legal entities (cooperative societies, trade unions, etc.). Thus the membership of the fustian weaving-mill in Hebden Bridge is distributed into 294 workers who constitute the personnel of the factory with a capital share of 147,960 marks, 200 outside individuals with 140,640 marks, and 300 associations with 208,300 marks. The loan capital consists mostly of credits which the members leave standing and which yields an interest of 5 per cent. The distribution of the surplus takes place in accordance with rather varied principles. In some factories a somewhat higher rate of profit is paid on the share capital than as a bonus on wages. However, for the first half year of 1896, the shoe-factory in Kettering paid the shareholders a dividend of only $7\frac{1}{2}$ per cent and the workers 40 per cent (on their wages). The customers got the same rate on goods purchased (thus bringing the society closer to being a purchasers' cooperative).[*]

There is a similar distribution in one of the smaller cooperative shoe-factories in Leicester. Most producers' cooperatives find a large part of their market, if not their whole market, within the cooperative world itself.

I need not enlarge here on other forms of the cooperative system (loan and credit societies, raw materials and warehouse associations, dairy cooperatives, etc.) as they are of no significance to the wage-labouring classes. However, in view of the importance which the question of the peasantry (who, though not wage-earners, also belong to the working class) has for Social Democracy, and in view of the

---

[*] By way of illustration, here are the figures. In the half year, it distributed:

To shareholders (excluding tax)	1,164 marks
To customers	8,325 marks
To workers	8,068 marks
To the management committee	700 marks
To the educational fund	525 marks
To the relief fund	1,050 marks

fact that handicrafts and small businesses still play a very noticeable role, at least in terms of the number of persons involved, we must draw attention to the progress which the cooperative movement has achieved in these areas. The benefits achieved by purchasing seed, procuring machinery, and selling produce communally, as well as the possibility of cheap credit, cannot rescue peasants already ruined. They are, however, a means of protecting thousands and thousands of small peasants from ruin. There can be no doubt about it. There is unusually good evidence for the tenacity and productivity of the peasant economy (which does not need to be that of very small peasants) quite apart from the figures which the trade statistics present. It would be rash to say, as some writers do, that in agriculture the law regarding the advantages of large as against small units is exactly the opposite to what it is in industry. But it is not too much to say that the difference is quite extraordinary and that the advantages which the large concern, strong in capital and well equipped, has over the small are not so significant that the small concern could not, to a large extent, compensate for them by making fuller use of the cooperative system. The use of mechanical power, the procuring of credit, a more secure market – the cooperative can make all this available to the peasant, whilst the nature of his economy makes it easier for him to overcome occasional losses than it is for the large farmer. For the great majority of peasants are not merely producers of commodities; they also produce for themselves a considerable portion of the food they need.

In all advanced civilised countries, the cooperative system is rapidly growing in scope and extent. The picture is no different in Belgium, Denmark, France, Holland, and recently also in Ireland, than in a large part of Germany. It is important for Social Democracy that, instead of picking over the statistics for evidence to support the preconceived theory of the ruin of the peasantry, it should urgently examine this question of the cooperative movement in the countryside and its significance. The statistical evidence for forced sales, mortgage burdens, etc., is in many respects misleading. Undoubtedly, property is more mobile nowadays than previously, but this mobility does not work one way only. So far, the gaps caused by public auctions have always been filled again.

These general remarks will have to suffice. I have no specific agrarian programme to propound. It is, however, my firm conviction that such a programme ought to take much more cognizance of the experiences available with regard to agricultural cooperatives than has hitherto been the case, and that, if this is done, it will be less a matter of explaining that ultimately the small peasants can not be saved than of pointing out the manner in which they can be rescued and their number increased. Where a small peasant economy predominates, the organisation of agricultural labourers into trade unions and the like is, on all possible counts, a chimera. Only through the spread of the cooperative system can they be lifted out of the wage relationship.

The facts which Dr O. Wiedfeldt (Dresden) imparts in number 13, volume VIII of *Sozialen Praxis* on the activity and success of *agricultural syndicates in France* are well worth noting. According to him, there are approximately 1,700 agricultural (peasant) syndicates grouped in ten associations with a total of more than 700,000 members in France. 'These craft associations began, in the first instance, as purchasing associations for agricultural *fodder* and *fertiliser*, and their central office (*Coopératives Agricoles*) has already got a certain influence on the trade in these articles. They have furthermore collectively procured *threshing-machines, reaping-machines*, etc., or carried out *drainage, irrigation*, and so forth. They have established *breeding-cooperatives, dairies, cheese-factories,*[r] *bakeries, flour-mills, canneries*, etc., and in some areas they have successfully taken the marketing of their agricultural products in hand.' In pursuit of this end, they have not been content to establish a connection with the consumer cooperatives which are also spreading in France, but they have *founded their own*. 'Thus in La Rochelle, Lyon, Dijon, Avignon, Tornelle, etc., we have the establishment of cooperatives such as butcher's shops, flour-mills, bakeries, which are *half agricultural producers' cooperatives and half consumers' cooperatives*.' In the Departement of Charente Inférieure alone there are 130 cooperative bakeries of this kind. Furthermore, the syndicates have also established canneries, and sausage, starch, and macaroni factories, 'so that, in a certain sense, a *localisation of industry*, insofar as it is connected with agriculture, is being attempted'. Most of the syndicates accept *the workers as members*. The 1,000 members of the Castelnaudardy syndicate include 600 workers. Moreover, the syndicates have turned to setting

---

[r] According to *Emancipation*, 13 November 1898, in France alone there are 2,000 cooperative dairies, most of them in the Jura and the two Savoys.

up all kinds of mutual aid institutions: insurance, arbitration, people's secretariat, agricultural schools, and recreational associations.

Thus far the report in *Sozialen Praxis*.

The question springs to mind as to the rights of the workers in these cooperatives. The report speaks only of profit-sharing between management and workers, but this allows for very many interpretations. In any case, the admission of workers into the cooperatives has so far not changed the fact that, as agricultural associations, they are essentially *entrepreneurial* syndicates. This is evident from the fact that, however many cooperative arrangements they have hit upon, there is one area of cooperation which has until now been denied to the workers: agriculture itself, that is, the cultivation of field and pasture and the actual rearing of livestock. Work connected with, or attached to, agriculture is done cooperatively, or at least for cooperatives; but here and elsewhere agriculture itself is out of bounds for cooperative work.[*] Is cooperative work less favourable to agriculture than to other industries? Or is it simply peasant landed property that stands in the way?

It has often been emphasised that peasant property, the division of the land amongst many owners, is a major obstacle to working the land cooperatively. But it is not the only difficulty; or to put it differently, it *increases* the *real* difficulties but is not generally their cause. The spatial isolation of the workers, as well as the individualistic nature of a great deal of agricultural work, also plays a part. It is possible that the peasants' syndicates, which are still very young, may, in their further development, overcome these obstacles or – which seems to me to be most likely – that they will gradually extend their present limits. For the moment, however, this is something we cannot count on.

Even agricultural production *for* cooperatives is, at present, an unsolved problem. The English consumers' cooperatives have done no worse business with any enterprises than with their own farms. The third annual report of the British Labour Department (1896) gives 106 producers' cooperatives an average profit of 8.4 per cent. Of these, the six cooperative farms and dairies had an average profit of only 2.8 per cent. Nowhere do the peasants get a greater return

[*] Thus, e.g. in the fast rising *Irish agricultural cooperatives*, which began in the year 1889 with a small association of 50 members, but which in March 1898 already numbered 243 associations with 27,332 members, including many agricultural labourers (cottiers).

from the land than in Scotland. The amount of profit for wheat, oats, etc., per acre is much greater in Scotland than in England. Nevertheless, a Scottish farming cooperative furnished with good machines and representing a capital of a quarter of a million marks has turned out to be a great failure. In 1894 it made a profit of 0.6 per cent, and in 1895 it made a loss of 8.1 per cent. However, how does it stand with actual *agricultural workers' cooperatives*? Does a producers' cooperative of agricultural workers offer better prospects than one of industrial workers?

The question is all the more difficult to answer because practical experience provides no satisfactory examples. The classical case of such a cooperative, the celebrated Ralahine Cooperative,[29] lasted too short a time (1831 to 1833) and, whilst it lasted, it was too much under the influence of its founder, Vandeleur, and his agent, Craig, to serve as a valid proof of the ability of independent cooperatives of agricultural workers to survive.[*] All it demonstrates is the great advantage of collective management under certain circumstances and assumptions.

The same holds for the experience of communist colonies. They often prosper for a long time in physical or psychological isolation under circumstances one would consider most unfavourable. However, as soon as they achieved a greater degree of prosperity and entered into a more intimate intercourse with the outside world, they soon deteriorated. Only a strong religious bond or the like, a sectarian wall raised between them and the surrounding world, will keep such a colony together when it has become prosperous. But the fact that men must in some way or another remain at a primitive level of

---

[*] As the gifted Owenite, Finch, humorously put it in 1838, its constitution was a combination of all the advantages of Toryism, Whiggism, and Radicalism, without any of their faults. 'It had all the power and unity of purpose and action of a monarchy and Torydom, all the moderation, the inventiveness, the preventive and precautionary measures of Whiggery, and much more than the freedom and equality of Radicalism.'[30] Mr Vandeleur was 'king', the management consisting of treasurer, secretary, and storehouse superintendent was the 'upper house', and the committee of workers was the popular assembly.

[29] The Ralahine Community in County Clare was an Owenite agricultural cooperative established by the landowner, J. S. Vandeleur, in 1831. John Finch discussed it in a series of letters published in the *Liverpool Mercury*. For a more recent account, see S. Pollard and J. Salt (eds.), *Robert Owen, Prophet of the Poor* (London and Basingstoke, 1971), pp. 47–52.

[30] See note 33 below.

development in order to feel at home in such colonies shows that they can never become the normal type of cooperative work. For socialism, they are on a par with the pure industrial producers' cooperative. However, they have provided a brilliant demonstration of the advantages of collective management.

On the basis of all these facts and the experiments which intelligent landlords have made with shared tenancies, profit-sharing with agricultural workers, etc., Dr F. Oppenheimer, in the book we have already mentioned, has developed the idea of an agricultural cooperative which he calls a 'colonising cooperative'. It is to be a cooperative of agricultural workers, or is to begin as such, and is to combine individual with collective management, that is, small farming with cooperative large-scale farming, as is the case today on large estates where separate allotments are let out to the agricultural workers at a more or less substantial rent, which the workers often manage in a truly exemplary fashion. Oppenheimer has a similar division in mind for the colonising cooperative; only here the point is, naturally, not to lower the price of labour power for the benefit of the central establishment around which those small holdings are grouped, but simply to give each individual member the opportunity to enjoy, on an adequate piece of land, the mental satisfaction of owning his own establishment and to employ in its cultivation all the labour power not required by the central establishment of the cooperative, which either promises him the best returns or otherwise best suits his individuality. But for the rest, the cooperative is to exploit all the advantages of modern large-scale enterprise and to make all possible cooperative or mutual arrangements for the business needs of its members. By working up its own products and by admitting craftsmen to membership, the cooperative will increasingly acquire the character of an organisation combining agriculture and industry – which is what Owen had in mind with his home colonies and other socialists envisaged with their communist projects. But Oppenheimer tries to stay strictly within the bounds set by the principle of free cooperation. The only criterion for joining a colonising cooperative should be economic interest; this alone protects it from the exclusiveness of industrial producers' cooperatives. In contrast to the latter, it is not just a producers' (or selling) cooperative but also a consumers' (or purchasing) cooperative; and this circumstance is the basis on which it obtains credit, and protects it from those convulsions to which large capitalist agricultural enterprises are nowadays exposed.

This is not the place for a closer examination of Oppenheimer's proposals and the theory on which they are based. But I think I must say that they do not strike me as deserving the contemptuous reception they have been given in some of the party press. We may doubt whether the matter can or will be dealt with in exactly the way Oppenheimer describes. But the basic notion he develops rests so securely on scientific analysis of economic forms and agrees so closely with all the experience of cooperative practice that we may indeed say that, if cooperative management is ever achieved in agriculture, it is unlikely to be materially different in form from that developed by Oppenheimer.[*]

Expropriation across the board, which most critics of such proposals have in mind, cannot in any case conjure up organic creations overnight, and therefore even the most powerful revolutionary government would have to cast about for a theory of cooperative work in agriculture. Oppenheimer has collected abundant material for such a theory and has subjected it to a rigorous and systematic analysis which does complete justice to the basic ideas of historical materialism. This alone makes the 'colonising cooperative' seem worth studying.

There is still one more point to be made on the subject of agricultural cooperatives. Insofar as socialists are party politicians, they can greet the present migration from country to town only with satisfaction. It concentrates the masses of workers, revolutionises their minds, and in any case furthers political emancipation. However, as a theorist who looks beyond the immediate present, the socialist must add that, in the long run, this migration can become too much of a good thing. It is well known that it is infinitely easier to draw country people into the towns than to draw town people into the country and

---

[*] At the most recent conference of the British cooperatives (Peterborough, May 1898) a delegate, Mr J. C. Gray of Manchester, read a report on 'co-operation and agriculture' in which, after an objective examination of all the experiments made in England, he finally made a suggestion which is remarkably similar to Oppenheimer's project. 'The soil should be cooperative property, the procurement of all supplies should be cooperative, and the sale of all products should be cooperative. But in the cultivation of the soil, an individual interest must be catered for, with appropriate precautions against encroachment on the interest of the collectivity.' (*Co-operation and Agriculture*, Manchester, 1898, p. 9).

accustom them to agricultural work. So the flood of migrants into the towns and industrial centres is not only a problem for the present government. Take the case of a victory of working-class democracy which brings the socialist party to the helm. All our experience so far suggests that the direct consequence would probably be a significant increase in the flood of migrants into the large towns; and it is rather doubtful whether 'industrial armies for agriculture' would be any more prepared to be sent into the countryside than they were in France in 1848. But apart from this, the creation of viable and efficient cooperatives will, under all circumstances, be a more difficult task the further the depopulation of the countryside has advanced. The advantage of having prototypes of such cooperatives to hand would be well worth the price of having a somewhat slower expansion of the very large towns.^v

^v I see with pleasure that, in his work on the agrarian question, which has just appeared,[31] Karl Kautsky has seriously investigated the question of agricultural cooperatives. What he says about the obstacles that hinder the conversion of peasants' small holdings into agricultural cooperatives fully agrees with Oppenheimer's exposition of the same topic. Kautsky looks to industry and to the seizure of political power by the proletariat for a solution to the problem. Current developments make the peasant ever more dependent on capitalist distilleries, breweries, sugar refineries, grinding mills, butter and cheese factories, wine cellarage businesses, etc., and turns them into casual workers in other kinds of capitalist enterprise such as brickworks, mines, etc., where, at present, small peasants take temporary work to make up the deficit on their establishments. With the socialisation of all these enterprises peasants would become 'collective workers', casual workers in socialist cooperative undertakings, while, on the other side, the proletarian revolution would necessarily lead to the conversion of large agricultural enterprises, on which a large number of small peasants nowadays depend, into cooperative undertakings. Thus small peasant undertakings would increasingly lose their hold, and their amalgamation into cooperative enterprises would meet with fewer and fewer difficulties. The nationalisation of mortgages and the abolition of militarism would further facilitate this development.

In all this there is a great deal that is correct. However Kautsky seems to me to fall into the error of greatly overestimating the forces working in the direction which has his sympathy and, equally, underestimating the forces working in the other direction. Some of the industrial enterprises he enumerates are well on the way to becoming not masters of peasant businesses but dependencies of peasant cooperatives, and, with others such as, for instance, the breweries, the connection with agriculture is too loose for a change in their nature to have a powerful effect on the industrial shape of the latter. Further, Kautsky, in my view, too frequently allows the strong words which he occasionally employs to lure him into conclusions which would be correct if those words were universally true; but since they apply to only a part of the real world, they can not claim universal validity. To make it clearer: in Kautsky, the existence of the small peasant seems a kind of hell. There is a great number of small peasants of whom this can fairly be said, but there is also a great number of whom it is a gross exaggeration,

[31] Kautsky, *Die Agrarfrage*, pp. 116ff and 404ff.

134

For the industrial worker, however, cooperatives offer the possibility of, on the one hand, counteracting commercial exploitation and, on the other, raising the resources which in various ways smooth the path of liberation. The support workers are able to get from cooperative stores in difficult times, during lock-outs, etc., is now generally well known. To the classical example of the support the big English consumers' cooperatives provided for the locked-out miners, textile workers, and engineers, we might add that producers' cooperatives can also be of great service to the workers in their struggle for a living. In Leicester and Kettering, the cooperative shoe-factories maintained the standard rate of wages in the whole region at the level they themselves set. The cooperative repair shop in Walsall did the same; a lock-out is impossible in Walsall. Throughout the lock-out from 1892 to 1893, the spinning and weaving cooperative, 'Self Help', in Burnley stopped work and thus, in conjunction with the cooperative shops, helped force the employers to give way. In short, as *Trade Unionist*, 2 November 1898, puts it: 'Wherever in the country these (producers') cooperatives exist, people become accustomed to engage in manufacture, not just for the sake of profit, but in such a fashion that the worker does not have to lay down his manhood at the factory gate but carries himself with that sense of freedom and that civility which the public spirit in a free community based on equal rights breeds.'[*]

However, up till now producers' cooperatives have proved viable only where they have been supported by cooperative shops or have resembled them in their form of organisation. This points in the

just as the description of small peasants as modern 'barbarians' is in many cases now overtaken by developments. It is also an exaggeration to describe as 'slave labour' the work which a small peasant does on neighbouring farms because his own farm does not keep him fully occupied. The use of such expressions establishes ideas which encourage the assumption that those classes have certain perceptions and tendencies when, in fact, they have them only in exceptional cases.

If I can not accept all of Kautsky's statements on the probable development of the peasant economy, I am all the more at one with him on the principles of his programme of agrarian policy to be followed by Social Democracy today. However, I will deal with this elsewhere.

[*] 'I have publicly stated more than once at trade-union conferences that the cooperatives are, in general, the best friends which the bakery workers have in this country, and I stand by this statement ... Both I and my union stand on the best footing with the big consumers' cooperatives and their bakeries, and we hope that this will remain the case' (J. Jenkins, Secretary of the Union of British Bakery Workers in *Labour Co-partnership*, November 1898).

direction in which we must look for the most successful further development of workers' cooperatives.

(c) Democracy and socialism

The 24th February 1848 saw the first light of the dawning of a new historical era.

He who says universal suffrage utters a cry of reconciliation.
Lassalle, *Workers' Programme*

Just as consumers' cooperatives are concerned with the rate of profit in trade, so trade unions are concerned with the rate of profit in production. The struggle of trade unionists for an improvement in their living standard is, from the capitalist point of view, a struggle of the wage rate against the rate of profit. It would, indeed, be pushing a generalisation too far to say that changes in the level of wages and the hours of work have no influence at all on prices. The amount of labour expended upon a unit of a certain class of goods remains, of course, unchanged, as long as the method of production remains the same, regardless of whether the wage rises or falls. However, so far as the market is concerned, the quantity of labour without the price of labour is an empty concept, for in the market it is a matter, not of the abstract value of total production, but of the relative value of the various kinds of goods compared with one another; and here the level of wages is a not unimportant factor. If the wages of workers in certain industries rise, the value of the products in question also rises in relationship to the value of the products of all those industries which experience no such rise in wages; and if the class of employers concerned does not succeed in compensating for this rise by an improvement in technology, it must either raise the price of the product accordingly or suffer a loss in the rate of profit. In this respect, different industries are very differently placed. There are industries which, on account of the nature of their product or of their monopolistic organisation, are fairly independent of the world market; and in them a rise in wages is for the most part accompanied by a rise in prices, so that the profit rate does not only not need to fall but can even rise.[*] On the other hand, in industries which operate on the

---

[*] Carey relies *inter alia* on this partial truth in his doctrine of harmony.[32] Certain extractive industries – mines, etc. – afford examples of it.

[32] Henry Charles Carey, *Principles of Political Economy* (Philadelphia, 1837).

world market, as in all other industries where commodities produced under various conditions compete and the cheapest commands the market, rises in wages almost always result in a lowering of the rate of profit. The same result occurs when competition makes a lowering of prices necessary and an attempt to compensate by a proportional reduction in wages is defeated by the resistance of the organised workers. As a rule, compensating by improved technology means a proportionally larger outlay of capital on machinery and the like, and this means a corresponding fall in the rate of profit. Finally, the workers' struggle for wages can, in fact, only be a matter of preventing a rise in the rate of profit at the expense of the rate of wages, however little the combatants are aware of it at the moment.

There is no need to show that the conflict about the working day is, at the same time, also a conflict about the rate of profit. Although the shorter working day does not directly cause a reduction in the work done for the current wage – it is well known that in many cases the opposite occurs – it does indirectly lead to an increase in demands for a better standard of living for the workers, and so makes a rise in wages necessary.

In certain circumstances, a rise in wages leading to a rise in prices need not be to the disadvantage of the community as a whole. However, it is more often harmful than beneficial in its effect. For instance, so far as society is concerned, it makes no difference whether an industry extracts monopolist prices simply for the benefit of a handful of entrepreneurs or whether the workers concerned also get a certain share of the booty. It is still worth resisting a monopoly price, just as it is worth resisting the low price of products achieved only by reducing wages below the average minimum rate.ʸ But, in

---

ʸ The above was already written when Kautsky's article in no. 14 of *Die Neue Zeit* reached me. In it, Kautsky characterises the industrial alliances which have recently arisen in the English Midlands (and which I described in an earlier article) as trade unions which 'unite with capitalist circles to plunder the public', and are a 'means employed by English manufacturers to corrupt the trade-union movement'. The struggle against capital is, according to him, replaced by 'the struggle against society, hand in hand with capital' (*Die Neue Zeit*, xvii, 1, p. 421). As is evident from my notes to the text and from my remarks upon the nature of the cooperative movement, I am by no means blind to the tendency which Kautsky here denounces, and I am on principle just as opposed to coalitions directed against the public as he is, be they coalitions of capitalists or of workers. Nevertheless, I think his critique goes too far. I can not, in principle, condemn the kind of industrial organisation designed to counter unfair competition and unregulated undercutting, exemplified in the industrial alliances in question, as associations to plunder the public. So far, there has been very little evidence of such exploitation, even in a large number of trusts. On the contrary, it is often enough the case that the

general, a rise in wages that affects only the rate of profit will, under present conditions, be only advantageous for the community. I expressly say 'in general' because there are also cases where the opposite applies. If the rate of profit in a certain industry is forced down well below the general minimum, this can mean that the country in question loses this industry and that it goes to countries with much lower wages and inferior conditions of work. From the standpoint of the world economy, this can be regarded as being of no importance because, in one way or another, all things are equalised over time. However, this is of little comfort to the parties concerned. At first, and sometimes for a long time thereafter, such 'expatriation' is a positive loss both for the people concerned and for the community as a whole.

Fortunately, such extreme cases are very rare. Usually, the workers know full well how far they can push their demands. The rate of profit can, indeed, withstand fairly heavy pressure. Before the capitalist abandons his enterprise, he will try every conceivable means to get a greater output for wages. The great differences in the rate of profit actually achieved in different spheres of production demonstrate that the average rate of profit is more easily calculated in theory than achieved, even approximately, in practice. Indeed there are cases of new capital seeking investment in the market and turning its back on enterprises offering the highest rate of profit because, like a man choosing his occupation, it is guided by considerations in which the amount of profit takes second place. So even this very significant factor in the equalisation of profit-rates has an irregular effect. How-

exploitation of unfair competition in order to reduce prices constitutes, in my view, a wholly unacceptable exploitation of the producers. In short, I see in industrial alliances, which seem to be increasingly prevalent (at present, negotiations for their introduction into the glass industry and the potteries are in train), and which have a counterpart in the German customs union, a phenomenon which is certainly not above suspicion, but which will, just as its predecessors (joint wages committees, sliding pay scales, etc.), be judged to be a natural product of the movement against industrial anarchy. They threaten the interests of the community no more than do a whole range of other shifts of trade-union policy which have, for a long time, been used by organised workers and which have hitherto been quietly accepted, if not supported, by Social Democracy, from the mere fact that they are formally – not in reality – directed against capital.

Furthermore, Kautsky is mistaken if he supposes that the English trade unions have set themselves, as a matter of principle, against the sliding wage scale. They are opposed only to the 'bottomless' fluctuating tariff. They have no objection whatsoever to a fluctuating tariff with a minimum living wage as a 'bottom' and with stipulations that take account of technical changes in production.

138

ever, for purely material reasons, capital already invested (which far outweighs the rest) cannot follow the movement of the rate of profit from one sphere of production to another. In short, an increase in the cost of human labour produces, in most cases, either technological improvement and better organisation of industry or a more equitable division of the proceeds of labour. Both are advantageous to general well-being. With certain limitations, Destutt de Tracy's well-known dictum can be modified to say: 'Low profit-rates indicate a high degree of well-being among the mass of the people.'[33]

By virtue of their socio-political position, the trade unions are the democratic element in industry. Their tendency is to erode the absolute power of capital and to give the worker a direct influence in the management of industry. It is only natural that there should be great differences of opinion as to the degree of influence to be desired. To one way of thinking, it is a breach of principle to suggest that a trade union has anything less than an unconditional right to make decisions in its industry. However, the awareness that such a right is as utopian in present circumstances as it would be nonsensical in a socialist society has led others to deny trade unions any permanent role in economic life and to see them as being, temporarily, the lesser of various unavoidable evils. Indeed, for some socialists the trade unions are nothing more than an object-lesson demonstrating in a practical way the uselessness of any action other than revolutionary politics. In fact the trade unions have at present, and will have for the foreseeable future, very important industrial–political tasks to perform, which do not require – indeed, would not be consistent with – their being omnipotent.

The credit for being the first to grasp the fact that trade unions are indispensable organs of democracy and not merely transient coalitions belongs to a group of English writers. This is, incidentally, not surprising, considering that trade unions became important in England earlier than elsewhere and that, in the last third of our century, England has been transformed from being an oligarchy into being an almost democratically governed state. The most recent and most thorough work on this subject, *The Theory and Practice of the British Trade Unions* by Sydney and Beatrice Webb, has been rightly

[33] In his *Traité de la volonté et de ses effets* (Paris, 1826), p. 231, Destutt de Tracy says: 'In poor nations the people are comfortable, in rich nations they are generally poor.' Marx quotes the dictum in *Capital* I, p. 802, which is where Bernstein probably got it.

described by the authors as a treatise on *Industrial Democracy*. Previously, the late Thorold Rogers in his lectures on the economic interpretation of history (which, by the way, has little in common with the materialist conception of history and only touches upon it at one or two points) called the trade union a *Labour Partnership* – which comes to the same thing in principle, but which at the same time indicates the limit to which trade-union activities can extend, but beyond which they should not go, in a democratic community.[34] Regardless of whether the employers are the state, the community, or the capitalists, the trade union as an organisation of everyone employed in a particular trade, can protect the interest of its members and simultaneously foster the common good only so long as it is content to remain a partner. Above and beyond this, it always runs the risk of degenerating into a closed corporation with all the unpleasant characteristics of a monopoly. It is the same with cooperatives. A trade union controlling a whole branch of industry (the ideal of various older socialists) would in fact be simply a monopolist producers' cooperative, and as soon as it asserted and implemented its monopoly it would be in conflict with socialism and democracy, whatever its internal constitution might be. Why it would be in conflict with socialism needs no further explanation. Association against the community has no more to do with socialism than does the oligarchic management of public affairs. However, why is a trade union of this kind contrary to democracy?

This question raises another: what is democracy?

The answer to this appears very simple. It is translated as 'government by the people' and, at first glance, this would seem to settle it. But even a brief consideration tells us that this gives us only a very superficial and purely formal definition. Almost everyone who uses the term 'democracy' nowadays takes it to mean something more than just a form of government. We shall come much closer to the heart of the matter if we express ourselves negatively and define democracy as the absence of class government. This indicates a state of society in which no class has a political privilege which is opposed to the community as a whole. This also makes it immediately clear why a monopolistic corporation is anti-democratic. Furthermore, this negative definition has the advantage over the phrase 'government by the

[34] James E. Thorold Rogers, *The Economic Interpretation of History* (Lectures Delivered in Worcester College Hall, Oxford, 1887–8) (London, 1888), p. 313.

people' that it leaves less room for the idea of the oppression of the individual by the majority, which is absolutely repugnant to the modern mind. Nowadays we find the oppression of a minority by the majority 'undemocratic', although it was originally held to be quite consistent with government by the people.[z] As we understand it today, the concept of democracy includes an idea of justice, that is, equality of rights for all members of the community, and this sets limits to the rule of the majority – which is what government by the people amounts to, in any concrete case. The more democracy prevails and determines public opinion, the more it will come to mean the greatest possible degree of freedom for all.

Of course, democracy and lawlessness are not one and the same. Democracy is distinguished from other political systems not by the absence of law as such but only by the absence of laws which create or sanction exceptions on the grounds of property, birth, or religious confession. And it is distinguished not by the absence of laws which limit individual rights, but by the abolition of all laws which limit the

---

[z] Consistent advocates of Blanquism also invariably conceived of democracy as being primarily a repressive force. Thus Hyppolyte Castille begins his history of the Second Republic[35] with an introduction which culminates in a veritable glorification of the Reign of Terror. 'The most perfect society,' he says, 'would be one in which tyranny was exercised by the whole community. That proves fundamentally that the most perfect society would be one where there is least freedom in the satanic (i.e. individualistic) sense of the word . . . The phrase "political freedom" is only a nice way of describing the legitimate tyranny of the many. Political liberties are only the sacrifice of a number of individual liberties to the despotic god of human societies, to social reason, to the contract.' 'From this epoch (the time from October 1793 to April 1794 when Girondists, Hébertists, Dantonists were beheaded one after the other) dates in truth the rebirth of the principle of authority, this eternal bulwark of human societies. Freed from the moderates and the ultras, secured against any conflict of authorities, the Committee of Public Safety acquires the form of government dictated by the circumstances, the strength and unity necessary to maintain its position and to protect France from the danger of imminent anarchy . . . No, it is not the government that killed the first French republic but the parliamentarians, the traitors of Thermidor. The hordes of anarchists and liberal republicans swarming all over France persist in vain with the old calumny. Robespierre remains a remarkable man, not on account of his talents and virtues, which are here incidental, but on account of his feeling for authority, on account of his powerful political instinct.'

This cult of Robespierre was not to survive the Second Empire. The younger generation of Blanquist social revolutionaries who took the stage in the mid 1860s, and who were, above all, anti-clerical, found Robespierre too petty bourgeois on account of his deism. They swore by Hébert and Anacharsis Cloots. But otherwise they reasoned like Castille, i.e. like him, they carried to extremes the correct idea of subordinating individual interests to the general interest.

[35] Hyppolyte Castille, *Histoire de la seconde République française*, 4 vols. (Paris, 1854–6).

141

universal equality of rights, the equal right of all. So if democracy and anarchy are completely different, it is, or would be, a tasteless play on words, in which all distinctions are lost, to use expressions such as despotism, tyranny, etc., with reference to democracy as a social order merely because, in it, the decision of the majority prevails and everyone is required to acknowledge the law decreed by the majority. Of course, democracy is not an infallible defence against laws which will be perceived as tyrannical by some individuals. However, in our times, there is an almost unconditional guarantee that the majority in a democratic community will make no law that does lasting injury to personal freedom, for today's majority can easily become tomorrow's minority and every law oppressing a minority is thus a threat to members of the current majority. The tyranny of the majority, as manifested in conditions of civil war, is fundamentally different from majority rule in a modern democracy. Indeed, experience has shown that the longer democratic arrangements persist in a modern state the more respect and consideration for minority rights increases and the more party conflicts lose their animosity.[aa] Those who cannot imagine the achievement of socialism without an act of violence will see this as an argument against democracy; and, in fact, there has been no lack of such views expressed in socialist literature. But anyone who has not succumbed to the utopian idea that, under the impact of a prolonged revolutionary catastrophe, the nations of today will dissolve into a multitude of mutually independent communities, will regard democracy as more than a political expedient the only use of which, insofar as it serves as an instrument for the working class, is to complete the ruin of capital. Democracy is both means and end. It is a weapon in the struggle for socialism, and it is the form in which socialism will be realised. It is true that it cannot perform miracles. In a country such as Switzerland, where the industrial proletariat constitutes a minority of the population (not yet half of 2 million adults), it cannot help this proletariat gain political power. Nor in a country such as England, where the proletariat constitutes by far the most numerous class in the population, can it make this

---

[aa] From this point of view, it is significant that the most violent attacks on my sins against the idea of the dictatorship of the proletariat came from natives of the most despotic state in Europe, Russia, and met with approval mostly in Saxony, where, in the interests of order, the rulers have sacrificed a tolerably democratic franchise for the unjust three-class franchise, whereas from socialists of more democratic countries the article in question met partly with unreserved approval and partly with widespread acceptance.

proletariat master of industry, partly because it feels no inclination for such a role, but partly also because it is not, or is not yet, ready for the tasks it would involve. However, in England, as in Switzerland, and also in France, the United States, the Scandinavian countries, etc., it has proved to be a powerful lever of social progress. Whoever looks not at the label but at the content will find – if he examines the legislation in England since the electoral reform of 1867, which gave the urban workers the vote – a very significant advance in the direction of socialism, if not in socialism itself. It is only since that time that state schools have existed at all in three-quarters of the country; until then, there were only private and church schools. In 1865 school attendance amounted to 4.38 per cent of the population; but in 1896 it was 14.2 per cent. In 1872, the state spent only 15 million marks annually on elementary schools; in 1896, it spent 127 million marks. The administration of schools and poor relief at both county and municipal level has ceased to be the monopoly of the propertied and the privileged; here the mass of the workers has the same electoral right as the greatest landlord and the richest capitalist. Indirect taxes are steadily reduced and direct taxes are steadily increased (in 1866, about 120 million marks were raised by income tax; in 1898, it was about 330 million marks, to which we must add at least 80 to 100 million marks in increased inheritance tax). Agrarian legislation has rendered the property-absolutism of the landowner less overwhelming; and the right of public appropriation, hitherto recognised only for the purposes of communications and sanitation, is claimed as a matter of principle also for economic changes. The fundamental change in the policy of the state with regard to the workers it employs, both directly and indirectly, is well known, and so is the expansion which factory legislation has undergone since 1870. All that, and similar developments on the Continent, is due, not exclusively, but essentially to democracy – or to that element of democracy which the countries in question have instituted. And if, in some areas, the legislation of politically advanced countries does not proceed as expeditiously as it occasionally does under the influence of energetic monarchs or their ministers in countries that are relatively backward politically, then at least there is no backsliding in these matters where democracy is established.

In principle, democracy is the abolition of class government, although it is not yet the actual abolition of classes. We speak of the conservative nature of democracy, and, in a certain respect, with justice. Absolutism, or semi-absolutism, deceives both its supporters and its opponents as to the extent of its capabilities. In countries where it prevails, or its traditions still persist, we therefore have whimsical planning, exaggerated language, erratic policy-making, fear of revolution, and hope of oppression. In a democracy, the parties and the classes supporting them soon learn to recognise the limits of their power and, on each occasion, to undertake only as much as they can reasonably hope to achieve under the circumstances. Even if they make their demands rather higher than they seriously intend in order to have room for concessions in the inevitable compromise – and democracy is the school of compromise – it is done with moderation. In a democracy, therefore, even the extreme left appears in a conservative light, and reform, because it is kept in proportion, appears to move more slowly than it does in reality. However, its direction is unmistakable. The right to vote in a democracy makes its members virtual partners in the community, and this virtual partnership must in the end lead to real partnership. With a working class undeveloped in numbers and culture, universal suffrage may for a long while seem no more than the right to choose 'the butcher'. However, as the workers grow in numbers and awareness, it becomes an instrument for transforming the people's representatives from being the masters into being the real servants of the people. Although the English workers vote for members of the old parties in parliamentary elections and thus superficially appear to be the 'tail' of the bourgeois parties, in industrial constituencies it is nonetheless this 'tail' that wags the dog rather than the other way round – not to mention the fact that the extension of the suffrage in 1884, together with the reform of local government, has given Social Democracy full rights as a political party in England.

And is it really any different elsewhere? In Germany, it was for a while possible for universal suffrage to serve as Bismarck's instrument, but in the end it compelled Bismarck to serve as *its* instrument. It did temporarily serve the purposes of the junkers east of the Elbe, but it has long since been the terror of these very same junkers. In 1878, it enabled Bismarck to forge the weapon of the anti-socialist law, but it was also the means by which this weapon was rendered blunt and broken until, with its help, Bismarck was decisively beaten. If, in 1878, Bismarck had used his majority to pass a political exceptional law rather than a police measure, a law excluding the workers from the franchise, he would for a while have inflicted much more damage on Social Democracy than he did. He would, of course, have hit other people as well. There are two senses in which the universal franchise is the alternative to revolution.

However, universal suffrage is only a part of democracy, albeit a part which must, in due course, draw the other parts to it as a magnet draws bits of iron. It does indeed proceed more slowly than many would wish, but it is nonetheless at work. And Social Democracy cannot further this work better than by taking an unqualified stand on the democratic doctrine of universal suffrage, with all the resulting consequences for its tactics.

In practice, that is, in its actions, it has in the end always done so. However, its literary advocates have often offended against this doctrine in their pronouncements, and such offences still continue. Phrases which were coined at a time when the privilege of property reigned unchecked all over Europe, and which were understandable and even to some extent justified under these circumstances, but which are nowadays only a dead weight, are treated with as much reverence as though the progress of the movement depended on them, and not on direct perception of what can and should be done. Is there any sense, for example, in maintaining the phrase 'dictatorship of the proletariat' at a time when representatives of Social Democracy have in practice placed themselves wherever possible in the arena of parliamentary work, in the struggle for a representation of the people which adequately reflects their numbers, and in the struggle for popular participation in legislation, all of which are inconsistent with dictatorship.[*] The phrase is nowadays so out of date that it can be reconciled with reality only by stripping the word dictatorship of its actual meaning and giving it some kind of diluted signification. All the practical activity of Social Democracy is aimed at creating the circumstances and conditions which will enable and ensure the transition from the modern social order to a higher one – without convulsive upheavals. Social Democrats are constantly generating fresh zeal and inspiration from the awareness that they are

---

[*] See e.g. the statement of the Offenbach socialists against the assault on the non-socialist minority in the municipal representative body and the support it received at the conference of socialist municipal representatives of the province of Brandenburg (*Vorwärts*, 28 December 1898).

the pioneers of a higher civilisation; and herein lies also the moral justification for the social expropriation which they endeavour to achieve. But class dictatorship belongs to a lower civilisation and, apart from the question of the expediency and practicability of the matter, it can only be regarded as a retrograde step, as political atavism, if it encourages the idea that the transition from capitalist to socialist society must necessarily be accomplished in the manner of an age which had no idea – or only a very imperfect idea – of the present methods of propagating and implementing legislation and which lacked organisations fit for the purpose.

I say expressly transition from capitalist to socialist society and not 'from civil [*bürgerlich*] society', as it is so frequently expressed these days. This use of the word *bürgerlich* is much more of an atavism, or at least a verbal ambiguity, which must be considered a liability in the technical language of German Social Democracy. It provides an excellent basis for misinterpretations by both friend and foe. This is partly the fault of the German language, which has no special word for the concept of a citizen with equal rights in a community, as distinct from the concept of a privileged citizen. Since all attempts to devise a special word for either the former or the latter concept have so far failed, it always seems to me to be preferable to use the loan-word *bourgeois* for the privileged citizen and what pertains to him, for to translate it as *Bürger* or *bürgerlich* opens the door to all kinds of misunderstandings and misinterpretations.

Nowadays everyone in the end knows what is meant when we speak of opposing the bourgeoisie and abolishing bourgeois society. But what does opposing or abolishing civil (*bürgerlich*) society mean? In particular, what does it mean in Germany? In Prussia, the largest and most important state in Germany, the priority is still to get rid of significant elements of feudalism which stand in the way of civil (*bürgerlich*) development. No one thinks of destroying civil society as a community ordered in a civilised way. Quite the contrary, Social Democracy does not want to break up civil society and make all its members proletarians together; rather, it ceaselessly labours to raise the worker from the social position of a proletarian to that of a citizen (*Bürger*) and thus to make citizenship universal. It does not want to replace a civil society with a proletarian society but a capitalist order of society with a socialist one. It would be a good thing if, instead of using the former ambiguous expression, we confined ourselves to the latter which is quite unambiguous. We would then be rid of a large proportion of the other contradictions between the phraseology and the practice of Social Democracy, which our opponents, not entirely without reason, identify. A few socialist newspapers nowadays are pleased to indulge in exaggerated anti-*bürgerlich* language which would perhaps be appropriate if we were sectarian anchorites; but it is absurd in an age which deems it to be no offence to socialist sentiment to conduct one's life in a thoroughly 'bourgeois' fashion.*

Finally, a certain measure of restraint is to be recommended in declaring war on 'liberalism'. It is indeed true that the great liberal movement of modern times has, in the first instance, benefited the capitalist bourgeoisie, and that the parties which took the name of Liberal were, or became in time, nothing but straightforward defenders of capitalism. There can, of course, be nothing but enmity between these parties and Social Democracy. But with respect to liberalism as a historical movement, socialism is its legitimate heir, not only chronologically, but also intellectually. Moreover, this receives practical confirmation in every question of principle on which Social Democracy has had to take a stand. Whenever an economic demand in the socialist programme was to be met in a manner, or under circumstances, which appeared seriously to endanger the development of freedom, Social Democracy has never shied away from opposing it. For Social Democracy, the defence of civil liberty has always taken precedence over the fulfilment of any economic postulate. The aim of all socialist measures, even of those that outwardly appear to be coercive measures, is the development and protection of the free personality. A closer examination of such measures always

---

* Lassalle was much more logical on this point than we are today. It was indeed very one-sided to derive the concept 'bourgeois' from political privilege alone without taking at least equal account of economic power. But otherwise he was enough of a realist to defuse the above contradiction at the very beginning by stating in *The Workers' Programme*: 'In the German language the word bourgeoisie has to be translated as *Bürgerthum* [citizenry]. But it does not have this meaning for me. We are *all citizens*: the worker, the petty bourgeois, the big bourgeois, etc. In the course of history, the word bourgeoisie has rather acquired a meaning which denotes a well defined political tendency' (*Collected Works*, ii, p. 27). What Lassalle goes on to say about the distorted logic of Sansculottism is to be recommended particularly to the belletrists who study the bourgeoisie 'in the field' in the café and then judge the entire class according to these exceptional cases, just as the philistine thinks that he is witnessing the archetype of the modern worker in the taproom habitué. I do not hesitate to declare that I regard the bourgeoisie, including the German, as being, on the whole, in a fairly healthy state, not only economically but also morally.

shows that the coercion in question will *increase* the sum total of liberty in society, and will give *more* freedom over a *more extended* area than it takes away. For instance, the legally enforced maximum working day is actually a delimitation of minimum freedom, a prohibition against selling your freedom for longer than a certain number of hours daily, and as such it stands, in principle, on the same ground as the prohibition, accepted by all liberals, against selling oneself permanently into personal servitude. It is thus no accident that the first country in which the maximum working day was implemented was Switzerland, the most democratically advanced country in Europe; and democracy is merely the political form of liberalism. As a movement opposed to the subjection of nations to institutions which are either imposed from without or which have no justification but tradition, liberalism first sought its realisation as the sovereignty of the age and of the people, both of which principles were endlessly discussed by the political philosophers of the seventeenth and eighteenth centuries, until Rousseau, in *The Social Contract*, established them as the basic conditions of the legitimacy of any constitution; and in the democratic constitution of 1793, imbued with the spirit of Rousseau, the French Revolution proclaimed them the inalienable rights of man.[dd]

The constitution of 1793 was the logical expression of the liberal ideas of the epoch, and a cursory glance at its contents shows how little it was, or is, an obstacle to socialism. Babeuf and the Equals saw in it an excellent starting point for the realisation of their communist aspirations, and accordingly inscribed the restoration of the constitution of 1793 at the head of their demands. What later passed for political liberalism was a matter of dilutions and adaptations to conform with, or made necessary by, the requirements of the capitalist middle class after the fall of the old regime, just as so-called Manchesterism[36] is a dilution and one-sided statement of the basic principles of the classics of economic liberalism. In fact, there is no liberal thought that is not also part of the intellectual equipment of socialism. Even the principle of the economic responsibility of the individual

[dd] 'Sovereignty rests with the people. It is indivisible, imprescriptible, inalienable' (Article 25). 'A people has at any time the right to revise, reform and alter its constitution. No generation can bind the next to its laws' (Article 28).

[36] The doctrine of laissez-faire and self-interest advocated by Cobden and Bright. Disraeli dubbed it 'the Manchester school'.

for himself, which appears to be completely Manchesterish, cannot, in my judgment, be denied in theory by socialism, nor are there any conceivable circumstances in which it could be suspended. There is no freedom without responsibility. In theory, we can think what we like about man's freedom of action but, in practice, we must take it as the foundation of the moral law, for only on this condition is social morality possible. Similarly, in the age of commerce, no healthy social life is possible in states which number their inhabitants in millions unless the individual economic responsibility of everyone capable of working is presupposed. Recognition of his responsibility for his own economic welfare is the return the individual makes to society for the services it has rendered or made available to him.

Perhaps I may be permitted to quote some passages from my above-mentioned article, 'The Social and Political Significance of Space and Number'.[37]

'And for the foreseeable future, the *responsibility for economic self-reliance* laid on those who are able to work can be changed only in *degree*. Employment *statistics* can be greatly extended in scope, the *exchange* and *mobility* of *labour* can be much improved and facilitated, and a system of labour *law* can be developed which would give the individual much greater security and a more flexible choice of occupation than at present. In this respect, the most advanced organisations of economic self-help, the large trade unions, are already showing the way things are likely to develop ... As we have said, there are already some indications that a democratic system of labour law is emerging. Strong unions are able to secure a kind of right to employment for their able-bodied members by pointing out to the employers that they would be very ill advised to dismiss a union member without a very good cause acknowledged as such by the union; and in the allocation of work they take both the order of registration and the need of the worker into account' (*Die Neue Zeit*, xv, 2, p. 141). There are other promising developments in the form of industrial courts, trades councils, and similar institutions in which democratic self-government has taken shape, though still often imperfectly. On the other hand, the expansion of public services, especially the educational system and mutual-aid institutions (insurance, etc.), will undoubtedly contribute a great deal towards

---

[37] Tudor and Tudor, p. 94.

divesting individual economic responsibility of its harshness. But a right to work, in the sense that the state guarantees everyone employment in his trade, is utterly unlikely to be implemented in the foreseeable future, and it is not even desirable. What its advocates intend can only be achieved to the advantage of the community in the way I have described, by the combination of various agencies; and equally it is only by this method that a universal obligation to work can be implemented without a stultifying bureaucracy. In such large and complicated organisms as our modern civilised states and their centres of industry, an absolute right to work would simply result in disorganisation; it is inconceivable except as 'a source of vindictive wilfulness and endless strife' (ibid.).

Historically, liberalism had the task of breaking the chains which the restrictive medieval economy and its characteristic legal institutions had imposed on the further development of society. The circumstance that, at first, it strictly maintained the form of bourgeois liberalism did not prevent it from expressing, in actual fact, a much more far-reaching general principle of society, the fulfilment of which will be socialism. Socialism will create no new bondage of any kind whatever. The individual will be free, not in the metaphysical sense dreamed of by the anarchists – that is, free from all duties towards the community – but free from any economic compulsion in his actions and choice of vocation. Such freedom is only possible for all by means of organisation. In this sense, one might call socialism 'organised liberalism', for if we examine more closely the organisations that socialism wants, and how it wants them, we will find that what primarily distinguishes them from the superficially similar feudal institutions is nothing other than their liberalism: their democratic constitution and their openness. Therefore, while a trade union's attempt to limit the number of workers in a trade, as the guilds used to do, is, for socialists, an understandable product of the defence against capitalism's tendency to overstock the labour market, the very tendency to seek such controls, and the degree to which it is governed by this tendency, makes it an unsocialist organisation. And the same would be true of a union which was the owner of a whole branch of industry, since it would inevitably tend to be exclusive in the same way as a 'pure' productive cooperative.^α

^α In my view, the much discussed question of having a choice of doctors under health insurance should also be assessed according to the above criterion. Whatever local

In this context, let me quote a passage from Lassalle's *System of Acquired Rights* which has always seemed to me to be an excellent guide to the problems in question: 'That against which the underlying tendencies of our time are directed, and with which they are still struggling', says Lassalle, 'is not the moment of *individuality* – this could be on their side just as well as the moment of *universality* – it is the thorn of *particularity* which we have inherited from the Middle Ages and which still sticks in our flesh' (*System*, 2nd edn, part 1, p. 221). Applied to our subject, this means that organisation should unite particularity and universality, not separate them. When, in the passage quoted, Lassalle objects that liberalism wants the rights it proclaims, not for the individual as such, but only for the individual who finds himself in a particular situation, this is aimed at what was the liberal party at the time, 'our so-called liberalism', not at theoretical liberalism – as is, in fact, expressly stated in the immediately preceding passage.

The problem indicated by what I have said above is not a simple one; indeed, many dangers lurk in its bosom. In itself political equality has not so far sufficed to ensure the healthy development of communities concentrated in large cities. As the examples of France and the United States demonstrate, it is not an infallible remedy against the uncontrolled growth of social parasitism and corruption of every kind. Were a large part of the French people not imbued with such an extraordinary sense of solidarity, and were the country not so well favoured geographically, France would long since have succumbed to the scourge of the bureaucratic class which has gained a foothold there. As it is, this scourge is one of the reasons why, despite the great mental agility of the French, the industrial development of France lags further and further behind that of neighbouring countries. If democracy is not to outdo centralised absolutism in fostering bureaucracy, it must be based on a highly differentiated system of self-government with the relevant economic responsibilities devolved to all units of government as well as to all adult citizens. Nothing is more harmful to the healthy development of democracy than enforced

conditions might cause health insurers to limit the choice of doctors, such limitation is in principle definitely unsocialist. The doctor should be an official, not of a closed corporation, but of the community. Otherwise, we would gradually reach the point at which the proposition in *The Communist Manifesto*, 'The bourgeoisie has turned the doctor, the lawyer, the scientist into its paid wage-labourer', would have to suffer a peculiar revision.

uniformity and excessive protectionism. They impede or prevent any rational distinction between viable institutions and parasitical institutions. If, on the one hand, the state abolishes all legal obstacles to producers' organisations and transfers certain powers with regard to the control of industry to professional associations, under certain conditions which would prevent them from degenerating into monopolistic corporations, so that full guarantees against wage reductions and overwork are provided, and if, on the other hand, care is taken, by means of the arrangements sketched earlier, that nobody is compelled by extreme need to sell his labour under conditions that are unacceptable, then it is a matter of indifference to society whether, in addition to public enterprises and cooperative enterprises, there are enterprises run by private individuals for their own gain. In time, they will of their own accord acquire a cooperative character.

To create the organisations described or, where they already exist, to develop them further is the indispensable precondition for what we call the socialisation of production. Without this, it is evident that the so-called social appropriation of the means of production would result in nothing but a massive devastation of productive forces, senseless experimentation, and pointless violence. The political rule of the working class could, in fact, be implemented only in the form of a dictatorial, revolutionary central power supported by the terrorist dictatorship of revolutionary clubs. It was thus that the Blanquists imagined it; and it was thus that it was represented in *The Communist Manifesto* and in the works published by its authors at the time it was composed. But 'in view of the practical experience gained, first in the February Revolution, and then, still more, in the Paris Commune, where the proletariat for the first time held power for two whole months', the revolutionary programme set forth in the *Manifesto* has 'in some details become antiquated'. 'One thing especially was proved by the Commune, viz., that the working class cannot simply lay hold of the ready-made State machinery and wield it for its own purposes.'[38]

Thus Marx and Engels in the preface to the new edition of the *Manifesto* in 1872. And they refer to the *The Civil War in France* where this is developed more fully. However, if we open the work in question and read the part referred to (it is the third), we find a

---

[38] MECW, vol. XXIII, p. 175; MEW, vol. XVIII, p. 96.

programme outlined the political content of which displays, in all material respects, the greatest similarity to the federalism of – Proudhon!

'The unity of the nation was not to be broken, but, on the contrary, to be organised by the Communal Constitution and to become a reality by the destruction of the State power which claimed to be the embodiment of that unity independent of, and superior to, the nation itself, from which it was but a parasitic excrescence. While the merely repressive organs of the old governmental power were to be amputated, its legitimate functions were to be wrested from an authority usurping pre-eminence over society itself, and restored to the responsible agents of society. Instead of deciding once in three or six years which member of the ruling class was to misrepresent the people in Parliament, universal suffrage was to serve the people, constituted in Communes, as individual suffrage serves every other employer in the search for the workmen and managers in his business.

'The antagonism of the Commune against the State power has been mistaken for an exaggerated form of the ancient struggle against over-centralisation ... The Communal Constitution would have restored to the social body all the forces hitherto absorbed by the State parasite feeding upon, and clogging the free movement of, society. By this one act it would have initiated the regeneration of France.'[39]

Thus Marx in *The Civil War in France*.

Let us now hear Proudhon. As I do not have his book on federalism to hand, what follows is a few passages from his work on the political potentiality of the working class, in which, by the way, he urges the workers to form a political party of their own.

'In a democracy organised according to the true ideas of the sovereignty of the people, that is, according to the fundamental principles of the right of representation, every oppressive and corrupting action of the central authority on the nation is rendered impossible. The mere supposition of such a thing is absurd.

'And why?

'Because in a truly free democracy the central authority is not separated from the assembly of delegates, the natural organs of local

---

[39] MECW, vol. XXII, pp. 332–3; MEW, vol. XVII, pp. 340–1.

153

interests called together for agreement. Because every deputy is, first of all, the man of the locality which named him its representative, its emissary, one of its fellow-citizens, its special agent to defend its special interests, or to bring them as much as possible into union with the interests of the whole community before the great jury (the nation); because the combined delegates, if they choose from their midst a central executive committee of management, do not separate it from themselves or make it their commander who can carry on a conflict with them.

'There is no middle course; the commune must be sovereign or only a branch (of the state) – everything or nothing. Give it however pleasant a part to play, from the moment when it does not create its rights out of itself, when it must recognise a higher law, when the great group to which it belongs is declared to be superior to it and is not the expression of its federated relations, they will unavoidably find themselves one day in opposition to each other and war will break out.' But then both logic and power will be on the side of the central authority. 'The idea of a limitation of the power of the state by means of groups, when the principle of subordination and centralisation rules in regard to these groups themselves, is inconsistent, not to say contradictory.' It is the municipal principle of bourgeois liberalism. A 'federated France' on the other hand, 'a regime which represents the ideal of independence and whose first act would be to restore to the municipalities their full independence and to the provinces their self-government' – that is the municipal freedom which the working class must inscribe on its banner, (*Capacité Politique des Classes Ouvrières*, pp. 224, 225, 231, 235). And while, in *The Civil War*, it says that 'the political rule of the producer cannot coexist with the perpetuation of his social slavery',[40] in *Capacité Politique* we read: 'When political equality is once given by means of universal suffrage, the tendency of the nation will be towards economic equality. That is just how the workers' candidates understood the matter. But this is also what their bourgeois rivals did not want' (ibid., p. 214). In short, whatever other differences there may be between Marx and 'petty-bourgeois' Proudhon, on this point their way of thinking is as nearly as possible the same.

There is not the slightest doubt – and so far practical experience

---

[40] MECW, vol. XXII, p. 334; MEW, vol. XVII, p. 342.

has repeatedly confirmed it – that the general development of modern society is marked by a steady increase in the duties of local government and an extension of municipal freedom, and that local government will be an increasingly important instrument of social emancipation. Needless to say, I have my doubts as to whether the primary task of democracy is, as envisaged by Marx and Proudhon, necessarily to abolish the modern state system and completely transform its organisation, so that the current form of national representation disappears (i.e. constituting the national assembly out of delegates from provincial or district assemblies, which in their turn are composed of delegates from the municipalities). Modern developments have produced so many institutions which have expanded beyond the control of municipal and even district and provincial government that we can not dispense with the control of central management without first reorganising them. Furthermore, I do not regard the absolute sovereignty of local communities, etc., as one of my ideals. The local community is an integral part of the nation and therefore has duties towards it as well as rights in it. We can not, for instance, grant a local community an unconditional and exclusive right to the land, any more than we can grant such a right to an individual. Valuable royalties, forestry and river rights, etc., belong, in the last instance, not to local communities and districts, which have indeed only the use of them, but to the nation. Hence a representative body in which the national interest, and not the provincial or local interest, comes to the fore in the sense that it is the first duty of the representatives seems to be indispensable, particularly at a time of transition. At the same time, other assemblies and representative bodies will become increasingly important with the result that, whether or not there is a revolution, the functions of the central representative body will diminish and thus lessen the danger which it and other such authorities pose for democracy. In advanced countries, this danger is nowadays already very slight.

For the moment, however, we are concerned not so much with criticising the details of this programme as with highlighting the great importance it attaches to self-government as the precondition of social emancipation, and with showing how it depicts grass roots democracy as the way to actualise socialism, and how the antagonists, Proudhon and Marx, come together again in – liberalism.

The future alone will tell us how the municipalities and other self-governing bodies will discharge their duties under complete democracy, and how far they will make use of these duties. But this much is clear: the more suddenly they come into possession of their freedom, the more liable they will be to frequent and violent experimentation and therefore to making greater mistakes; and they will proceed all the more cautiously and pragmatically and preserve the general good all the better, the more experience working-class democracy has had in the school of self-government.

Simple as democracy appears to be at first glance, its problems in so complex society as ours are by no means easy to solve. We need only read Mr and Mrs Webb's *Industrial Democracy* to see how much experimentation it took, and is still taking, for the English trade unions just to find an effective form of government and administration, and how important this constitutional question is to them. In this respect, the English trade unions have been able to evolve in perfect freedom for more than seventy years. They began with the most elementary form of self-government and had to learn from practical experience that this form is suitable only for the most elementary organisms, that is, for very small local unions. As they grew, they gradually learned to reject as harmful to their successful development certain cherished ideas of doctrinaire democracy (the tied mandate, the unpaid official, the powerless central representative body) and to develop instead an efficient democracy with representative assemblies, paid officials, and central government with full powers. This part of the history of 'industrial democracy' is extremely instructive. Although not everything that has stood the test for trade unions would be suitable for organs of national administration, much of it would be. Incidentally, this particular chapter in the Webbs' book is a contribution to democratic administrative theory which agrees on many points with Kautsky's conclusions in his book on direct popular legislation.[41] The history of the development of the trade unions shows how their central executive bodies – their state government – can arise simply from the division of labour made necessary by its geographical expansion and the growth in the number of its members. It is possible that later on, with the socialist development of society, this centralisation will once again become superfluous. But for the

---

[41] Bernstein is presumably referring to chapter 2 ('Representative Institutions') of Sidney and Beatrice Webb, *Industrial Democracy*, 2 vols. (London, 1897) and to Kautsky's *Der Parlamentarismus, die Volksgesetzgebung und die Sozialdemokratie* (Stuttgart, 1893).

time being, it cannot be dispensed with, even in a democracy. As has already been explained at the end of the first section of this chapter, it is impossible for the municipalities of large towns or industrial centres to take control of all local production and trading establishments. It is also on practical grounds unlikely – not to mention the grounds of equity against it – that, in a revolutionary upheaval, they would, without further ado, 'expropriate' each and every one of these establishments. But even if they did (and in most cases they would find themselves holding nothing but empty shells) they would be compelled to lease the bulk of the companies either to individual cooperatives or to trade unions for cooperative management.*ff*

In each of these cases, as also *vis-à-vis* local and national independent enterprises, certain interests common to individual professions would need to be respected; and there would therefore still be room for the trade unions to exercise a monitoring function. The diversity of available agencies is of particular value at times of transition.

However, we have not yet got that far, and it is not my intention to expound visions of the future. I am not concerned with what will happen in the more distant future, but with what can and ought to happen in the present, for the present and the immediate future. And so the conclusion of this exposition is the very banal statement that the victory of democracy, the creation of democratic social and political organisations, is the indispensable precondition for the realisation of socialism. It may be argued that the prospect of achieving this in Germany without a political catastrophe is very remote, if not non-existent, and that the German bourgeoisie will become increasingly reactionary. This might perhaps be true for the moment, although there is much evidence to the contrary. But even so, it cannot last long. What we call the bourgeoisie is a very complex class consisting of all kinds of groups with diverse or differing interests. These groups stand together for a time only if they see themselves as groaning under a common oppressor or facing a common threat. At present, of course, only the latter applies. That is, the bourgeoisie constitutes a uniformly reactionary mass because all its elements feel themselves to be equally threatened by Social Democracy, some in their material, others in their ideological interests: that is, in their

---

ff This would certainly cause very complicated problems. One thinks of the many joint enterprises of modern times which employ members of a great variety of trades.

religion, their patriotism, and their hopes to save the country from the horrors of a violent revolution.

But this is no longer necessary. For Social Democracy does not threaten all equally, and it threatens nobody personally; and it has no enthusiasm for a violent revolution against the entire non-proletarian world. The more clearly this is said and substantiated, the sooner will this generalised fear be dissipated, for many elements of the bourgeoisie experience oppression from other quarters and would rather make common cause against these oppressors (who also oppress the working class) than against the workers; they would rather align themselves with the latter than with the former. They tend to be unreliable customers. But we will certainly make them bad allies if we tell them that we want to help them destroy the enemy but that immediately afterwards we will destroy them as well. Since there can be no question of a universal, instantaneous, and violent expropriation but only of a piecemeal settlement by means of organisation and legislation, it would certainly not interrupt the development of democracy to bid farewell to outdated militancy in our language as well as in our practice.

Nearly everywhere it took force to destroy feudalism with its rigid corporate institutions. The liberal institutions of modern society differ from these precisely in being flexible and capable of change and development. They do not need to be destroyed; they need only to be further developed. For that we require organisation and energetic action, but not necessarily a revolutionary dictatorship. A while ago (October 1897) a Swiss Social Democratic paper, the Basle *Vorwärts*, wrote: 'As the object of the class struggle is to abolish class distinctions altogether, there must logically be a period in which the realisation of this object, this ideal, is to be begun. This beginning, these successive periods, are already inherent in our democratic development; they come to our aid in absorbing the class struggle and gradually replacing it with the building up of social democracy.' The Spanish socialist Pablo Iglesias recently remarked: 'The bourgeoisie, of whatever shade of opinion it may be, must be persuaded that we do not want to take power forcibly by the same means that were once employed, by violence and bloodshed, but by legal means appropriate to civilisation' (*Vorwärts*, 16 October 1898). From a similar point of view, the *Labour Leader*, the leading organ of the English Independent Labour Party, agreed unreservedly with Vollmar's remarks on the Paris Commune. But no one will accuse this paper of timidity in its opposition to capitalism and the capitalist parties. And another organ of English socialist workers' democracy, the *Clarion*, accompanied an extract from my article on the theory of collapse, which it endorsed, with the following commentary:

> The formation of a true democracy – I am quite convinced that that is the most pressing and most important duty which lies before us. This is the lesson which the socialist campaign of the last ten years has taught us. That is the doctrine which emerges out of all my knowledge and experience of politics. We must build up a nation of democrats before socialism is possible.

(d) The most immediate tasks of Social Democracy

> And what she is, that dares she to appear.
>
> Schiller, Maria Stuart

The tasks of a party are determined by many factors: by the state of the general economic, political, intellectual, and moral development within its sphere of operation, by the nature of the parties that work beside it or against it, by the nature of the resources at its command, and by a range of subjective, ideological factors, foremost among which is the main aim of the party and its conception of the best way to achieve this aim. With regard to the first of these factors, it is well known that there are great differences between different countries. Even in countries at an approximately equal level of industrial development we find very significant political differences and great differences in the intellectual tendency of the mass of the people. Peculiarities of geographical situation, rooted customs of national life, inherited institutions, and traditions of all kinds create ideological differences which take a long while to succumb to the influence of that industrial development. Even where socialist parties began by accepting the same presuppositions as the starting point of their operation, they have, in the course of time, been compelled to adapt their activity to the special conditions of their various countries. So, at any given time, we could draw up a set of general political principles of Social Democracy which could claim universal validity, but we could not draw up a programme of action which would be equally valid for all countries.

As I argued in the previous section, democracy is a precondition of socialism to a much greater degree than is often supposed, that is, it is not only the means but also the substance. Without a certain number of democratic institutions or traditions, the socialist doctrine of our time would be completely impossible. There might well be a labour movement, but there would be no Social Democracy. The modern socialist movement, as well as its theoretical expression, is in fact the product of the great French Revolution and of the conceptions of right which, through its influence, gained general acceptance in the wages and labour movement of the industrial workers. This movement would have existed without these conceptions. There was, after all, a tradition of popular communism linked to primitive Christianity which was independent of these conceptions and which existed before they were propounded.[g] But this popular communism was ill-defined and semi-mystical, and the labour movement would have lacked inner cohesion had it not rested on the basis of those legal institutions and conceptions which are, at least to a great extent, the necessary accompaniment of capitalist development. It would have been very much like the situation in Oriental countries today. A working class without political rights, steeped in superstition and with deficient education will indeed revolt from time to time and engage in conspiracies on a small scale, but it will never develop a socialist movement. It takes a certain breadth of vision and a fairly well-developed consciousness of rights to make a socialist out of an occasionally rebellious worker. So political rights and education have a prominent position in every socialist programme of action.

This is all very general. Indeed, it is no part of my purpose in this book to evaluate the detailed points in the socialist programme of action. I am not in any way tempted to propose changes to the immediate demands of the Erfurt Programme of German Social Democracy. Probably like all other Social Democrats, I do not regard all the points as being equally important or expedient. For example, it is my opinion that, under present circumstances, the administration of justice and legal aid free of charge is to be recommended only

---

[g] Over the years it has been my repeated experience (and no doubt that of others) that, at the end of a political meeting, workers or artisans who had heard the socialist case for the first time would come to me and declare that what I had said was already to be found in the Bible; they could show me the passages, sentence for sentence.

within limits. Arrangements must certainly be made to enable those without means to get justice. However, there is no pressing need to take over the bulk of present-day property cases and to bring the bar under state control. Meanwhile, since socialist legislation can not be carried through without a complete reform of the legal system, or can be carried through only in step with the creation of new legal institutions (such as the industrial arbitration courts already in existence), the said demand may keep its place in the programme as an indication of a development we hope to see, despite the fact that our present legislators will not contemplate it, albeit for different reasons.

Incidentally, I explicitly expressed my doubt as to the expediency of this demand in its present form as early as 1891 in an essay on the draft programme then under discussion, and I declared that the paragraph in question gave 'too much and too little' (*Die Neue Zeit*, ix, 2, p. 821). The article belongs to a series on the programme which Kautsky and I produced jointly, and of which the first three pieces were almost entirely the work of Kautsky, whilst the fourth was composed by me. Let me here quote two propositions from it which indicate the point of view I upheld at that time with regard to praxis in Social Democracy, and which will show how much or how little my opinions have changed since then.

'Simply to demand state maintenance for all the unemployed means giving, not only those who cannot find work, but also those who refuse to look for work, access to the public trough . . . It really does not take an anarchist to see the endless heaping up of public responsibilities as too much of a good thing . . . We want to maintain the basic principle that the modern proletarian is indeed impoverished but that he is not a pauper. There is a whole world in this distinction; it is the essence of our struggle, the hope of our victory.'

'We propose the formula, "transformation of the standing army into a people's militia", instead of "people's militia in the place of a standing army", because, at a time when it is simply not possible to disband standing armies, it maintains the aim and yet leaves the party a free hand to press for a series of measures which at least reduce as much as possible the antagonism between the army and the people: for example, the abolition of special military courts of justice, reduction of time of service, etc.' (pp. 819, 824, 825).

As the question, '*standing army or militia*', has recently become the subject of heated debate, it is appropriate at this point to offer a few remarks on the topic.

First, it seems to me that the question as worded above is wrongly put. It should read: government army or people's army. This would, from the start, unambiguously identify the political side of the question. Should the army be the tool of the government or the armed defence force of the nation? Should it take its final orders from the crown or from the representatives of the people? Should it take its oath to some person or other standing at the head of the nation or to the constitution and the representatives of the people? No Social Democrat can be in any doubt as to the answer. Of course, if the representatives of the people are not socialist and if the constitution is not democratic, then an army subordinate to the popular representative could still occasionally be used to oppress minorities or an actual majority that has only a minority in parliament. However, there is no formula that will guard against such eventualities, as long as a part of the nation is under arms and is obliged to follow the national representative. In my opinion, even the so-called 'mobilisation of the whole people' would, given present technology, be only an illusory defence against organised armed force. And if the composition of this force did not already safeguard the people against attack (which it increasingly does, thanks to universal conscription) a mobilisation of the whole people would serve only to cause needless sacrifices on both sides. Even where it is still necessary today, it would, for political reasons, not be carried out; and where it could be carried out, it would not be necessary. Much as I wish to see the creation of a hardy and valiant race, I do not regard the mobilisation of the whole people as a socialist ideal. Fortunately, we are increasingly becoming accustomed to settle political differences in ways other than by the use of firearms.

So much for the political side of the question. As for the technical side (training, length of service under arms, etc.), I frankly confess that I am not sufficiently expert to make a definitive judgment. Those examples from earlier times that speak in favour of quickly trained armies (revolutionary wars, wars of liberation, etc.) can not be directly applied to the completely transformed conditions of warfare today; and our experience with volunteers in the recent Greek–Turkish and Spanish–American wars does not seem to me to be applicable to the eventualities with which Germany has to reckon, at least not directly. For, although it is my view that we sometimes exaggerate 'the Russian peril', or that we look for it where it is least to be found, nonetheless I concede that a country the great bulk of whose population consists of politically apathetic and very ignorant peasants can always be a danger to its neighbours. In such cases, it would therefore be shrewd to carry the war as quickly as possible to the enemy's territory and to wage it there, since in modern countries a war on one's own territory is a war already half lost. Consequently, the question is whether a militia army would possess the combat readiness, the confidence, and the cohesion to guarantee that result, or how long a training under the colours it would require. On this matter, I believe that all we can say with certainty is that if the young are properly trained in valour and if the legacy of square-bashing is eliminated, then a very significant reduction in the length of military service should be possible without in the slightest impairing the military potential of the nation. Here, of course, the good-will of whoever is at the head of the army at the time plays a major role, but already now the representatives of the people can effectively lend this good-will a helping hand by pressure on the military budget. As with the factory acts, an enforced reduction in the length of military service would make many things possible which pedantry and special interests now declare to be 'impossible'. So, insofar as any value at all is attached to the maintenance of armed forces prepared for attack as well as defence, the first question (apart from the essential transformation in the political position of the army) is not 'militia or no militia' but what reduction in the length of military service is possible immediately and, step by step, later on, without putting Germany at a disadvantage *vis-à-vis* neighbouring states.

But has Social Democracy, as the party of the working class and of peace, an interest in maintaining the nation's readiness to fight? From many points of view, it is tempting to answer the question in the negative, especially if one starts from the proposition in *The Communist Manifesto*: 'The proletarian has no fatherland.'[42] However, although this proposition might perhaps apply to the worker of the 1840s, deprived of rights and excluded from public life, nowadays it has already lost much of its truth, despite the enormous increase in

[42] MECW, vol. VI, p. 502; MEW, vol. IV, p. 479.

the intercourse between nations, and it will lose even more, the more the worker ceases to be a proletarian and becomes a citizen through the influence of Social Democracy. The worker who has equal voting rights in state and municipality, etc., and thus shares in the common good of the nation, whose children the community educates, whose health it protects, and whom it insures against injury, will have a fatherland without therefore ceasing to be a citizen of the world, just as nations draw closer to one another without thereby ceasing to have a life of their own. It might seem a great convenience if everyone were to end up speaking only one language. But what a stimulus, what a source of intellectual enjoyment, would thus be lost to future generations! The total disintegration of nations is not an attractive prospect and is, in any case, not to be expected in the foreseeable future. But if it is not desirable that any of the other major civilised nations lose its independence, neither is it a matter of indifference to Social Democracy whether the German nation – which has indeed borne, and is still bearing, its fair share in the civilising work of nations – be eclipsed in the council of nations.

There is much talk nowadays about the conquest of political power by Social Democracy, and the strong position Social Democracy has gained in Germany makes it at least not impossible that, in the near future, some political event or other will assign it the decisive role. Since neighboring countries are not so far advanced, it is precisely in such circumstances that, like the Independents in the English Revolution and the Jacobins in the French Revolution, Social Democracy would be forced to be national, that is, it would have to establish its fitness to be the leading party or class by showing that it has just as clear a view of national interests as it does of class interests.

I write this with no inclination to chauvinism (for which I have in truth no cause or occasion) but rather by way of an objective investigation of the duties which Social Democracy would have to assume in such a situation. My esteem for internationalism is as high today as it ever was, and I do not believe that the principles developed in these pages will in any way contravene it. Only if Social Democracy were to confine itself to doctrinaire propaganda and the socialist experiment would it be able to maintain a purely negative attitude to national questions in politics. However, political action is already in itself a compromise with the non-socialist world and forces us to take measures that are not a priori socialistic. In the long run, however, national action is just as socialistic as municipal action. Even today, socialists in democratic states like to call themselves nationalists and speak freely of nationalising the land, etc., instead of confining themselves to the expression 'socialisation', which is much less precise and constitutes more of a make-shift than an improvement on the former word.

In the foregoing, I have indicated the point of view which, under present conditions, Social Democracy should in principle take as the basis of its position on questions of *foreign policy*. Though the worker is not yet a full citizen, he is not so bereft of rights that national interests are of no importance to him. Also, though Social Democracy is not yet in power, it nevertheless occupies a position of power which imposes certain obligations upon it. Its voice carries great weight. Given the present composition of the army and the complete uncertainty as to the effect of introducing small bore fire-arms, the government of the Reich will think ten times before venturing on a war against the determined opposition of Social Democracy. Even without the famous general strike, Social Democracy can speak with a weighty if not a decisive voice in favour of peace, and it will do so in conformity with the time-honoured motto of the International[43] as often and as energetically as is necessary and possible. Also, in cases where conflicts arise with other nations and direct agreement can not be reached, it will, in accordance with its programme, stand up for settling the difference by means of arbitration. But it is not called upon to insist that the present or future interests of Germany be abandoned if or because English, French, or Russian chauvinists take umbrage at certain policies. Where it is not just a question of partiality on the part of Germany or of the special interests of particular groups which are indifferent or even detrimental to the welfare of the people, where really important national interests are at stake, internationalism is no reason for yielding weakly to the pretensions of foreign interested parties.

This is not a new idea. It is simply a recapitulation of the train of thought which underpins almost all the declarations of Marx, Engels, and Lassalle on questions of foreign policy. Furthermore, the position recommended here is not one that endangers peace. Nations nowadays no longer go lightly to war, and a firm stand can, under some

---

[43] Undoubtedly a reference to: 'Proletarians of all countries, unite!'

circumstances, be more serviceable to peace than continuously giving way.

Nowadays many regard the doctrine of the European balance of power as being out of date – and so it is, in its old form. However, in a changed form the balance of power still plays a major role in the resolution of international controversies. Whether a particular measure is implemented or blocked is still, at times, a matter of how strong a combination of powers supports it. I regard it as a legitimate objective of German imperial policy to ensure that, in such cases, the voice of Germany is heard; and I do not regard it as the business of Social Democracy to oppose the appropriate measures as a matter of principle.

Let us take a specific example. The leasing of Kiaochow Bay was, at the time, criticised very severely in the German socialist press.[44] Insofar as the criticism referred to the circumstances in which the lease was granted, the Social Democratic press had a right, nay a duty, to make its point. It was equally correct to mount a determined opposition to the introduction or promotion of a policy for the partition of China, for such a partition is in no way in the interests of Germany. But when some papers went still further and declared that the party must under all circumstances and as a matter of principle condemn the acquisition of the Bay, I cannot by any means agree.

It is a matter of no interest to the German people that China be divided up and Germany acquire a piece of the Celestial Empire. But the German people does have a great interest in China not becoming the prey of other nations; it has a great interest in China's commercial policy not becoming subordinate to the interests of a single foreign power or a coalition of foreign powers; in short, it has an interest in Germany having a decisive word to say in all questions concerning China. Its trade with China requires that it have a right of veto. Now, the circumstance that the acquisition of Kiaochow Bay is a means of guaranteeing and enforcing this right of veto – and it will be difficult to deny that it does contribute to it – is, in my view, a reason why Social Democracy should not object to it in principle. Apart from the manner in which the Bay was acquired and the pious

---

[44] In November 1897, the Germans occupied Kiaochow Bay, using the murder of two missionaries in Shantung as the pretext. The move precipitated a general scramble among the European powers to obtain, or force, concessions from the Chinese government. It also precipitated a lively debate in the German press.

words which accompanied the act, it was not the worst blow struck by German foreign policy.

It was a matter of ensuring free trade with, and in, China. For there can be no doubt that, without that acquisition, China would have been drawn increasingly into the orbit of the capitalist economy and that Russia would have continued its policy of encirclement and would have occupied the Manchurian ports at the first opportunity. It was thus only a question as to whether Germany should look calmly on while, by one *fait accompli* after another, China fell into an ever greater dependence on Russia, or whether Germany should secure for itself a position on the basis of which it could at any time, and under normal conditions, make its influence felt on the shape of things in China, instead of having to be content with *ex post facto* protests. To the extent that the leasing of Kiaochow Bay guaranteed, and still guarantees, the future interests of Germany in China (whatever the official explanation) Social Democracy can give its approval without compromising its principles in the slightest.

However, since those who conduct German foreign policy are not accountable, there can be no question of Social Democracy giving positive support. The only question is that of finding the right basis for a negative position. Without some guarantee that such enterprises will not be diverted behind the backs of the people's representatives to purposes other than those announced (say as a means to achieve some small temporary success at the expense of greater future interests) Social Democracy can accept no part of the responsibility for foreign-policy measures.

As is evident, the rule unfolded here for taking a position on foreign-policy questions amounts pretty much to the stance which Social Democracy has, until now, been observed to adopt in practice. It is not for me to discuss how far its basic assumptions agree with the way of thinking that prevails in the party.

On the whole, tradition plays a greater role in these things than we think. It is in the nature of all forward-moving parties to attach little importance to changes already accomplished. Attention is always focussed mainly on what has not yet been changed. To strive for certain goals, to set objectives, is a perfectly justifiable and useful tendency. However, parties imbued with this spirit easily fall into the habit of upholding, longer than is necessary or useful, received opinions based on conditions which have to a large extent changed. They

167

disregard or underestimate these changes. They search out facts which will give those opinions an appearance of validity, rather than examine the question whether, on the basis of all the relevant facts, the opinion in question has not over time degenerated into a prejudice.

Such a priori political reasoning often seems to me to play a part when *the question of colonies* is being discussed.

At present, it is in principle a matter of complete indifference to socialism and to the labour movement whether new colonies are successful or not. The notion that colonial expansion will delay the realisation of socialism rests at bottom on the completely out-dated idea that the realisation of socialism depends on an increasingly rapid reduction in the number of the very rich and on the growing impoverishment of the masses. It has been shown in earlier chapters that the first is a fairy-tale; and the immiseration theory has now been abandoned nearly everywhere – if not outright and with all its consequences, then at least in that it is explained away as much as possible.[hh] But even if the theory were correct, the colonies in question

[hh] H. Cunow makes just such an attempt to explain things away in his article on the collapse. He writes that when Marx, at the end of the first volume of *Capital*, speaks of 'the increasing mass of misery', this is to be understood 'not as a simple, absolute decline in the economic living conditions of the worker' but 'only as a decline in his social condition as a whole relative to the forward moving cultural development, i.e. relative to the increase in productivity and the growth in general cultural requirements'. The concept of misery is not a fixed one. 'What appears to one worker in a certain category, separated from his employer by a great difference in education, as a state of affairs worth striving for may appear to the skilled worker of another category, who is perhaps intellectually superior to his employer, as such a mass of "misery and oppression" that he rises in revolt against it' (*Die Neue Zeit*, xvii, 1, pp. 402–3).

Unfortunately, in the sentence referred to, Marx speaks not only of the growing mass of misery, of oppression, but also of 'slavery, degradation and exploitation'.[45] Are we to understand these also in the aforesaid – Pickwickian – sense? Are we to accept a deterioration of the worker which is only a deterioration relative to the rise in the general level of culture? I am not inclined to do so, and neither, probably, is Cunow. No, in the passage referred to, Marx speaks quite positively of '*the constant decrease in the number* of capitalist magnates, who "usurp ... *all the advantages* of the capitalist process of transformation", and of the growth of "the mass of misery, oppression" etc.' (*Capital*, i, ch. 24, 7.) The theory of collapse can be based on this antithesis; but it can not be based on the poor morale produced by intellectually inferior employers, as is to be found in any office in any hierarchical organisation.

Incidentally, it gives me a little satisfaction to see that Cunow can reconcile the propositions on which the theory of collapse rests with reality only by suddenly introducing workers of different categories with fundamentally different social ideas. Are these, then, also 'English workers'?

[45] *Capital* I, p. 929.

168

with regard to present day Germany, are not remotely in a position to influence social conditions at home quickly enough to delay a possible collapse, even for just a year. In this respect, German Social Democracy would have nothing whatsoever to fear from the colonial policy of the German Reich. The development of the colonies Germany has acquired (and the same holds for those which it might still acquire) will take so much time that there can be no question of any influence worth mentioning on social conditions in Germany for many a long year. German Social Democracy can therefore deal with the question of these colonies without prejudice. Colonial possessions can not even have any serious effect on political conditions in Germany. Naval chauvinism, for instance, is without doubt closely connected with colonial chauvinism and is to a certain extent nourished by it. But it would exist without it. After all, Germany had a navy long before it thought of acquiring colonies. It must nevertheless be granted that this connection is the most appropriate ground on which to justify a principled opposition to colonial policy.

Otherwise, when colonies are acquired, there is some justification for examining carefully their value and prospects and tightly controlling the indemnification and treatment of the natives as well as other matters of administration; but there is no reason to regard such acquisitions as being reprehensible as such. The political position which Social Democracy is allowed within the present system of government precludes anything other than a negative stance on such matters; and the question as to whether Germany needs colonies at present can with good reason be answered in the negative, particularly with regard to those colonies still to be obtained. But the future also has rights which we must consider. If we take into account the fact that Germany now annually imports a considerable amount of colonial produce, we must note that the time may come when it might be desirable to procure at least a part of these products from our own colonies. However fast we may think that Germany is developing, we can not be blind to the fact that it will be a long time before a large number of other countries go over to socialism. However, if there is nothing wrong with enjoying the produce of tropical plantations, there can be nothing wrong with cultivating such plantations ourselves. The decisive question is not *whether* but *how*? It is not inevitable that the occupation of tropical countries by Europeans should harm the natives in their enjoyment of life, nor has it usually been the case up till now. Moreover, we can recognise only a conditional right of savages to the land they occupy. Higher civilisation has ultimately a higher right. It is not conquest but the cultivation of the land that confers an historical right to its use.[i]

These are, in my judgment, the essential points of view which ought to determine the position of Social Democracy on the question of colonial policy. They too would not, in practice, bring about any change worth mentioning in the way the party votes; but I repeat that it is a question, not only of how we vote on any given issue, but also of why we vote the way we do.

There are some Social Democrats who regard any intercession for national interests as chauvinism or as a violation of the internationalism and class policy of the proletariat. Just as, in time past, Domela Nieuwenhuis declared Bebel's well-known assertion – that in case of an attack from Russia Social Democracy would call its men to the defence of Germany – to be chauvinism, so Mr Belfort Bax recently detected reprehensible jingoism in a similar statement by H. M. Hyndman.[ii] Now, it must be admitted that it is not always easy to determine the point at which advocacy of the interests of one's own nation ceases to be justified and becomes pseudo-patriotism; but the remedy for exaggerations in this direction certainly does not consist in greater exaggerations in the other. The remedy is, rather, to be sought in an exchange of ideas between the democracies of the civilised countries and in support for all factors and institutions working for peace.

However let us return to the question of the immediate demands of the party's programme. Although some of these demands have not been put on the agenda of party agitation and parliamentary action at all, or have appeared only in modified form, in other cases the objectives laid down in the programme have, here and there, already

---

[i] 'Even a whole society, a nation, nay, all contemporary societies taken together are not proprietors of the earth. They are only its possessors, its usufructuaries, and have to leave it improved as *boni patres familias* to the following generation' (Marx, *Capital*, iii, 2, p. 309).[46]

[ii] Hyndman energetically promotes the idea that, for the protection of its imports of food, England requires a navy large enough for every possible combination of adversaries. 'Our existence as a nation of free men depends on our supremacy at sea. This can be said of no other people of the present day. However much we socialists are naturally opposed to armaments, we must, however, recognise facts' (*Justice*, 31 December 1898).

[46] *Capital* III, p. 911.

been pushed beyond their original limits. Thus the programme demands that the employment of children under fourteen be forbidden. However, at the workers' protection conference at Zurich in 1897, fifteen years was designated as the lowest limit for the employment of children; and even this is too low for some socialists. I am, however, convinced that, in present circumstances, this extension is not to be regarded as an improvement. Provided that the working day is short enough to inflict no physical damage on the young and to leave sufficient time for play, recreation, and further education, then the circumstance that young people begin productive work when they have passed their fourteenth year is not so great an evil that it would be necessary to forbid it altogether. It depends entirely on the nature and conditions of the work – which, incidentally, current legislation already recognises in principle, in that it forbids completely the employment of young workers in some trades, and in others narrowly restricts the time per day during which it is allowed to occur. I believe that the rational development of protection for the young lies in the further improvement of these regulations, as well as in perfecting the public educational system, and not in mechanical increases in the age limit for industrial labour.

It is, of course, generally acknowledged that this question is connected with the question of education. The question of child labour must start with schooling and must be regulated with constant reference to it, if the result is to be satisfactory.[*] Wherever industrial employment is detrimental to health and to the intellectual and moral educational objectives of schooling, it is to be forbidden. On the other

---

[*] In a book, *How It Can Be Done*, an English engineer, John Richardson, a member of the Social Democratic Federation, works out a plan for the realisation of socialism according to which instruction is made compulsory until the age of twenty-one and is combined with the completely free maintenance of the student. However, from the age of fourteen, four hours a day is devoted to productive work, and from the age of nineteen, six hours. In this and on various other points, the plan, much as it underestimates the economic difficulties of the matter, at least proceeds from thoroughly sensible principles. 'For a Social Reform to be successful', says the author, 'the following conditions must be complied with: First, it must be possible, that is, it must deal with human nature as it is, and not as it ought to be. Second, it must make no violent and sudden change in the constitution of society. Third, while the application is gradual, the effect should be immediate and certain. Fourth, it must be permanent in its effect; and, as far as possible, automatic in its operation, when once started. Fifth, it must be just and equitable in its action, and equal in its application. Sixth, it must be elastic, so as to permit of indefinite expansion, modification, and perfection' (*How it Can be Done, or Constructive Socialism*, London, The Twentieth Century Press [1895, p. 17]).

hand, any general prohibition which also affects age groups above school-leaving age is to be firmly rejected. It is absolutely wrong to let economic considerations such as the restriction of production or competition among workers intrude upon the question. Conversely, it is always well to bear in mind that productive or, to use a less ambiguous expression, socially useful work has great educational value and, for this reason alone, is not in itself something to be opposed.

At present, the question of what to *add* to the party programme is more important than that of pressing for demands already on the programme. Practical experience has put a large number of questions on the agenda which, when the programme was first drawn up, were in part regarded as lying too far in the future to be of any immediate concern to Social Democracy, but it is also the case that their implications were not fully appreciated. These include the *agrarian question*, questions of *municipal politics*, the *cooperatives question*, and various questions of *industrial law*. The great growth of Social Democracy in the eight years since the Erfurt Programme was drawn up, its effect on the domestic politics of Germany, as well as the experience gained from other countries, have made a closer consideration of all these questions unavoidable, and many views which were formerly held about them have undergone substantial revision.

As regards the *agrarian question*, even those who regard the peasant economy as doomed to destruction have changed their views quite significantly as to the time it will take for this to happen. Indeed, major differences of opinion on this point played a part in recent debates on what agrarian policy Social Democracy should pursue; but the point of principle on which these debates turned was whether and, in any given case, to what extent Social Democracy should give assistance to the peasant as such, that is, as an independent agricultural entrepreneur, against capitalism.[47]

It is easier to ask the question than to answer it. To begin with, the fact that the great majority of peasants, although they are not wage-earners, nonetheless belong to the working classes – that is,

---

[47] In 1894, Vollmar and Schoenlank persuaded the party conference at Breslau to establish a commission to see if an acceptable agrarian programme could be worked out. The commission reported to the conference at Frankfurt in 1895 where, after a long debate, its proposals were rejected. However the controversy rumbled on, and it surfaced again at the Stuttgart Conference. See e.g. the speeches by Scheidemann and Ulrich, *Protokoll*, 1898, pp. 86 and 88.

their livelihood does not depend merely on title of possession or inherited privilege – places them closer to the wage-earning classes. Then again, they constitute so significant a part of the population in Germany that, at elections, their votes decide the issue between capitalist and socialist parties in a great many constituencies. If Social Democracy does not want to limit itself to being a workers' party in the sense of being merely the political wing of the trade-union movement, then it must consider how to interest at least a large proportion of the peasants in the victory of its candidates. In the long run, we can do this only by committing ourselves to measures which offer the small peasant the prospect of improvement in the near future, measures which bring him immediate relief. But many legislative measures which have this as their objective cannot distinguish between the small and the medium peasant; and furthermore they cannot assist the peasant as citizen and worker without also supporting him, at least indirectly, as an 'entrepreneur'.

This is evident in, among other places, the programme of socialist agrarian policy which Kautsky has outlined under the rubric 'The Neutralisation of the Peasantry' at the end of his book on the agrarian question.[48] Kautsky shows convincingly that, even after a Social Democratic victory, there would be no reason to set about abolishing the landed property of the peasantry. But at the same time he strongly opposes supporting measures or demands aimed at 'protecting peasants' in the sense of artificially maintaining the peasant as an entrepreneur. He then suggests a whole series of reforms – or declares it permissible to support them – which provide relief for rural municipalities and increase their sources of income. However, which class would these measures benefit in the first instance? According to Kautsky's account of the matter, it would be the peasants. For, as he emphasises elsewhere in his work, there can be no question of the proletariat in the countryside having any influence worth mentioning on the business of municipalities, even where universal suffrage prevails. The rural proletariat is too isolated, too backward, and too dependent on the few employers of labour who control it. 'A communal policy other than one in the interest of the landowner is unthinkable.' And nowadays, 'modern management of the land in a large cooperative farming enterprise controlled by a village commune'

---

[48] Karl Kautsky, *Die Agrarfrage: eine Uebersicht über die Tendenzen der modernen Landwirthschaft und die Agrarpolitik der Sozialdemokratie* (Stuttgart, 1899), pp. 436ff.

is equally unthinkable (*The Agrarian Question*, pp. 337 and 338). But insofar, and for as long, as this is correct, measures such as 'annexation of the hunting preserves of the large landowners by the rural municipalities', 'nationalisation of responsibility for schools, roads, and poor relief' would obviously contribute to the improvement of the economic position of the peasant and thus also contribute to shoring up his property. In practice, then, it would operate as a 'protection for peasants'.

Support for peasant protection of this kind seems to me to be unobjectionable, under two preconditions: first, that it is accompanied by strong protection for agricultural labourers and second, as a *sine qua non* for its realisation, that democracy is established on both the state and municipal levels.[″] Indeed, both are assumed by Kautsky. But he underestimates the influence of the agricultural labourer in rural municipalities. Agricultural labourers are as powerless as he suggests in the passage quoted only in those communities which lie outside the sphere of commercial intercourse, and the number of these is steadily diminishing. In general, the agricultural labourer, for whom Kautsky himself produces material enough, is nowadays reasonably well aware of his interests and would, with universal suffrage, become even more so. Besides, there are, in most municipalities, all kinds of conflicts of interest among the peasants themselves; and village communities contain elements, in craftsmen and small businessmen, which, on many matters, have more interests in common with agricultural labourers than with the peasant aristocracy. All this means that, except in very few cases, the agricultural labourers would not wind up standing alone against a solid 'reactionary mass'. In time, democracy, in the socialist sense, must have its effect in the rural municipalities. I regard democracy, combined with the effects of the great revolution in communications and transport, as a more

---

[″] I am disregarding the technical questions of management connected with this topic. Obviously, it would be contradictory to oblige one body (the state) to provide the means and give the other body (the municipality) an unchecked right to dispose of these means. Either the state, as the organ which provides the resources, must be allowed extensive financial control over municipal expenditure, or the municipality must itself be responsible for at least a part of the costs of carrying out specified duties, so that it must face the consequences of injudicious expenditure. So far as I am concerned, my view is that the state should be the subsidiary and not the primary financial authority in these matters.

powerful instrument for the emancipation of the agricultural labourer than the technological changes in the peasant economy.

Moreover, Kautsky's programme is in fact chiefly – and indeed precisely on the points to which he attaches the greatest importance – just an application of the demands of bourgeois democracy to agrarian conditions, reinforced by extensive regulations for the protection of agricultural labourers. It is obvious from what has gone before that, in my view, this is anything but a negative criticism. And in saying this, I say nothing that Kautsky himself has not expressly emphasised. What is more, he thinks that his programme must forego the title of a Social Democratic agrarian programme, partly because those of its demands which benefit the agricultural labourer in rural self-government are, in essence, already contained in the demands for workers' protection and in the immediate political demands of Social Democracy, and partly also because they are – if we discount the demands for the nationalisation of forestry management and water utilities – 'minor measures' which have already been implemented elsewhere and with regard to which Social Democracy is distinguished from other parties only by the ruthlessness with which it defends the public interest against the interests of private property. However, whether or not a programme can be described as Social Democratic depends, not on the significance of individual demands, but on the character and significance of all the demands in their inter-connection. Social Democracy can put forward only those immediate demands which are suited to present conditions, the proviso being that they bear within themselves the seed for further development towards that social order which is Social Democracy's objective. However, there is no demand of this kind to which one or other non-socialist party could and would not also subscribe. A demand which all bourgeois parties would necessarily oppose on principle would, by that fact alone, be branded as utopian. On the other hand, Social Democracy can not put forward demands which, under the given economic and political conditions, would serve to consolidate present property and power relations rather than to loosen them up in such a way that the relevant measures could, under different circumstances and at a more advanced stage of development, become the instrument of the socialist transformation of production. An example of such a demand – from which Kautsky, after careful examination, distances himself – would be the nationalisation of mortgages. At present, it is not an issue for Social Democracy.

I will not go through all the details of Kautsky's programme – with which, as I have already remarked, I agree thoroughly in principle – but there are, I believe, a few observations on it which ought not to be suppressed. As I have already observed, I think that the main current duties of Social Democracy with regard to the agricultural population fall into three groups. Namely: (1) *Opposition to all remaining remnants and supports of land-owning feudalism* and *the fight for democracy in municipality and province*. In other words, action for the abolition of entail, manorial holdings, hunting privileges, etc., as laid down by Kautsky. The word 'fullest' in Kautsky's formulation, 'fullest self-government in municipality and province', is not in my view well chosen, and I would replace it with the word 'democratic'. Superlatives are nearly always misleading. 'Fullest self-government' could suggest a closed circle of privileged participants, whereas what is actually meant is better expressed by 'democratic self-government'. It could also suggest *rights of administration*, and then it would signify a municipal absolutism which is unnecessary and incapable of being reconciled with the requirements of sound democracy. Municipalities are subject to the general legislation of the nation, which allots them their particular functions and represents the general interest against their particular interests. (2) *Protection and relief for the agricultural working classes*. This includes workers' protection in the more restricted sense: abolition of regulations governing the rights and duties of servants, limitation of the working day of various categories of wage-earners, health regulations, public education, as well as measures to bring tax relief to the small peasant. As regards workers' protection, Kautsky's suggestion that child labour between 7.00 p.m. and 7.00 a.m. be prohibited does not seem to me to be practical. In the summer months, this would mean transferring work from the morning hours to the hottest time of the day, when normally work ceases completely. In the countryside, people generally get up early in the summer, and for certain jobs at harvest-time an early start is unavoidable.[mm] A normal working day can not be implemented in the

---

[mm] For instance, when the grass is mown in the meadows, youngsters are given the job of spreading out the mown grass so that it dries in the sun during the day. If we are not going to deny them this work and the supplementary work of turning the grass and

countryside in the same way as in industry. As Kautsky himself explains, it is possible only through a plan of work established for the whole year and taking account of the nature of the various kinds of seasonal work depending on the weather etc. It must also be a plan based on the average of the maximum hours of work permitted for the youngest workers as well as adults. A standard working day of eight hours for adults would then correspond to a standard working day of six hours for young people. (3) *Opposition to the absolutism of property and the encouragement of cooperation.* This includes demands such as 'limitation of private property rights in land in order to encourage (1) suppression of the aggregation of land, (2) the cultivation of the land, (3) the prevention of infectious diseases' (Kautsky). 'Reduction of exorbitant rents by courts of justice set up for the purpose' (Kautsky). The building of healthier and more comfortable workers' accommodation by municipalities. 'The facilitation of cooperative mergers by legislation' (Kautsky). Enabling municipalities to acquire land by purchase or expropriation for lease to workers or workers' cooperatives at a low rate.'''

This latter demand brings us to the *question of cooperatives.* After what has been said in the section on the economic potentialities of cooperatives, little more needs to be said here. Nowadays, the question is no longer whether cooperatives ought to exist. They exist and will continue to exist whether Social Democracy likes it or not. By dint of its influence on the working class, Social Democracy could indeed retard the spread of workers' cooperatives, but this would be no service either to itself or to the working class. Nor can we recommend the rigid Manchesterism which is often manifested in the party with regard to the cooperative movement and which is based on the proposition that there can be no socialist cooperatives within a capitalist society. It is, rather, a matter of taking a definite position and being clear as to what cooperatives Social Democracy can recommend and to which it can give moral support, according to its means, and to which it can not. The resolution which the Berlin party confer-

stacking it, then it is better for them and for the work itself to let them do it from about 6 to 10 in the mornings and from 4 to 8 in the afternoons during the hottest months.
''' The new English Local Government Act includes a similar paragraph, albeit with rather too many qualifications. The original draft, proposed by the Liberal government in 1894, was much more radical, but it had to be watered down, thanks to the opposition of the Conservatives backed by the House of Lords.

ence in 1892 passed on the subject of cooperatives is therefore already inadequate because it refers to only one kind of cooperative, the industrial production cooperative. Moreover this is a form of cooperative which, because it is meant as an independent enterprise competing with capitalist factories, should be given the coolest possible reception. But what holds for the economic potentialities of production cooperatives does not hold for other forms of cooperative enterprise. It does not hold for consumers' cooperatives and the production units associated with them. And it is questionable whether it is not also untenable with regard to agricultural cooperatives.

We have seen what extraordinary progress credit-, purchasing-, dairy-, work-, and business-cooperatives have made amongst the rural populations of all modern countries. However in Germany, these cooperatives are generally peasant cooperatives, representatives of the 'middle class movement' in the countryside. I consider it incontrovertible that, in conjunction with the lowering of interest rates which accompanies the growing accumulation of capital, they could in fact contribute much towards keeping peasant enterprises competitive *vis-à-vis* big business. Consequently, these peasant cooperatives are for the most part the playground of anti-socialist elements, of petty-bourgeois liberals, clericals, and anti-semites. So far as Social Democracy is concerned, they are at present out of the reckoning almost everywhere, even though their ranks may include many small peasants who are nearer to Social Democracy than to the other parties. Their tone is set by the middle peasantry. If Social Democracy ever had any prospect of using cooperatives to increase its influence on the class of the rural population referred to, it has let the opportunity slip. Today, only cooperatives of agricultural workers and very small peasants can, or could, come into consideration, and the form of such cooperatives is not yet discovered, or at least not yet tested. However, if we consider that established trade-union organisations have not so far been practicable, even in England where no service regulations or combination laws prohibit them, and that their prospects are therefore very slim in our own country, whereas on the other hand all kinds of agencies are at present labouring to bind the agricultural worker to the soil by means of rented accommodation and similar creations, then we must admit that the task of at least showing the agricultural labourer a way to turn the methods of cooperation to his advantage in his own way falls to Social Democracy. The most

178

important requisites for this are: sufficient land and the opening up of the market. With regard to the former, it seems to me that the demand formulated above, according to which municipalities would get the right to acquire land by expropriation and to lease it on favourable terms to cooperatives, is the next stage in democratic development. And the urban consumers' cooperatives would be able to provide the rural workers' cooperatives with a market – inasmuch as they have to overcome a boycott by the capitalist business world.

However, cooperatives of agricultural labourers will remain mere paper realities, if the battle for democracy is not won first. At present, the establishment of such cooperatives by self help or through private means might be on the cards, as F. Oppenheimer suggests. However, like the establishment of consumers' cooperatives, that is a matter that lies outside the brief of Social Democracy as a party. As a militant political party, it cannot embark on economic experiments. Its task is to clear away the legal impediments which stand in the way of the workers' cooperative movement and to fight for the effective transformation of those administrative organs which will eventually be called upon to further the movement.

But if it is not the vocation of Social Democracy as a party to found consumers' cooperatives, that does not mean that it should take no interest in them. The popular saying that consumers' cooperatives are not socialist enterprises depends on the self-same formalism which for a long time was used against the trade unions and which now begins to give way to the opposite extreme. Whether a trade union or a workers' consumer association is socialist or not depends not on its form but on its substance, on the spirit that permeates it. They are certainly not the wood itself, but they are trees that can be very useful parts of, and genuine assets to, the wood. To speak unmetaphorically, they are not socialism, but as workers' organisations they have in them enough of the socialist element for them to be developed into valuable and indispensable instruments of socialist emancipation. They will certainly best discharge their economic tasks if they are left completely to themselves in their organisation and administration. But just as the aversion and even hostility to the trade-union movement which many socialists once felt has gradually changed into friendly neutrality and then into a feeling of solidarity, so it will happen with consumers' cooperatives – so, in part, it has already happened. Here too, practice is the best guide.

By campaigning against consumers' cooperatives for workers, those elements which are hostile not only to the revolutionary movement but to every workers' emancipation movement have compelled Social Democracy to intervene in their support. Experience has also shown that fears that, for instance, the cooperative movement would drain away the intellectual or other strength of the political labour movement, are completely unfounded. It might happen in a few places and in the short run; but in the long run exactly the opposite invariably occurs. Where the appropriate economic and legal preconditions are present Social Democracy can contemplate with equanimity the establishment of consumers' cooperatives for workers, and it will do well to accord such initiatives its unstinting good-will and to give them whatever help is possible.[∞]

Only from one point of view could consumers' cooperatives for workers seem to be questionable as a matter of principle, namely, as a good thing which stands in the way of a better, where the better consists in the organisation of the procurement and distribution of goods by the municipality, as is prescribed in nearly all socialist systems. But, first, a democratic consumers' association needs no alteration in principle in order to include all the members of the community in which it is located. It needs only to broaden its constitution, which is completely in accord with its natural tendencies. (In some smaller localities, consumers' cooperatives are already close to counting all the inhabitants of the place as members.) And second, the implementation of this idea is still so far distant, presupposes so many political and economic changes and intermediate stages of development, that it would be foolish to forego, for its sake, the advantages which workers might at present derive from consumers' associations. At the moment, so far as the municipality as a political unit is concerned, it can only be a question of providing for a few clearly defined general needs.

This brings us, finally, to the *municipal policy of Social Democracy*. This too was, for a long time, a step-child of the socialist movement. It is, for example, not too long ago that a foreign socialist paper edited by very intelligent people (it is now defunct) scornfully rejected as petty bourgeois the idea of using municipal government, here and now, as an instrument of socialist reform and of using the municipal-

---

[∞] This assistance, however, must not take the form of allowing the consumers' association to carry sub-standard goods, etc.

ity as the basis for the actualisation of socialist demands, without at the same time neglecting parliamentary action. The irony of fate decreed that the chief editor of that paper was able to get into the parliament of his country only on a wave of municipal socialism. Similarly in England, before Social Democracy succeeded in getting its own representatives into Parliament, it found a rich field of fruitful activity in municipal government. In Germany, the development was different. Here Social Democracy had achieved parliamentary representation long before it gained a footing in municipal government to any extent worth mentioning. However, with its continued expansion, its successes in municipal elections also increased, so that the need to develop a socialist municipal programme, such as those which have already been agreed for individual states or provinces, has become ever more evident. Thus, quite recently, on 27 and 28 December 1898, a conference of socialist municipal representatives from the province of Brandenburg agreed on a programme for municipal elections which should, on the whole, serve its purpose extremely well and which at no point invites criticism on any matter of principle. However, it limits itself to demands that fall within the existing rights of municipalities, without embarking on any discussion of what, on a socialist view, the rights and duties of a municipality ought in principle to be – and nothing other can be expected from an action programme. On the other hand, a general Social Democratic municipal programme would have to say something on the question. What does Social Democracy demand *for* the municipalities, and what does it expect *from* them?

On this matter, the Erfurt Programme says only: 'Self-determination and self-government of the people in Reich, state, province, and municipality; election of officials by the people', and it goes on to demand universal, equal, and direct adult suffrage for all elections.[49] It says nothing about the legal relationship between the governmental bodies mentioned. No doubt, most of the delegates, like the author of this demand, assumed at the time that the order in which the bodies were enumerated indicated their legal ranking, so that, in cases of conflict, Reich legislation should take precedence over state legislation, etc. But this would, for example, again partly abolish, or limit, the self-determination of the people in the municip-

---

[49] For the full text see Susan Miller and Heinrich Potthoff, *A History of German Social Democracy: from 1848 to the Present* (New York, 1986), p. 241.

alities. As stated above, I do in fact maintain, even now, that national laws or decrees must be the highest court of appeal in any community. However, that does not mean that the rights and powers of state and municipal government should be the same as they are today.

Nowadays, for instance, municipalities have very limited rights of expropriation. A whole range of politico-economic measures would consequently meet with a positively insurmountable barrier in the opposition or exaggerated demands of landowners. An extension of the right of expropriation would accordingly be one of the first demands of municipal socialism. It is, however, not necessary to demand an absolute and completely unlimited right of expropriation. In matters of expropriation, the municipality would always be bound to keep to those rules of common law which protect the individual against the arbitrary action of fortuitous majorities. In any community, the property rights which common law allows must be inviolable as long as, and to the extent that, common law allows them. To take away lawful property otherwise than by compensation is confiscation, which can be justified only in cases of extreme pressure of circumstances (war, epidemics).*

So, besides the democratisation of the franchise, Social Democracy must demand an extension of municipal rights of expropriation (still very limited in various German states) if a socialist municipal policy is to be possible. Moreover, it must demand that the administration

---

* I have already expressed this thought very forcefully some years ago in my preface to extracts from Lassalle's *System of Acquired Rights*, which work is itself, as Lassalle writes, intended to reconcile revolutionary law with positive law, i.e. to take adequate account of positive law even in formulating revolutionary law.[50] At the risk of being accused of petty-bourgeois sentiments, I do not hesitate to state that the thought or idea of an expropriation that would only be confiscation dressed up in legal form – not to speak of expropriation as prescribed by Barère – seems to me to be thoroughly objectionable, quite apart from the fact that such expropriation would be objectionable on purely economic, utilitarian grounds. 'Whatever far-reaching encroachments on existing property privileges one may presuppose, in the period of transition to a socialist society, they cannot be the senseless application of brutal force but must be the expression of a definite legal idea, albeit one which is new and which is asserted with elemental force' (Lassalle, *Collected Works*, vol. III, p. 791). The form of the expropriation of the expropriators which corresponds most closely to the legal principles characteristic of socialism is that of their replacement by organisations and institutions.

50 The basic theme of Lassalle's work was, as he put it, 'the transition from an old legal system to a new', *Das System der erworbene Rechte* (Leipzig, 1861), p. 49. The problem was: how can acquired rights be legally abolished if a law can not have retrospective effect? Lassalle argued that there were circumstances in which a law could, in fact, have retrospective effect.

of this policy, and especially the enforcement of it, be completely independent of the state. What is to be expected from municipalities with regard to taxation and education policy is, essentially, already laid down in the general programme of the Party, but it has received some valuable amplifications in the Brandenburg programme (provision of school canteens, appointment of school doctors, etc.). Furthermore, demands respecting the creation of *communal enterprises* as well as *public services* and a *labour policy* for municipalities are nowadays rightly brought to the fore. With regard to the first, the demand should be made on principle that all enterprises serving the *general* needs of members of the community and having a monopolistic character should be conducted under the authority of the municipality itself and that, for the rest, the municipality should constantly strive to increase the range of services for its members. As regards *labour policy*, we must demand that municipalities, as employers of labour, whether under their own management or under contract, maintain as a minimum condition the wages and hours of work accepted by the relevant workers' organisations, and that they guarantee the right of combination for these workers. However, let us note that, while it is only right to endeavour to make municipalities, as employers of labour, set a good example by providing better working conditions and welfare arrangements than private enterprise, it would be a short-sighted policy to demand conditions for municipal workers so favourable that it puts them in a position of being an unusually privileged class compared with their fellow workers, and to make the costs of municipal production considerably higher than those of private enterprise. That would, in the long run, lead to corruption and to a weakening of public spirit.

Modern developments have assigned further duties to municipal government: the establishment and supervision of local health insurance, to which, perhaps in the not-very-distant future, responsibility for invalidity insurance will be added. There has also been added the establishment of labour exchanges and industrial tribunals. The minimum demand of Social Democracy with regard to labour exchanges is that their balanced character be guaranteed and, with regard to industrial tribunals, that their establishment be compulsory and their powers be extended. Social Democracy is sceptical, if not dismissive, of municipal unemployment insurance, since the view prevails that such insurance is one of the legitimate tasks of trade unions and can best be dealt with by them. However, that can hold good only for well-organised trades, which unfortunately still comprise a small minority of the working population. The great mass of workers is still unorganised and the question arises whether municipal unemployment insurance can, in conjunction with the trade unions, be so organised that, so far from being an encroachment on their legitimate functions, it becomes precisely a way of encouraging them. In any case, where such insurance is instituted, it would be the duty of Social Democratic municipal representatives to press with all their energy for bringing the trade unions into play.

By its very nature, municipal socialism is an indispensable instrument for the development, or complete actualisation, of what in the previous chapter we called the *democratic right to work*. But it is, and must remain, less than perfect where the municipal franchise is a class franchise. But such is the case in much more than three-quarters of Germany. So here too, as with the state parliaments – on which the municipalities are to a high degree dependent – and the other organs of self-government, we face the question: how can Social Democracy put an end to the existing class franchise and achieve its democratisation?

In Germany at present, Social Democracy's most effective means of asserting its demands, apart from propaganda by voice and pen, is the Reichstag franchise. The influence of this franchise is so great that it has extended even to those bodies from which the working class is excluded by a property qualification or a system of class franchise; for even here the parties must pay attention to the Reichstag electors. If the Reichstag franchise were immune from attack, there might be some justification for treating the question of the franchise for the other bodies as relatively unimportant, though even then it would be a mistake to make light of it. But the Reichstag franchise is not secure at all. Governments and government parties will certainly not take the decision to change it lightly, for they will be aware that such a step would inevitably cause hatred and bitterness amongst the mass of German workers, which they would show in a very uncomfortable way on suitable occasions. The socialist movement is too strong, and the political self-consciousness of the German workers is too highly developed, to be dealt with in a cavalier fashion. Also, we may assume that a great many of those who oppose universal franchise on principle would, on moral grounds, hesitate to deprive the people of this right. However, although curtailing the franchise would, under normal circumstances, create a revolutionary crisis with all its attendant dangers for the governing classes, there are no serious technical difficulties in changing the franchise so that the victory of an independent socialist candidate would be the exception. It is only political considerations which decide the issue on this matter. And there is no need for any elaborate demonstration that situations can arise in which such scruples would be scattered like chaff before the wind, or that Social Democracy would be powerless to prevent it. For its part, Social Democracy may well persist in its resolve not to be provoked into a violent confrontation, whatever the consequences; but it can not, in all circumstances, restrain the politically unorganised masses from engaging in such confrontations.

On this and other grounds, it does not seem advisable to make the policy of Social Democracy wholly dependent on the conditions and opportunities provided by the Reichstag franchise. We have, more-over, seen that we are not making as rapid progress with it as might have been expected from the successes of 1890 and 1893. While the socialist vote in the three year period from 1887 to 1890 rose by 87 per cent, and from 1890 to 1893 by 25 per cent, it only rose by 18 per cent in the five years from 1893 to 1898 – a significant increase in itself, but not one that would justify expecting anything extraordin-ary from the near future.

It is true that Social Democracy does not depend exclusively on the franchise and parliamentary activity. It also has a large and fertile field of activity outside parliament. Indeed, the socialist labour move-ment would exist even if it were excluded from parliament. Nothing demonstrates this better than the present gratifying activity among the Russian workers. But if the German labour movement were excluded from representative bodies, it would lose much of the inner cohesion which at present binds together its various sections; it would acquire a chaotic character, and the steady, unremitting march for-ward with firm steps would be replaced by fitful advances with the inevitable reverses and exhaustion.

Such a development is not in the interest of the working class. Nor can it be attractive to those opponents of Social Democracy who have realised that the present social order is not created for all eternity but is subject to the law of change, and that a catastrophic develop-ment with all its horrors and devastation can be averted only if changes in the relations of production and exchange and in the development of classes are taken into account in legislation. And the number of those who realise this is steadily increasing. Their influence would be much greater than it is today, if Social Democracy could find the courage to emancipate itself from phraseology that is, in fact, obsolete and to make up its mind to appear what it is in reality today: a democratic socialist party of reform.

It is not a matter of renouncing the so-called right of revolution – this purely speculative right which no constitution can enshrine and no statute book can prohibit and which will endure as long as the law of nature forces us to die if we renounce the right to breathe. This unwritten and imprescriptible right is no more affected if we take our stand on the ground of reform than the right of self-defence is abolished if we make laws to regulate our personal and property disputes.

But is Social Democracy today something other than a party that strives to achieve the socialist transformation of society by means of democratic and economic reform? According to some of the statements that were made against me at the Stuttgart Conference, it seems that perhaps it is. However, in Stuttgart my letter to the conference was seen as an indictment of the party for following the course of Blanquism, whereas in actual fact it was aimed only at a few individuals who had attacked me with Blanquist arguments and modes of speech and who wanted to get the conference to make a pronouncement against me.[51] The circumstance that a few otherwise steady and objective individuals allowed the commotion which my article caused (quite contrary to my intent and expectation) to seduce them into opposing me, and thus apparently endorsing the call for an anathema, could not for a moment deceive me as to the ephemeral nature of this consensus. And how could I see Cunow's refutation of my statements against catastrophe speculation[52] as being anything other than the product of a passing mood when, in the spring of 1897, the same Cunow wrote:

We are still very far from the final end of capitalist development.

---

[51] Parvus in particular tried to get the 'Bernstein question' put on the agenda of the conference with a view to having Bernstein's position formally repudiated. He did not succeed. However, the 'Bernstein question' was nonetheless debated (under the agenda item 'Press') and the weight of opinion at the conference was clearly against Bernstein.

[52] Cunow, 'Zur Zusammenbruchstheorie'.

Because we live in the main centres of trade and industry with the enormous increase in production and the decay of the liberal bourgeoisie taking place before our eyes, we are all too ready to underestimate the distance and the obstacles that separate us from our goal. In what country is the economic self-destruction of capitalism already so far advanced that it can be regarded as being ripe for a socialist form of economy? Not in England, and even less in Germany and France.

(H. Cunow, 'Our Interests in East Asia', *Die Neue Zeit*, xv, 1, p. 806)

Even a definite verdict by the Stuttgart Conference against my statement would not have shaken my conviction that the great mass of German Social Democrats is far removed from being liable to fits of Blanquism. After the speech at Oeynhausen,[53] I knew that I could expect the conference to take no other position that the one it did in fact adopt, and I explicitly said so beforehand in my correspondence.

Since then, the Oeynhausen speech has suffered the fate of so many other speeches by extraordinary men; it has been semi-officially corrected, and black has been declared to be white. And what has been the spirit manifested by the party since Stuttgart? Bebel, speaking on the assassination attempts, has protested most vigorously against the idea that Social Democracy pursues a policy of violence, and all the party papers have reported these speeches with applause; no protest against them has been voiced anywhere. In *The Agrarian Question*, Kautsky develops principles for a Social Democratic agrarian policy which are entirely those of democratic reform, just as the municipal programme adopted in Brandenburg is a democratic programme of reform. In the Reichstag, the party supports the compulsory establishment of industrial tribunals and the extension of their powers – these being organisations for the promotion of industrial peace. In Stuttgart shortly after the conference, where according to Klara Zetkin the 'Bernsteiniade' received its death blow, the Social Democrats formed an electoral alliance with bourgeois democracy for the municipal elections; and their example was followed in other Würtemberg cities. In the trade-union movement, one union after

---

[53] Shortly before the Stuttgart Conference, the Kaiser gave a speech at Oeynhausen in which he announced forthcoming legislation to make it an offence punishable by imprisonment to prevent a man from working or to incite him to strike. In the event, the bill was rejected by the Reichstag.

187

the other introduces unemployment insurance – thus, in practice, abandoning its character as a pure trade union – and declares itself in favour of municipal labour exchanges with employers and employees equally represented; while in various party strongholds – Hamburg, Elberfeld – socialists and trade unionists have established consumers' cooperatives. Everywhere there is action for reform, action for social progress, action for the victory of democracy. 'They study the details of topical problems and look for ways and means of using them to push the development of society in a socialist direction.' I wrote this just a year ago,⁴⁴ and I know of no facts that might induce me to delete a word of it.

For the rest, let me repeat that the more Social Democracy decides to appear to be what it really is, the more will it improve its prospects of achieving political reforms. Fear is certainly a major factor in politics, but we deceive ourselves if we think that causing fear can accomplish everything. The English workers gained the right to vote not when the Chartist movement was at its most revolutionary but when they abandoned revolutionary slogans and forged an alliance with the radical bourgeoisie for the achievement of reforms. And I beseech anyone who objects that this is impossible in Germany to look again at the way in which the Liberal press wrote about the trade-union struggle and labour legislation just fifteen or twenty years ago and at how the representatives of the Liberal parties in the Reichstag voted when the issues in question were to be resolved. He will then, perhaps, agree that political reaction is by no means the most prominent phenomenon in bourgeois Germany.

---

⁴⁴ 'The Struggle of Social Democracy and the Social Revolution', *Die Neue Zeit*, xvi, 1, p. 451 [*sic*; should be 484].

Conclusion: final goal and movement

Kant against cant

I have, at various points in this book, already referred to the great influence tradition has on the evaluation of facts and ideas, even in Social Democracy. I say expressly 'even in Social Democracy', because the power of tradition is a very widespread phenomenon from which no party, no literary or artistic tendency, is free, and which has a profound influence even on most of the sciences. Moreover, it is unlikely that it will ever be completely rooted out. There is always a lapse of time before people recognise that tradition is so far distant from the actual facts that they are prepared to discard it. Until this happens, or until it can happen without damage to the case in hand, tradition is normally the most powerful means of uniting those not otherwise bound together by any strong and continuous interest or external pressure. Hence the intuitive preference which all men of action have for tradition, however revolutionary their objectives may be. 'Never swop horses whilst crossing a stream.' This saying of Lincoln's is rooted in the same thought as Lassalle's well-known condemnation of 'the nagging spirit of liberalism', the 'disease of individual opining and wanting to know better'. While tradition is essentially preservative, criticism is almost always destructive. When, therefore, the time comes to take important action, even criticism fully justified by the facts can be wrong and therefore reprehensible.

To recognise this is, of course, not to make a fetish of tradition and to forbid criticism. Parties are not always in the midst of a raging torrent where all attention is concentrated on one task alone. For a party which wants to keep in step with the course of events, criticism is indispensable, and tradition can become an oppressive burden, a fetter and restraint rather than a motive force.

But people are rarely prepared to take full account of the significance of the changes that have taken place in the preconditions of

189

their traditions. Usually they prefer to take into account only changes vouched for by undeniable facts and then to bring them as far as possible into harmony with traditional slogans. The method is called pettifogging, and the verbal result is, as a rule, cant.

Cant – the word is English and is said to have been first used in the sixteenth century as a description of the saintly singsong of the Puritans. More generally it denotes an unreal manner of speech, either thoughtlessly repetitive or used with the consciousness of its untruth to attain any kind of object, whether it be a matter of religion or politics, dead theory or living reality. In this wider sense, cant is very ancient – there were no worse cant-peddlers, for example, than the Greeks of the post-classical period – and in countless forms it permeates our entire cultural life. Every nation, every class, and every group united by doctrine or interest has its own cant. In part, it has become so much a matter of mere form and convention that no one is any longer deceived by its emptiness, and to mount a campaign against it is to take a sledgehammer to crack a nut. This, however, does not apply to cant that appears in the guise of science, or to cant that has become a political catchword.

My proposition 'that what is usually termed the final goal of socialism is nothing to me, the movement is everything'[1] has often been seen as a rejection of every definite goal of the socialist movement, and Mr George Plekhanov has even discovered that I have quoted this 'famous sentence' from the book *Towards Social Peace* by Gerhard von Schulze-Gavernitz.ᵃ There, indeed, a passage states that it is

---

ᵃ In a series of articles, 'What Should we Thank him for? An Open Letter to Karl Kautsky', published in nos. 253 to 255 of the *Sächsische Arbeiter-Zeitung* of 1898. At the Stuttgart Conference, Kautsky had said that, although Social Democracy could not accept my views, it should nevertheless be grateful for the stimulus I had given it through my essays. In the view of Mr Plekhanov, that was much too mild a criticism. It was not sufficient for him that, at Stuttgart, I was disavowed by the overwhelming majority of party delegates as an ignoramus of 'striking poverty of thought' and as an 'uncritical adherent' of bourgeois reforms who 'has dealt such a savage blow at socialist theory and (consciously or unconsciously – that makes no difference) is out to bury that theory to the delight of the united "reactionary mass"', that I must be expelled with scorn and contempt or, as Mr Plekhanov puts it, 'buried by Social Democracy'.[2]

I refrain from using the proverbial expression usually applied to this kind of communication. Everyone acts according to his own nature, and no one expects dulcet tones from a peacock. However, the suggestion that my murderous handiwork 'delights' the 'united reactionary mass' compels me to make a brief riposte.

---

[1] Tudor and Tudor, pp. 168–9.
[2] Plekhanov, *Selected Philosophical Works*, vol. II, p. 351.

certainly necessary for revolutionary socialism to take as its final goal
the nationalisation of all means of production, but not for practical
political socialism which gives goals which are nearer at hand priority
over more distant ones. Because a kind of final goal is here regarded
as being unnecessary for practical purposes, and because I too have
professed little interest in a kind of final goal, I am an 'uncritical
follower' of Schulze-Gavernitz. One has to confess that this argument
displays remarkable intellectual sophistication.

Although my criticism was still strongly influenced by assumptions
I no longer hold, when I reviewed Schulze-Gavernitz's book in *Die
Neue Zeit* eight years ago,[3] I discarded as irrelevant the notion that
the final goal and practical reform work are mutually exclusive –
without encountering any protest – and I agreed that for England a
further peaceful development of the kind Schulze-Gavernitz predicts
is at least not improbable. I expressed the view that if free development were to continue, the English working class would certainly
increase its demands, but would not demand anything which could
not always be shown to be unquestionably necessary and attainable.
That is at bottom nothing other than what I say today. And if anyone
wishes to bring against me the progress Social Democracy has
achieved in England since then, I reply that this expansion has been
accompanied, and made possible, by English Social Democracy's
development from a utopian-revolutionary sect, as Engels himself

Elsewhere in this book I have mentioned various socialist papers which have accepted
my conclusions or have expressed views similar to mine. The list could be made much
longer. However, I am not concerned to strengthen my arguments with the weight of
numbers and the reputation of those who share my views. Nevertheless, in order to put
Mr Plekhanov's style of disputation in its proper light, I must mention that a large, if
not the largest, part of Russian Social Democrats active in Russia, including the editors
of the Russian workers' paper, have declared themselves firmly in favour of a standpoint
very similar to mine, and that various of my 'contentless' articles have been translated
by them and distributed in special editions.[4] Not, it may be, to Plekhanov's 'delight'.
But, under these circumstances, of which he is very well aware, how tasteful it is to
speak of a 'united' reactionary mass – an expression which, incidentally, is ten times
more absurd than the phrase, a single reactionary mass, which Marx and Engels always
rejected.[5]

[3] *NZ*, 9, 1 (1891).
[4] A reference to the legal Marxists and the 'Economists' in the Russian Social Democratic
Movement. See Samuel H. Baron, *Plekhanov, the Father of Russian Marxism* (London,
1963) pp. 195ff.
[5] Lassalle's phrase. For Marx's views see his 'Critique of the Gotha Programme',
MECW, vol. XXIV, pp. 88–9; MEW, vol. XIX, pp. 22–4.

repeatedly represented it to be,[6] into a party of practical reform. In England nowadays, no responsible socialist dreams of an imminent victory for socialism through a great catastrophe; none dreams of a quick seizure of Parliament by the revolutionary proletariat. However, for that reason they rely more and more on work in the municipalities and other organs of self-government; the earlier contempt for the trade-union movement has been abandoned, and a closer sympathy for it has taken hold – and, here and there, also for the cooperative movement.

And the final goal? Well, that just remains a *final* goal. 'The working class . . . has no ready-made utopias to introduce *par décret du peuple*. They know that in order to work out their own emancipation, and along with it that higher form to which present society is irresistibly tending by its own economical agencies, they will have to pass through long struggles, through a series of historic processes, transforming circumstances and men. They have no ideals to realise, but to set free the elements of the new society with which old collapsing bourgeois society itself is pregnant.' Thus Marx in *The Civil War in France*.[7] When I penned the sentence about the final goal, I had this passage in mind, not in its every detail but in its basic line of thought. For, after all, what does it say but that the movement, the series of processes, is everything, while in comparison any goal fixed in detail before the event is immaterial? I have, on a previous occasion, already stated that I am prepared to abandon the form of the proposition about the final goal, insofar as it admits the interpretation that any general goal of the labour movement formulated as a principle should be declared worthless.[8] But preconceived theories about the outcome of the movement which go beyond such a generally conceived goal, and which determine the fundamental direction and character of the movement, will always be forced into utopianism and will, at some time or other, stand in the way of the real theoretical and practical progress of the movement, obstructing and constricting it.

Anyone who knows even a little about the history of Social Democracy will also know that the party has become great by continuously

---

[6] See, for instance, Engels to Kautsky, 12. 8. 1892 (MEW, vol. XXXVIII, pp. 422–3) and Engels to Ludwig Schorlemmer, 25. 7. 1892 (MEW, vol. XXXVIII, p. 412).
[7] MECW, vol. XXII, p. 335; MEW, vol. XVII, p. 343.
[8] Present volume, p. 5.

contravening such theories and infringing resolutions based upon them. What Engels says about the Blanquists and the Proudhonists in the Commune in his preface to the new edition of *The Civil War*,[9] namely, that they were both compelled, in practice, to act contrary to their own dogma, has been repeated often enough in other forms. A theory or a statement of basic principle which is not sufficiently broad to permit the protection of the manifest interests of the working class at each stage of development will always be breached, just as all renunciations of petty reform work and support for friendly bourgeois parties will be forgotten time and again. And time and again party conferences will have to hear the complaint that here and there in the election campaign the final goal of socialism was not brought sufficiently to the fore.

The quotation from Schulze-Gavernitz which Plekhanov flings at me[10] states that, in abandoning the proposition that the condition of the worker [in modern society] is hopeless, socialism loses its revolutionary edge and becomes occupied with the initiation of legislative demands. It is clear from this antithesis that Schulze-Gavernitz always used the concept 'revolutionary', in the sense of an endeavour to achieve a violent revolution. Mr Plekhanov turns the thing around and, because I do not represent the condition of the workers as being hopeless, because I recognise their capacity for improvement and other facts which bourgeois economists have established, he lumps me together with 'the opponents of scientific socialism'.

'Scientific socialism' – indeed! If ever the word, science, has been degraded to pure cant, this is a case in point. The proposition about the 'hopelessness' of the condition of the workers was advanced more than fifty years ago. It runs through the entire radical-socialist literature of the 1830s and 1840s, and many established facts seem to provide it with justification. It is therefore understandable if, in *The Poverty of Philosophy*, Marx stated that the natural wage for labour is the minimum necessary for subsistence[11] – if *The Communist Manifesto* says categorically: 'The modern labourer, on the contrary, instead of rising with the progress of industry, sinks deeper and deeper below the conditions of existence of his own class. He becomes a pauper,

[9] MESW, vol. I, pp. 481–2; MEW, vol. XXII, pp. 195–6.
[10] In his open letter to Kautsky, 'What should we thank him for?', G. Plekhanov, *Selected Philosophical Works*, vol. II (Lawrence & Wishart, London, 1976), pp. 341–2.
[11] MECW, vol. VI, p. 125; MEW, vol. IV, p. 83.

and pauperism develops more rapidly than population and wealth'[12] – if, in *The Class Struggles*, it says that the smallest improvement in the condition of the workers 'remains a utopia within the bourgeois republic'.[13] Now, if the condition of the workers were still hopeless today, then this proposition would naturally also still be correct. Mr Plekhanov's reproach implies that it is. According to him, the hopelessness of the condition of the workers is an indisputable axiom of 'scientific socialism'. Recognising facts which speak against it means, according to him, following the bourgeois economists who have substantiated these facts. They therefore should be accorded the thanks which Kautsky accorded to me. 'Let us do so, in general, to all supporters and admirers of *"harmonies economiques"*, and, of course, first and foremost to the immortal Bastiat.'[14]

In one of his novels, the great English humourist, Dickens, has characterised this way of disputing very well. 'Your daughter has married a beggar', says a somewhat showy lady living in straitened circumstances to her husband, and when he replies that their new son-in-law is not exactly a beggar, he receives the devastatingly sarcastic answer: 'Indeed? I did not know that he possessed large estates.'[15] To deny an exaggeration is to maintain the opposite exaggeration.

Everywhere there are innocents on whom such subterfuges make an impression. To accept something which bourgeois economists have used as an objection to socialist presuppositions – what an aberration! I am, however, sufficiently hardened to regard the sarcasm of Mrs Wilfer as being simply childish. The fact that Marx and Engels once subscribed to an error does not justify continuing to maintain it; and a truth does not lose its force because it was first discovered or expounded by an anti-socialist or not completely socialist economist. In the field of science, bias has no claim to privilege or powers of expulsion. The one-sidedness of Schulze-Gavernitz's account of the historical development of modern England, which at the time I certainly pointed out with sufficient clarity, did not prevent him, both in his book *Towards Social Peace* and in his monograph *Big Business, An Economic and Social Advance*, from establishing facts which are of

[12] MECW, vol. VI, p. 495; MEW, vol. IV, p. 473.
[13] MECW, vol. X, p. 69; MEW, vol. VI, p. 33.
[14] Plekhanov, *Selected Philosophical Works*, vol. II, p. 343.
[15] Mrs Wilfer, 'the tragic muse with a toothache', is in *Our Mutual Friend*.

great value for understanding present economic development; and far from regarding it as a matter for reproach, I gladly acknowledge that Schulze-Gavernitz, as well as other economists from the school of Brentano (Herkner, Einzheimer), have drawn my attention to many facts which I had previously not appreciated or had not appreciated sufficiently. I am even not ashamed to confess that I have learned something from Julius Wolff's book, *Socialism and Socialist Social Order.*

Mr Plekhanov calls this 'an eclectic fusion [of scientific socialism] with the doctrines of bourgeois economists'.[16] As if nine-tenths of the elements of scientific socialism were not drawn from the works of 'bourgeois economists', as if scientific socialism were in any way a party science.[b]

---

[b] In a very perceptive article on the Stuttgart party conference, in the Belgian Social Democratic review, a Russian socialist whose views are close to mine, S. Prokopowitch, raises the objection that I am not being logical in my fight against the mischief of wanting to make science a matter of party politics. In admitting that theory has an influence on party tactics, I myself contribute to the confusion which, in this connection, reigns in Social Democracy. 'Party tactics', he writes, 'are determined much more by actual social conditions than by theoretical knowledge. It is not theoretical knowledge which exercises an influence on party tactics, but on the contrary, it is party tactics which undeniably influence the doctrines current in the party. For the modern mass movement . . . Science will always be a "party matter", if the men of action adhere to the idea that some conception or other of economic development can influence party tactics. Science will be free only from the moment it is acknowledged that it must *serve* the ends of the party, not *determine* them.' Instead of objecting that party tactics are made dependent on a doctrine which I regard as false, I should have objected to the fact that they are made dependent on any theory of social development at all (*Avenir Sociale*, 1899, i, pp. 15–16).

I can agree without reservation to a large part of what is said here, as indeed I have indicated in the first chapter when discussing the role of eclecticism, which was already in print when I received Prokopowitch's article. Where doctrine achieves a position of dominance, eclecticism mounts a rebellion on behalf of free scientific endeavour and opens a breach. However, I can not imagine a permanent collective will without a collective belief which, however much interests may contribute to its formation, is equally dependent on one or other commonly held view, or understanding of such a view, which is generally desirable and feasible. Without such a collective conviction there can be no sustained collective activity. It is this fact which is established by my proposition which is attacked by Prokopowitch. 'The second factor is intellectual in character; it is the extent to which social conditions are understood and the degree of insight into the nature and laws of development of the social organism and its elements' (*Die Neue Zeit*, xvi, 1, p. 485).[17] Assuming that this is the case, I can not exclude theoretical knowledge from all discussion of tactical questions. I only insist that science as such should be treated as a matter standing apart from the party. Besides, serving

[16] Plekhanov, *Selected Philosophical Works*, vol. II, p. 244.
[17] Tudor and Tudor, p. 150.

Unfortunately for Mr Plekhanov's scientific socialism, the Marxist propositions on the hopelessness of the condition of the workers quoted above have been overturned in a book that bears the title, *Capital, A Critique of Political Economy*. There we read of the 'physical and moral regeneration' of the Lancashire textile workers through the Factory Act of 1847, which 'struck the most imperceptive eye'.[18] So the achievement of a certain improvement in the condition of a large category of workers did not even require a bourgeois republic. In the same book it says that present society 'is no fixed crystal, but an organism capable of change and constantly engaged in change', and also that an 'improvement is unmistakable' in the treatment of economic questions by the official representatives of this society. Further, that the author had devoted so much space in his book to the results of English factory legislation in order to encourage those on the Continent to imitate them and thus help the process of social transformation to be accomplished in ever more humane forms (preface).[19] All of which suggests not hopelessness but capacity for improvement in the condition of the worker. And as the legislation described has been not weakened but improved and made more general since 1866 when this was written, and has further been supplemented by laws and institutions working in the same direction, there can be much less talk today of the hopelessness of the condition of the worker than there was at that time. If to state such facts means following the 'immortal Bastiat', then the first rank of the followers of this liberal economist includes – Karl Marx.

Mr Plekhanov gleefully quotes Liebknecht's pronouncement at the Stuttgart Conference: 'A man like Marx had to be in England in order to write *Capital*. But Bernstein has let himself be impressed by the colossal development of the English bourgeoisie.'[20] However, he finds this much too favourable to me. One does not need to be a Marx in order to remain true to scientific socialism (as understood by Marx and Engels) in England. My defection stems rather from the fact that I am 'ill acquainted' with that kind of socialism.[21]

the purposes of something also means influencing it. As Mephistopheles said, 'In the end, we are dependent on the creatures we have created.'[22]

[18] *Capital* I, p. 407.   [19] *Capital* I, p. 92.
[20] Tudor and Tudor, p. 302.
[21] Plekhanov, *Selected Philosophical Works*, vol. II, p. 347.
[22] Goethe, *Faust*, II, 7,003–4.

I would, of course, not think of entering into dispute on this latter point with someone whose science requires him to declare that, until the great revolution, the condition of the worker is hopeless under any conceivable circumstances. It is different with Liebknecht. If I understand his pronouncement correctly, it suggests that he recognises that there are mitigating circumstances for me. Much as I appreciate this, I must nonetheless state that I can not accept the mitigating circumstances. Naturally, I would not dream of comparing myself with Marx, the thinker. However, it is not a question of my greater or lesser inferiority to Marx. One can be in the right against Marx without being his equal in knowledge and intelligence. The question is whether or not the facts I have asserted are correct, and whether the consequences I have drawn from them are justified. As is clear from the above, even a mind like that of Marx is not spared the fate of making extensive modifications to his preconceived opinions in England; after arriving in England he too abandoned certain views he had held before.

Now, it can be asserted against me that Marx certainly acknowledged these improvements, but that the chapter on the historical tendency of capitalist accumulation at the end of the first volume of *Capital* shows how little these details influenced his fundamental view of things. To which I reply that, to the extent that it is correct, it speaks against the chapter in question and not against me.

This much quoted chapter can be understood in very different ways. I believe I was the first to point out – and, indeed, repeatedly – that it is a summary characterisation of a developmental *tendency* which is inherent in capitalist accumulation but which is not completely carried through in practice and which therefore need not be driven to the critical point of the antagonisms there depicted.[23] Engels never questioned this interpretation of mine; he never declared it to be false, either orally or in print. Nor did he have a word to say against what I wrote in 1891 about a work by Schulze-Gavernitz with reference to the questions under discussion: 'It is clear that where legislation, the systematic and conscious action of society, intervenes in an appropriate way, the working of the tendencies of economic development can be thwarted and, under certain circumstances, even eliminated. Marx and Engels have not only never denied this but

[23] Tudor and Tudor, p. 75.

197

have, on the contrary, always emphasised it' (*Die Neue Zeit*, ix, 1, p. 736). He who reads the chapter in question with this view in mind will quietly insert the word 'tendency' into its individual sentences and thus be spared the need of using the distorting arts of interpretation to bring it into accord with reality. But then the significance of the chapter itself would (or will) diminish as further development takes place. For its theoretical significance lies not in establishing the general tendency to capitalist centralisation and accumulation, which had been affirmed by bourgeois economists and socialists long before Marx, but in Marx's particular exposition of the circumstances and forms in which it actualises itself in higher stages, and of the results to which it should lead. But in this respect, the actual development is forever bringing forth new arrangements and forces, forever new facts, in the light of which that exposition seems inadequate and, to a corresponding extent, loses the ability to serve as a sketch of the development to come. That is my view.

However, the chapter can be interpreted differently. It can be understood as saying that all the improvements mentioned and some yet to come provide only temporary remedies for the oppressive tendencies of capitalism, that they are insignificant modifications which can not in the long run accomplish anything fundamental to counteract the heightening of antagonisms established by Marx, that indeed this heightening of antagonisms will finally occur in the manner described – if not literally, then in essence – and will lead to the catastrophic revolution intimated. This interpretation can refer to the categorical way the concluding sentences of the chapter are framed, and it receives a certain amount of support from the fact that at the end reference is once again made to *The Communist Manifesto*, shortly before which Hegel also appears with his negation of the negation – the restoration, on a new basis, of individual property negated by the capitalist mode of production.

In my view, it is impossible simply to declare the one interpretation correct and the other absolutely wrong. To me, the chapter illustrates a dualism which runs through the whole monumental work of Marx, and which also finds expression in a less pregnant fashion in other passages – a dualism which consists in the fact that the work aims at being a scientific investigation and also at proving a thesis laid down long before its conception, that it is based on a formula in which the result to which the exposition ought to lead is laid down beforehand.

The return to *The Communist Manifesto* points to an actual survival of utopianism in Marx's system. Marx had, in essentials, accepted the solution of the utopians, but he had recognised their means and their proofs as inadequate. He therefore undertook to revise them, and this with the zeal, the critical acumen, and the love of truth of a scientific genius. He suppressed no important facts, nor did he forcibly belittle the consequences of these facts, so long as the object of the investigation had no immediate bearing on the final goal of the formula to be proved. Up to that point, his work is free of any tendency necessarily detrimental to the scientific approach.ᶜ For in itself a general sympathy with the working-class struggle for emancipation does not stand in the way of being scientific. However, as Marx comes closer to those points at which the final goal becomes a serious issue, he becomes uncertain and unreliable; contradictions arise, such as those that were pointed out in the book under consideration, for example, in the section on the movement of incomes in modern society; and it is manifest that this great scientific mind was, in the end, nonetheless the prisoner of a doctrine. To put it metaphorically, he erected a mighty building within the framework of scaffolding which was already there, and in its erection he kept strictly to the laws of scientific architecture, as long as they did not collide with the conditions which the construction of the scaffolding prescribed, but he neglected or circumvented them when the constraints of the scaffolding did not permit their observance. Where the scaffolding imposed limits on the building, instead of destroying the scaffolding he changed the building itself at the expense of its proper proportions and so made it all the more dependent on the scaffolding. Was it the awareness of this irrational relation which, time and again, caused him to delay the completion of his work in order to improve particular parts of it? Whatever the case, I am convinced that wherever this dualism manifests itself the scaffolding must fall if the building is to come into its own. What deserves to survive in Marx lies in the building, not in the scaffolding.

Nothing confirms me in this view more than the anxiousness with which precisely the more devoted of those Marxists who have not yet been able to detach themselves from the dialectical framework of the

---

ᶜ I am, of course, disregarding the tendency which finds expression in the treatment of persons and the representation of events and which has no necessary connection with economic development.

book – the aforementioned scaffolding – seek to maintain certain positions in *Capital* which have been overtaken by events. At least, that is the only way I can explain how, when I remarked in Stuttgart that for years the number of property-owners has been increasing rather than decreasing, a man otherwise so open to facts as Kautsky could reply: 'If that were so, then the time of our victory would not only be long delayed, we would never reach our goal at all. If the capitalists rather than the unpropertied are on the increase, then we are moving further away from our goal as society develops; it is capitalism, not socialism, which is establishing itself.'[24]

This proposition, which Mr Plekhanov will naturally endorse as being 'excellent', would be incomprehensible to me, coming from the mouth of a Kautsky, were it not for the connection with Marx's expository framework. Miss Luxemburg took a similar view in the articles mentioned earlier – which are on the whole among the best of those that were written against me, so far as method is concerned. There she objected that on my interpretation socialism would cease to be an objective historical necessity and would be given an idealist basis.[25] Although her line of argument displays some hair-raising logical acrobatics and ends with a completely arbitrary identification of idealism with utopianism, she nevertheless hits the mark. I do not, indeed, make the victory of socialism depend on its 'immanent economic necessity'. On the contrary, I hold that it is neither possible nor necessary to give the victory of socialism a purely materialistic basis.

That the number of property-owners increases rather than diminishes is not an invention of bourgeois 'harmony economists' but a fact which is established by the tax authorities, often much to the chagrin of those concerned, and which can now no longer be disputed. But what does this fact signify for the victory of socialism? Why should the achievement of socialism depend on its denial? Well, simply because the dialectical scheme seems to prescribe it, because a plank threatens to break away from the scaffolding if one admits that the social surplus product is appropriated by an increasing instead of a decreasing number of property-owners. But it is only speculative theory that is affected by this question. It has no bearing whatsoever on the actual aspirations of the workers. It affects neither their

[24] Tudor and Tudor, p. 294.
[25] Tudor and Tudor, pp. 250–2.

struggle for political democracy, nor their struggle for democracy in industry. The prospects of this struggle do not depend on the concentration of capital in the hands of a diminishing number of magnates, nor on the whole dialectical scaffolding of which this is a plank. Rather, it depends on the growth of social wealth and of the social productive forces, in conjunction with general social progress, and in particular the intellectual and moral advance of the working class itself.

If the victory of socialism depended on the number of capitalist magnates constantly shrinking, the logical course for Social Democracy would be, if not to support by all possible means the heaping up of capital in ever fewer hands, then at least to refrain from anything that could impede it. In fact, Social Democracy more often than not does the opposite. These considerations, for instance, do not govern its votes on questions of taxation. From the standpoint of the theory of collapse, a great part of the practical activity of Social Democracy is a matter of undoing work that ought to be left alone. But it is not Social Democracy which is at fault in this respect. The fault lies in the doctrine which incorporates the idea that progress depends on a worsening of circumstances.

In the preface to his *Agrarian Question*, Kautsky turns on those who speak of the need to supersede Marxism. He says that he sees doubt and hesitation expressed but that this alone signifies no development beyond what has already been achieved.

That is correct inasmuch as doubt and hesitation alone do not constitute a positive refutation. They can, however, be the first step towards it. But is it really a matter of superseding Marxism? Or is it not rather a matter of rejecting certain remnants of utopianism which still adhere to Marxism and which are the source of the contradictions in theory and practice which have been pointed out in Marxism by its critics? This book is already longer than it should be, and I must therefore refrain from going into all the details of this subject. But I consider it all the more my duty to say that I regard a large number of objections to certain points of Marx's theory as unrefuted, and some as irrefutable. And I do this all the more easily as these objections have no bearing whatsoever on the aspirations of Social Democracy.

We ought to be less sensitive on this matter. It has repeatedly happened that Marxists have advanced propositions which they believed flatly contradicted Marx's theory, and which were attacked with the greatest of zeal, while in the end it transpired that, for the most part, there was no contradiction at all. Amongst others, I have in mind the controversy concerning the investigations of the late Dr Stiebeling on the effect of the concentration of capital on the rate of exploitation.[26] Stiebeling committed major errors in his manner of expression, as well as in some of his calculations, and Kautsky above all deserves the credit for having discovered them. On the other hand, the third volume of *Capital* has shown that, although Stiebeling's proof of the phenomenon is different from that of Marx, the basic idea of his works, the decrease of the rate of exploitation with the increasing concentration of capital, was not contrary to Marx's theory, as most of us then thought. However, at the time Stiebeling was told that, if what he said was correct, then the theoretical foundation of the contemporary labour movement, Marx's theory, was false. And, as a matter of fact, those who spoke thus could cite various passages from Marx. An analysis of the controversy over Stiebeling's treatises could very well serve to illustrate some of the contradictions in the theory of value.[d]

There are similar contradictions in the evaluation of the relationship between economics and the use of force in history, and they

---

[d] In this connection, I would like to draw attention to the very noteworthy article, subscribed 'Lxbg', on Stiebeling's work in *Die Neue Zeit* for the year 1887,[27] in which, amongst other things, the solution to the problem of the rate of profit was anticipated. The to me unknown author says pretty much the same about surplus value as I have argued in the section on the theory of value when he writes: 'The rate of surplus value, the ratio of total profit to total wages, is a concept that can not be applied to individual branches of production' (p. 129). At the time, Kautsky's objection was certainly the best that could be said on the basis of the available volumes of *Capital*, and also touched upon the *form* in which Lxbg clothed his thoughts. For the *concept* of the rate of surplus value can undoubtedly be applied to individual branches of production. But what Lxbg really meant was nevertheless correct. The rate of surplus value is a *measurable quantity* only for the economy taken as a whole, and therefore, so long as the latter is not actualised, it can not be ascertained for individual branches of production – at least, not until labour value is brought into direct connection with wages. In other words, there is no real way of measuring the rate of surplus value in individual branches of production.

[26] See G. C. Stiebeling, *Das Wertgesetz und die Profitrate* (New York, 1890) and Engels's reply: 'Bemerkung zu dem Aufsätze des Herrn Stiebeling', *NZ*, 3 (1887), 127–33. See also Engels's comments in *Capital* III, pp. 109–11.

[27] Lxbg, 'Bemerkung zu dem Aufsätze des Herrn Stiebeling: Ueber den Einfluss der Verdichtung des Kapitals auf den Lohn und die Ausbeutung der Arbeit', *NZ*, (1887), 127ff.

find their counterpart in the contradictions in the assessment of the practical tasks and opportunities of the labour movement, which has already been discussed elsewhere. This is, however, a point to which we must now return. But the question to be investigated is not the extent to which force originally, and in the subsequent course of history, determined the economy and *vice versa*, but simply the creative power of force in present society. Earlier, Marxists had, from time to time, assigned force a purely negative role in contemporary society, but nowadays an exaggeration in the opposite direction is in evidence; force is given what amounts to a creative omnipotence, and an emphasis on political action seems virtually the quintessence of 'scientific socialism' – or even 'scientific communism', to use the expression as 'improved' by a new fashion, not exactly with any advantage to its logic.

Now, it would be fatuous to go back to the prejudices of former generations with regard to what political power can do, for this would mean going back still further to explain these prejudices themselves. The prejudices which the utopians, for instance, cherished were well founded; indeed, one can scarcely say they were prejudices, for they rested on the real immaturity of the working class of the time, which meant that nothing was possible but transitory mob rule on the one hand and a return to class oligarchy on the other. Under these circumstances, advocating political action must have seemed a diversion from more pressing tasks. Nowadays, these conditions have been to some extent removed, and therefore no one who thinks twice will dream of criticising political action with the arguments of that period.

As we have seen, Marxism first turned the matter around, and, with the potentialities of the industrial proletariat in view, preached political action as the most important duty of the movement. But, in doing this, it got involved in major contradictions. It recognised – and this distinguished it from the demagogic parties – that the working class had not yet reached the maturity required for its emancipation, and also that the economic preconditions for this emancipation were not yet present. Nevertheless, it turned time and again to tactics which presupposed that both these conditions were almost fulfilled. In its publications, we come across passages where the immaturity of the worker is stressed with an emphasis that is little different from the doctrinaire attitude of the first socialists, and shortly afterwards we find passages which give us to suppose that all culture, all intelligence, all virtue is to be found only in the working class – which makes it incomprehensible why the most extreme social revolutionaries and violent anarchists should not be right. Corresponding with this, political action is always directed at the imminent revolutionary catastrophe, compared with which legislative work seemed for a long time only a *pis aller*, a merely temporary device. And we look in vain for any investigation into the question as to what can, in principle, be expected from legal and what from revolutionary action.

It is evident at first glance that there are major differences on this question. But they usually revolve around the point that law, or the path of legal reform, is the slower way and that of revolutionary force is the quicker and more radical.ᶜ But this is true only in a conditional sense. Whether the legislative or the revolutionary way is the more promising depends entirely on the nature of the measures and on their relation to the various classes and customs of the people.

In general, we can say that the revolutionary way (always in the sense of revolutionary force) works more quickly where it is a question of removing obstacles which a privileged minority places in the path of progress, that its strength lies on the negative side.

As a rule, constitutional legislation works more slowly. Its way is usually that of compromise; it does not abolish acquired rights but buys them out. But it is more powerful than revolution wherever the preconceptions, the limited horizon, of the great mass of the people stand as an obstacle in the way of social progress, and it offers greater advantages where it is a question of creating permanent and viable economic arrangements; in other words, it is better for positive sociopolitical work.

In legislation, the intellect governs emotion in quiet times; in a revolution, emotion governs the intellect. However, if emotion is often a poor guide, the intellect is often a slow and cumbersome driving force. Where revolution sins by being precipitate, workaday

---

ᶜ It is in this sense that Marx, in the chapter on the working day, speaks of 'the peculiar advantages of the French revolutionary method' which had been made manifest in the French twelve-hours' law of 1848.[28] It prescribes the same working day for all workers and all factories without distinction. That is correct. However, it has been established that this radical law remained a dead letter for a whole generation.

[28] *Capital* I, p. 413.

legislation sins by procrastinating. Legislation operates as a systematic force, revolution as an elemental force.

As soon as a nation has reached a political state of affairs where the rights of the propertied minority have ceased to be a serious impediment to social progress, where the negative tasks of political action take second place to the positive, the appeal to violent revolution becomes pointless.^f You can overthrow a government, a privileged minority, but not a people.

Even law, with all the influence of authority backed by armed force, is often powerless against the rooted customs and prejudices of the people. The basic cause of maladministration in Italy today is by no means ill-will, or lack of good-will, on the part of the House of Savoy. Against bureaucratic corruption which has become a tradition and the easygoing nature of the bulk of the people even the best-meant laws and ordinances often fail. Similarly in Spain, in Greece, and to an increasing extent in the East. Even in France where the Republic has accomplished a great deal for the progress of the nation, it has not only not rooted out certain major problems of national life; it has actually intensified them. What seemed outrageous corruption under the Bourgeois Monarchy is nowadays seen as a harmless game. A nation, a people, is only a conceptual unity; the legally proclaimed sovereignty of the people does not in reality turn this unity into the decisive factor. It can make the government dependent precisely on those compared with whom it ought to be strong: the bureaucracy, business politicians, the owners of the press. And that goes for revolutionary no less than for constitutional governments.

Where the working class does not possess strong economic organisations of its own and has not attained a high degree of mental independence through training in self-governing bodies, the dictatorship of the proletariat means the dictatorship of club orators and literati. There are those who regard the oppression and circumvention of workers' organisations and the exclusions of workers from legislation and administration as the pinnacle of statecraft, but I would not wish them to experience the difference in practice. Nor would I wish the labour movement itself to experience it.

Despite the great progress which the working class has made on

---

^f 'Fortunately, revolution in this country has ceased to be anything more than an affected phrase' (Monthly *News* of the Independent Labour Party in England, January, 1899).

205

the intellectual, political, and industrial fronts since the time when Marx and Engels were writing, I still regard it as being, even today, not yet sufficiently developed to take over political power. I am all the more inclined to say this openly as it is precisely on this topic that cant of a kind which threatens to stifle all sound judgment creeps into socialist literature; and I know that I am nowhere so certain to meet with an objective assessment of my remarks as among the workers who constitute the vanguard in the struggle for the emancipation of their class. None of the workers with whom I have discussed socialist problems have expressed any essential disagreement on these points. Only literati who have never had any close relationship with the real labour movement could make a different judgment on this matter. Hence the comic rage – to use a moderate expression – of Mr Plekhanov against all socialists who do not see the entire class of proletarians as being already what it is their historical vocation to become, who still see problems where he already has the solution. For – the proletariat is myself! Whoever does not think of the movement as he does is a pedant and a petty bourgeois. It is an old song which, however, gains nothing whatsoever with the passing of time.

Utopianism is not overcome by transferring or imputing to the present what is to be in the future. We must take the workers as they are. And they are neither universally pauperised, as was predicted in *The Communist Manifesto*, nor as free from prejudices and weaknesses as their flatterers would have us believe. They have the virtues and the vices of the economic and social conditions under which they live. And neither these conditions nor their effects can be removed overnight.

The most violent revolution can change the general level of the majority of a nation only very slowly. It is all very well to tell those opponents of socialism who make the celebrated calculation showing how little an equal distribution of incomes would change the incomes of the great majority that such an equal distribution constitutes the least part of what socialism seeks to achieve. But we must not then forget that the other part, the increase in production, is not something easily improvised. 'Only at a certain level of development of these social productive forces, even a very high level for our modern conditions, does it become possible to raise production to such an extent that the abolition of class distinctions can constitute real progress, can be lasting without bringing about stagnation or even decline in

206

the mode of social production.' What petty bourgeois, what pedant, wrote this, Mr Plekhanov? None other than Friedrich Engels.[g]

Have we yet reached the level of development of the productive forces which is required for the abolition of classes? In contrast with the incredible figures that were formerly produced on this subject, and which depended on generalisations from the development of particularly favoured industries, socialist writers have recently endeavoured to achieve, on the basis of careful and detailed calculations, proper evaluations of the productive potentialities of a socialist society, and their results are very different from the earlier figures.[h] In the foreseeable future, there can be no question of a general reduction in the hours of work per day to five or four or, indeed, three or two, as was previously supposed, if the general standard of living is not to be significantly reduced. Even with labour collectively organised, workers would have to begin work at a very young age and continue to a very advanced age if the same quantity of goods and services were to be achieved as under the eight-hour day.

In short, you can not in the course of a couple of years move the entire working class into conditions which are substantially different from those in which it finds itself at present. Actually, it is precisely those who indulge in the most extreme exaggerations regarding the numerical ratio of the propertyless to the propertied classes who ought to be the first to understand this. However, he who thinks irrationally on one point usually does so on another. And I am therefore not at all surprised when the same Plekhanov, who is outraged at seeing the position of the worker represented as not being hopeless, responds with the devastating epithet 'petty bourgeois' to my remark that there is no immediate likelihood of our abandoning the principle that those capable of work be economically responsible for themselves. It is not for nothing that one is the philosopher of irresponsibility.

However, anyone who looks about in the actual labour movement will find that the workers attach very little value to being liberated

---

[g] Compare 'Social Questions in Russia', *Vorwärts* edition, p. 50.

[h] Compare Atlanticus: *A Glance into the Future State: Production and Consumption in the Social State* (Stuttgart, Dietz) as well as the essays, *On Collectivism*, by Dr Joseph Ritter von Neupauer in Pernerstorfer's *Deutsche Worte* for 1897–8. Neither work is unobjectionable, but they are to be warmly recommended to those who wish to learn about the problems referred to. Neupauer thinks that if the average work done by all machines were reckoned, it would be shown that they barely save a third of human labour power.

from those characteristics which seem petty bourgeois to the pretended proletarian of bourgeois origin, that they by no means cherish the proletarian ethic but, on the contrary, are very interested in turning the proletarian into a 'petty bourgeois'. No permanent and solid trade-union movement would have been possible with the rootless proletarian bereft of home and family; it is no bourgeois prejudice, but a conviction gained through decades of labour organisation, which has turned so many of the English labour leaders – socialists and non-socialists – into zealous adherents of the temperance movement.[i] Working-class socialists know the faults of their class, and the most conscientious among them, far from glorifying these faults, seek to overcome them with all their might.

At this point I must once again refer to Liebknecht's suggestion that I have allowed myself to be impressed by the tremendous growth of the English bourgeoisie. It is correct only in that I have become convinced that assertions concerning the disappearance of the middle classes, once current in our literature and based on incomplete statistics, are erroneous. But this by itself was not sufficient to make me revise my views on the speed and nature of the evolution towards socialism. The lessons learned from closer acquaintance with the classic labour movement of modern times were much more important. And, without generalising in an uncritical way, I am convinced, and regard it as established in many ways, that the Continent is in principle no different from England. It is a question not of national but of social phenomena.

We cannot demand from a class the great majority of whose members live under crowded conditions, are badly educated, and have an uncertain and insufficient income, the high intellectual and moral standard which the organisation and existence of a socialist community presupposes. We will, therefore, not pretend that they do in fact possess it. Let us rejoice at the great stock of intelligence, self sacrifice, and energy which the modern labour movement has displayed and also produced, but we must not uncritically ascribe to the masses, to the millions, what holds good for the elite, for, say, hundreds of thousands. I will not repeat what workers have said to me on this point, both orally and in writing; I do not need to defend myself

---

[i] In a circular, even the executive committee of the Independent Socialist Labour Party warmly recommended that their sections not provide alcoholic drink in the premises of their clubs.

before reasonable people against the suspicion of Pharisaism and the arrogance of pedantry. But I am happy to confess that I am operating with two criteria here. It is precisely because I expect much from the working class that I censure everything that tends to corrupt its moral judgment much more severely than I do similar developments in the upper classes, and I view with the greatest regret the way in which a tone of literary decadence is appearing here and there in the socialist press, a tone which can only have a confusing and, in the end, corrupting effect. An up-and-coming class needs a healthy morality and no blasé decadence. Whether it sets itself a detailed final goal is of secondary importance, so long as it pursues its more immediate objectives in an energetic fashion. The important point is that its objectives are inspired by a definite principle which expresses a higher level of economy and of social life as a whole, that they are permeated by a social conception which points to an advance in cultural development and to a more elevated moral and legal standpoint.

From this point of view, I cannot subscribe to the proposition: 'The working class has no ideals to actualise'; rather, I see it only as the product of self-deception – if indeed it is not a mere play on words on the part of its author. It was with this in mind that I once invoked the spirit of the great Königsberg philosopher, the critic of pure reason, against the cant which sought to get a hold on the labour movement and to which the Hegelian dialectic offers a comfortable refuge. The fits of rage into which I thus threw Mr Plekhanov only strengthened me in the conviction that Social Democracy needs a Kant to judge the received judgment and subject it to the most trenchant criticism, to show where its apparent materialism is the highest and therefore most easily misleading ideology, and to show that contempt for the ideal and the magnifying of material factors until they become omnipotent forces of evolution is a self-deception which has been, and will be, exposed as such by the very actions of those who proclaim it. Such a mind, which laid bare with convincing clarity what is of value and destined to survive in the works of our great champions, and what must and can perish, would also make possible a more impartial judgment on those works which, while not starting from the premises which strike us as being decisive today, are nevertheless devoted to the ends for which Social Democracy is fighting. No impartial thinker will deny that socialist criticism often fails in this and that it displays the faults of epigonism. I have myself done my share towards this and I therefore cast no stone at anyone. But it is just because I belong to the school that I believe I have the right to express the need for reform. If I did not fear that what I write would be misunderstood (I am, of course, prepared for its being misinterpreted), I would translate 'back to Kant' as 'back to Lange'. For, just as the philosophers and natural scientists who stand by that motto propose to return not to the letter of what the Königsberg philosopher wrote but only to the fundamental principles of his criticism, so for Social Democracy there can be no question of going back to all the socio-political views and opinions of a Friedrich Albert Lange. What I have in mind is the characteristically Lange combination of sincere and intrepid championship of the working-class struggle for emancipation with a high degree of that scientific impartiality which is always ready to acknowledge errors and recognise new truths. Perhaps broad-mindedness of the magnitude that strikes us in Lange's writings is to be found only in persons who lack the penetrating sharpness of mind which is the property of pioneer spirits like Marx. But it is not every epoch that produces a Marx, and even for a man of equal genius the labour movement of today is too large for him to fill the position which Marx occupies in its history. In addition to militants, the labour movement today needs organising and co-ordinating thinkers who are of sufficiently high calibre to separate the chaff from the wheat, who are furthermore big enough in their thinking to recognise also the little plant that has grown on soil other than their own, and who, though perhaps not kings, are warm-hearted republicans in the domain of socialist thought.

Index

Cambridge Texts in The History of Political Thought

Titles published in the series thus far